# COMBAT VETERANS'

Stories of the Vietnam War

Volume 3 of 5

Norman Black

## Other books by Norman Black

*Combat Veterans' Stories of World War II*
*Volume I, North Africa and Europe*
*Volume 2, Pacific, China, and Burma*

*Combat Veterans' Stories of the Korean War*
*(Two volumes)*

*Ice, Fire, and Blood, a story of the Korean War*

The cover photo shows men of Alpha Company, 3rd Battalion, 7th Infantry Regiment, wading across a muddy Mekong Delta creek. The man in the foreground has a PRICK-25 radio on his back and a mosquito-repellant container on the left side of his helmet. The man behind him carries an M-79 grenade launcher.

*Photo by Thomas L. Reilly*

This work is dedicated to the men who fought in Vietnam and elsewhere in southeastern Asia, with special thanks to those men that shared their stories for inclusion in it.

# Content

VII  Foreword

IX  Acknowledgements

**1**  *Late October 1967* – **John David Blair** – U.S. Marine Corps rifleman: major battles at Mike's Hill, Foxtrot Ridge, and The Saddle. Skirmishes included Camp Carroll; Khe Sahn; Alpha 3; Cam Lo Hill; C-2; Hill 689; Con Thien; Dong Ha; Hill 552; Phui Nui; Firebase Shepherd; and LZ Stud, at Vandegrift Combat Base

**39**  *October 31, 1967* – **Cary Stuart King** – U.S. Army officer: artillery, aerial observer, forward observer; infantry intelligence officer; prisoner interrogation supervision; night aerial reconnaissance; Search and Seal operations; Tet Offensive: battles, including at Thu Duc water treatment plant; post-Tet Counter Offensive; artillery battery commander; numerous combat encounters

**64**  *December 1967* – **Marcus Gary Monk** – U.S. Marine Corps officer and Naval Aviator, helicopter pilot: troop insertions and removals, medevacs, recon unit inserts and extractions. Actions include Khe Sahn; I Corps, during Tet; and Con Thien. Shot down over Khe Sahn, but returned to duty.

**87**  *January 1968* – **Jonathan Tobias "Toby" Mack** – U.S. Navy, anti-submarine warfare officer aboard *USS Johnston* DD-821: carrier escort and air-crew rescue duty, in Gulf of Tonkin; off South Viet Nam's northern coast, as artillery support for US troops in I Corps area, including US Marines, in Battle of Hue, during Tet offensive

v

**100** *January 1968* – **Donald Terrance Dowd** – U.S. Army, medic and paratrooper: with 506th Paratroop Infantry Regiment, in numerous skirmishes and battles on search-and-destroy patrols, including at Cu Chi and Dak To on Laotian border; Long Range Reconnaissance Patrol missions with 2nd Battalion, 3rd Brigade, 101st Airborne Division; Dust off duty with air ambulance evacuation unit, including from Hamburger Hill

**107** *February 20, 1968* – **Thomas Joseph "Tom" Flaherty** – U.S. Marine Corps, infantry officer: patrols and ambushes south of Da Nang during Tet Offensive; battle at La Tho Bac 3; Battle of Cam Le and Can Do Bridges; Operation Allen Brook; Da Nang, during 1969 Tet attack; U.S.M.C. Reserve

**134** *March 1968* – **Robert B. "Bob" Humphries** – U.S. Army, infantry, 81mm mortars: at Di An, in III Corps, north of Saigon: search-and-destroy missions and ambushes, from Di An

**146** *Mid-March1968* – **Lee Wesley Sinnickson** – U.S. Army, infantry: M-60 machine gun crew member: search-and-destroy missions, from Lai Khe base, in III Corps; Graves Registration, in III Corps

**168** *May 1968* – **Ralph Howard Bigelow** – U.S. Navy: Mobile Riverine Force, machinist and gunner, on an armored troop carrier, on rivers and canals in the Mekong delta

**188** *May 21, 1968*, **Robert Clyde "Bob" Stephenson**, U.S. Army, infantry paratrooper: Detroit Riots, B Company, 1st Battalion, 505th Airborne Infantry Regiment, 82nd Airborne Division; Vietnam, 1968-1969, D Company, 2nd Battalion, 506th Airborne Infantry Regiment, 101st Airborne Division, radio telephone operator on patrols and fire fights in III, II, and I Corps areas; a four-day-long battle in Cu Chi area; and skirmishes and fire fights in the A Shau Valley and Central Highlands

**206** *Early August 1968* – **James Lee Patin** – U.S. Navy: Mobile Riverine Force, gunner's mate – Patrols and troop insertions and removals in III Corps and IV Corps

**216** *September 6, 1968* – **Thomas Lee Reilly, II** – U.S. Army, infantry: patrols, skirmishes, setting ambushes, and being ambushed, in the Mekong delta area of IV Corps; US Army war correspondent

**242** *First week of September 1968* – **Michael Albert Harris** – U.S. Navy: Mobile Riverine Force, radioman and gunner, on an armored troop carrier, on rivers and canals in Mekong Delta

**265** *September 1968* – **Kirk Steaven Baldwin Leavesley** – U.S. Marine Corps, artillery: in I Corps, doing fire support co-ordination control; mine clearing; forward observer with infantry patrols; patrols and night listening posts near the DMZ; night ambushes; monitoring in-ground sensors, identifying shell fragments, and determining shells' angles of penetration; and guarding medivac teams, in Vietnamese villages

**285** *First week of November 1968* – **Philip Leslie Spackman** – U.S. Army, armor officer: leader of an armored cavalry assault platoon, in I Corps: infantry support and reconnaissance in force

**308** **The author**

# Foreword

The autobiographies in *Combat Veterans' Stories of the Vietnam War* are told by Americans, Canadians, and Australians who fought during the Vietnam War. Their stories tell about dedication to comrades and duty, and of bravery, pain, suffering, and frustration, in a war without fronts, in which any Vietnamese civilian could have been an enemy when opportunity presented itself. Their stories tell with every step, on every patrol, every man risked death or injury by mines, booby traps, snipers, or mortar rounds, in ambushes and in skirmishes and major battles. Pilots and air crew members risked death or injury from ground fire, anti-aircraft missiles, and advanced enemy fighter aircraft.

This volume contains 15 autobiographical stories. The first begins in late October 1967, and is told by a Marine rifleman who fought in battles at Mike's Hill, Foxtrot Ridge, and numerous other battles. In this volume, the final story is told by an Army cavalry officer that led a platoon of armored personnel carriers with such ability and daring that he was awarded the Distinguished Service Cross, three Silver Stars, four Bronze Stars, and two Purple Hearts.

The other stories in Volume 3 include those told by a U.S. Army artillery officer, a Marine helicopter pilot, a naval officer on offshore fire support duty, and two men that served in the U.S. Navy's Mobile Riverine Force.

Photos used in this volume were supplied by the men interviewed.

There is a total of 57 stories in the four volumes. Forty-eight of the men that tell their stories are U.S. citizens, two are Australians, and three were Canadians, when they enlisted. One Canadian later became a U.S. citizen. With one exception, in volume 4, each man's story appears in chronological order according to the date on which he experienced his first combat.

Five of the U.S. veterans who tell their stories, were war prisoners of the Viet Cong and North Vietnamese. Their experiences let us know the mind-set and behavior of the people our forces were fighting. The history of their war prisoner treatment, told in volume five, tells that Vietnamese' war prisoner treatment was consistent from the French Indochina War to the Vietnam War. Their experiences, at the hands of what is now the government of Vietnam, reveal cultural barbarity similar to that of North Korean and Chinese Communists, during the Korean War.

Volume 4, in addition to combat veterans' stories, contains information about U.S. allies that fought in Vietnam.

Volume 5 contains the U.S.' explanation for the war, a review of the war and U.S. armed forces and various problems during the war. There is also information about POW treatment, POWs and MIAs, the CIA and the drug trade, war crimes, moral injury, and history lessons not learned. Volume 5 also contains a brief photo view of some aspects of events, in South Viet Nam, in 1968, a decisive year.

Norman Black
Marietta, Georgia

# Acknowledgements

I am thankful to the following people for identifying combat veterans that I was able to interview for these volumes: Mickey Christiason, Cerritos, California; Kevin M. Horgan of Roswell, Georgia; Michael Kelly of the Australian War Memorial, Canberra, Australia; Prof. Donald W. Livingston, McClellanville, South Carolina; David Martin, director of college relations, Wagner College, Staten Island, New York; Col. Bill Nisbet USAR (Ret.), assistant minister, Roswell Presbyterian Church, Roswell, Georgia Vincent Rios, president, 1st Marine Division Association; Capt. Kevin F. Spalding, USNR (Ret), of Gastonia, North Carolina; Maj. Richard T. Spooner, USMC (Ret.), of Quantico, Virginia; Wayne O. Witter of Dunwoody, Georgia;

I am grateful to Brian C. Cooper of Dianella, Western Australia, a Korean War combat veteran and retired, senior warrant officer of the Australian army, for help with several things. He interviewed Victor Kenneth Otway, an Australian army veteran of Korea; Malaya, and the Vietnam War. He also provided information about what Australia's Vietnam War veterans have experienced since they returned home from Vietnam. Additionally, he facilitated contact with a New Zealand combat veteran, which resulted in a section about New Zealand participation in the Vietnam War and its veterans' experience when they returned home.

I am thankful to Wayne O. Witter of Dunwoody, Georgia, a Vietnam War combat veteran, whose story is told in this work, for helping me to confirm that one interesting, exciting, and fantastic combat story was "stolen valor".

For other valuable help, I am grateful to Ronald Agnir, chief photographer, The Journal Newspaper, Martinsburg, West Virginia; Conrad C. Crane, chief of Historical Services and Support, U.S. Army Heritage and

Education Center, The U.S. Army War College, Carlisle Barracks, Pennsylvania; June Cornier, membership coordinator, First Marine Division Association; Lt. Col. Kerry A. Knowles, USMC (Ret), senior editor, Marine Corps Gazette, Quantico, Virginia; Kara Newcomer, historian, Historical Reference Branch, USMC History Division, Quantico, Virginia; Arthur G. Sharp, editor The Old Breed, the publication of the 1st Marine Division Association; Wayne O. Witter of Dunwoody, Georgia; Vince Rios, president, First Marine Division Association

Special mention must be made of Robert Winston Mercy, whose story is told in Volume 1 of Combat Veterans' Stories of the Korean War, who spent much time trying to track down a Vietnam veteran that was involved in capturing, disarming, and arresting a large number of U.S. military deserters, in a shanty town south of the U.S. Marine Corps air base, at Da Nang. The deserters were dealing in drugs, stealing U.S. military equipment, and trading with the Viet Cong. I greatly appreciate Mr. Mercy's help. Unfortunately, the trail was cold, and the only mention of this story to which I can refer readers is found in Douglas Valentine's book The Phoenix Program.

I appreciate *Armed Forces Journal* giving me permission to use an edited version of an article by Col. Robert D. Heinl, Jr., USMC (Ret), which appeared in its June 7, 1991 issue and to Janis Jorgensen, manager, Heritage Collection, U.S. Naval Institute, for the photo of Col. Heinl, which appears with it.

I am grateful to Michael Keating, editor of *The VVA Veteran*, for publicizing my interest in interviewing men that fought in the Vietnam War, and to Arthur Sharp, editor of *Old Breed News*, the publication of the First Marine Division Association, for letting his readers know of this interest. I am also grateful to Doris Williams of *Legion Magazine*, Kanata, Ontario, Canada, for insuring publication of my interest in interviewing Canadians that served, in combat, in U.S. forces, during the Vietnam War.

I am indebted to Allison Hackley Gahrmann of Benchmark II, LLC (benchmarkii.com) in Lincolnton, NC. for converting my manuscript into a publishable document, and to Capt. Kevin Spalding, USNR (Ret), who carefully read the manuscript and corrected my numerous keystroking errors.

I am also indebted to David L. Marchat of Ormond Beach, Florida, for ongoing help keeping my computer virus free, which enabled me to prepare the manuscript.

XII

# John David Blair
interview of February 21, 2016

My name is John D. Blair. The D is for David. I was born on November 7, 1945.

My father was James Marion Blair, and he was from Greensboro, North Carolina. He was career Army and stationed at Schofield Barracks, in Honolulu, on the island of Oahu, Hawaii. His specialty was ordnance. My mother was Elizabeth Arceo. She was Portuguese Hawaiian, from Hawaii, and her family lived on a pineapple plantation, where they worked. She had six brothers, and two of them joined the Air Force.

When my father met her, she was a hula dancer in the officers' club. He used to say that he bought her first pair of shoes. After she married my dad, she was a homemaker. He was a young chief warrant officer. He joined the Army when he was 17 and worked his way up. I think he was actually 16 when he joined. He got out as a chief warrant officer, after 23 years, and then died a couple of years later. He was at Pearl Harbor, during the Japanese attack, on December 7, 1941. My mother's relatives, that are alive now, still live in the Hawaiian Islands.

I have an older brother named James; we call him "Jim", and an older sister Sylvia Gorsuch. I'm the youngest. Each of us was born in the U.S., because my dad wanted us to be. I was born on Sullivan's Island, South Carolina, in a hospital. Each of us was carried back to Hawaii shortly after birth and lived on Oahu. I feel I was raised a native Portuguese Hawaiian. I lived in Oahu for my first 10 years and later, being an Army brat, moved to the States, to Okinawa, and back to the States.

Jim, my brother, served an enlistment in the Army. He was in combat, in Vietnam, with the 7th Cavalry, in 1965 and 1966. Vietnam affected him more than it did me. After his enlistment, he became a Methodist minister and served churches in northern Georgia for more than 30 years. He now serves as a supply minister.

I went to elementary school, at Schofield Barracks, up to the 6th grade. We lived at the entrance to Diamond Head. When my dad was stationed at Ft. Benning, we lived in Columbus, Georgia, and I went to St. Mary's Elementary School. Then we went back to Hawaii, and then to Okinawa, and then back to Columbus, Georgia, so I attended U.S. government schools in those places. I began my freshman year of high school at Columbus High School, and my dad retired at Ft. Benning I graduated in June 1963, which is why I call Columbus, Georgia, my home.

My father had a major heart attack, on December 21, 1962, and died when I was 16 and a senior in high school. After high school, I worked and went to Columbus College, on and off, and earned about 2-1/2-years of college credits. The Vietnam War was on, and everyone was patriotic and wanted to go, and I'd always wanted to be a marine. So, I joined the Marine Corps, in April of 1966, in Columbus, Georgia.

My brother had enlisted in the Army and was in Vietnam, at that time. I went to Parris Island, for recruit training. It was 13 weeks. From there, I went to Camp Geiger, for two weeks of individual combat training. I was classified as an 0311, a grunt, a rifleman, and the training we got was based on what we needed to know to fight the war in Vietnam. Ninety percent of the men I was trained with were sent to Vietnam, but not me.

When we finished, I got a top-secret clearance and was sent to the Marine Barracks, at Naval Air Station Cecil Field, in Jacksonville, Florida. My duty was at the ADT Center. The Marine detachment provided security there. We wore weapons and modified dress blues, on duty.

Above ground, the ADT Center was a room no more than 30-ft by 30-ft. To reach it people had to go through three sets of security gates and have special ID cards. There was one elevator in it. We searched everybody, and the groups of five or six would go down under ground in the elevator to an area that held about 100 people. It was like in a James Bond movie. It took an hour or so to get everyone that worked there underground every day. The people that worked under ground made conventional bombs and special weapons. When I was down there walking security, I saw them at work.

Above ground there were also igloos big enough to drive a semi in. They had about 20 of them, and they're all grassed-over, so you could not see them from the air, and they were fenced in with three security electric fences on about 100 acres. There was a road around them. Two platoons of Marines were stationed there. We ran security patrols over the igloos with bicycles with rifles stuck into a holster on each bicycle. The ADT Center was very unique, and it was stuck way back, in a wooded area, right across from the naval air station. You didn't know it was there. You had to drive a mile to get to the MP gate, and if you didn't have a clearance they would turn you around.

It really wasn't too bad living, being in the Marine Corps, at Cecil Field Marine Barracks. You worked eight hours and 16-hours off. You patrolled, and then we provided a security escort when the bombs and the warheads were carried to the aircraft carriers in Mayport Shipping Port, Jacksonville, Florida, to be loaded on the naval ships bound for Vietnam. We never knew what kind of bombs they were. They were all covered with canvas. Some of them were really big; some of them were not too big. We provided the escort for the tractor trailers that carried them to the naval station. We actually had loaded 50-cal. machine guns on each end of each trailer.

I was there from June of '66 to July of '67. Before I received orders for Vietnam, I had 30-days leave and went to Camp Pendleton, in California. At Camp Pendleton, you had 30 days of training for the type of fighting we would experience in Vietnam.

They had patrols and actually had one place where you were treated like a POW. In one of the mountains, they brought in a lot of mud, in a v-shaped area between two mountains. They built it up and put one little shack in it and barbed wire around it. It was probably no more than 20-yards deep and maybe 20-yards wide. They made you get in your boxer shorts with bare feet and dropped you off there at 12 o'clock at night. There were maybe 50 other guys in there. You couldn't leave for two days. They had big bowls of rice and some big bowls of carrots. The only thing that was really sanitary was they had portables where you could use a toilet outside. They treated you the way you would be treated, if you were POWs, except that they had a heated room and would let you go in there for a couple of hours. At the end of the two nights, at midnight, they gave you a pair of boots and they let you out, and they said, you've got to find your way back to the safe zone.

Then they taught you how to survive from snakes and insects. If you were out in the wilderness by yourself, this is what you could eat and this is how you prepare it. We learned to break down our weapon and put it together blindfolded within so many seconds.

From there we got shipped to Okinawa, in late October, on a commercial charter flight. They let us go into town for two days. It was like, 'Okay guys, enjoy these two days, 'cause some of you aren't gonna come back: maybe none of you come back.' Then we flew into Da Nang and it was quiet. There was no artillery coming in.

When we got off, we walked by troops that were waiting to get onto the plane to head home from Vietnam. The main thing I noticed, when I arrived, was the people waitin' to get on the plane. As I walked past them, even though they were young kids, they looked as if they had aged three years, and nobody was laughin'. They were serious.

From there they drove us up to Dong Ha, nearer to the Demilitarized Zone, the DMZ. It was nearer to the Marine rear area, and was where the 3rd Battalion, 4th Marine Regiment, 3rd Marine Division, was based, along with some other divisions. When I got there, I was by myself. I was going to India Company. The others on the truck went to other units. I noticed there were nice sandbags, and I walked to get a hot lunch under a tent. I was there for two days, and I was thinkin' this is a piece of cake. It was great. I was sleepin' in a cot, and I said Vietnam is not as bad as I thought.

The second morning, I got on a truck that took me up to Con Thien. Both were just south of the DMZ. There had just been a major battle at Con Thien. They were cleanin' up after it. The NVA, the North Vietnam Army tried to overrun 'em, and they had a big fight. It just ended before I got there. When I was at Da Nang, I noticed that there was a lot of wounded coming in, but I didn't know they were from Con Thien.

When I got to Con Thien we were in bunkers, because we were so close to North Vietnam that they would throw artillery in on you. It was pretty quiet, at that time. We were in a few skirmishes, but nothing major. I remember our Captain tellin' us this is not normal. I think the North Vietnam Army was preparin' for the Tet Offensive.

That's when I started eatin' C-Rations, and, after that, I ate nothin' but C-Rations, until I left. I ate C-Rations for 10 of my 13 months in Vietnam.

We ran patrols around Con Thien and up along the DMZ. Two weeks before Thanksgiving, India Company ran into a NVA company-size force. My platoon, the 3rd Platoon, provided rear security for the other platoons, in case the NVA decided to attack from the rear. We faced the rear and dug. It was scarier than being up front, because bullets would fly by us from behind. I was hoping I would not get hit in the back or head. A lot of casualties are caused by bullets passing you and hitting Marines coming up in support.

We were up in a free-fire zone. Where we were, if the bushes moved, I could unload a magazine on the bushes. I didn't have to ask permission. I could throw a grenade over there. We slept with our weapons. We always kept a loaded magazine with it. As long as you informed your squad leader and Lieutenant, you could go out to a fox hole and practice shootin' across the valley into the DMZ. Nobody did it regularly, but we could have. I remember one time when our platoon got a new 50-cal. machine gun. It was on a little hill, and we all went up and shot the 50-cal. across into the DMZ. There were no patrols in front of us, only the DMZ and the NVA.

There were no civilians up there. We fought strictly NVA: I mean people with uniforms. We didn't fight any black pajama people. We didn't have to worry about them or booby traps. This was by North Vietnam, on the border of Laos.

We heard rumors the NVA had Chinese advisors. We know the NVA had Chinese and Soviet weapons and ordnance, like the Chicom grenades, from China, that we could throw back, because it had a 10-second delay before exploding. They also had portable rocket launchers and the AK-47. The AK-47 was Soviet made and excellent. It never jammed the way our M16 rifles did. I have pictures of the Chinese and Soviet weapons we gathered after a battle.

My first kills came on December the 30th or 31st, 1967. We were goin' on patrol up to Camp Carroll. The company was on the move. We're leavin' Con Thien and goin' to Camp Carroll and Khe Sahn. I was walkin' point. When you walk point, you walk 100 yards ahead of the company, by yourself, going through the woods and the fields. And the reason you're that far out is that, if the enemy engages, you might be killed, but the company would know that you engaged, and you would save a lot of lives. And you had flankers too. Not everybody wanted to walk point, but when it came your time, you had to walk it.

Bein' a rookie Pfc. it was my time to walk point. As point, you go slow and quiet, about 100 yards ahead of your unit, through the jungle constantly lookin' for any sign of NVA and hopin' you see them before they see you. It is really intense being out there alone.

I was walkin' point, when we came up on the DMZ. Part of the DMZ is real tall grass and few trees. You knew that, on the other side, that's where the enemy was. It was kind of like patrolling the border of North Korea and South Korea. So, when I was walkin' point I see two NVA runnin' slow in the middle of the field, and they had the grass up on their helmets. I ran back to my company, to Capt. John Pritchard, and he said, 'Blair, what are you doin' back here? You're supposed to be up on point.'

I said, 'Sir, do we have any friendlies out here?'

He said, 'What do you mean?'

I said, 'I saw two NVA ahead in a field. What do you want me to do?'

He said, 'Kill the son of a bitches.'

As I'm goin' back up there through the woods, I'm thinkin', if there's two, there might be 20, or there might be a hundred. My father and I were hunters. He loved to deer hunt; he loved to rabbit hunt. My hunting skills came in then. I started sneakin' up real quiet and lookin', because I didn't know if I was goin' t' see 20 or 30 of 'em, or are they lookin' at me.

When I got up to the DMZ, about 30 yards ahead, I see them get up again and start coming towards a bush near me. We were wearin' big, heavy packs. You couldn't hardly even bring your gun up. They came up and I had a clear shot. The adrenaline was flowin', and I picked my M-16 to my shoulder, and I shot and killed both of them. They were probably 20, 25 yards away. I went up to them, and they were already dead, but I made sure they were. You don't just shoot 'em and leave 'em. You put a couple of more in them to make sure they're gone.

In those days, the thing was, if you took the belt from the first NVA soldier that you killed and wear it, you'll make it through Vietnam. First thing I did was take off that belt, and I put it on me and it fit. Of course, I weighed 150 or 145 lbs.

When I killed 'em, I moved back to the edge of the woods, and that's when the Company started coming up. I could hear them comin' up. I was just layin' there. They went over and looked at 'em and took information off of 'em. That night we camped near there, and they laid the two dead NVA soldiers right next to the path, and the word spread that Blair was the Marine who killed them.

We moved on to Camp Carroll, along Highway 9, which runs west to Khe Sahn. We would move for two or three days and sit for two or three days. We were kind of edging our way to Khe Sahn. It was reported there was high activity of NVA soldiers movin' south. The siege of Khe Sahn was goin' on, and we were on our way to reinforce Khe Sahn.

We stayed off Highway 9 and walked through some heavy terrain that you had to use machetes to cut through. A lot of people got leeches on them, but that's just part of combat. We were thinkin' it was to avoid bein' seen. We were thinkin' what difference does it make? They know we're comin' anyway. We wondered why we couldn't walk where it's normal to walk and just spread out.

We spent two days engaged in short skirmishes with the enemy, as we moved west along Highway 9. On January 25th, 1968, our 3rd Platoon was providing security, at the main bridge used by convoys bringin' supplies up Highway 9 to Khe Sahn. We were hit with small arms fire and mortar fire. There were two of our tanks there and the NVA were zeroed in on then. Several of our platoon members were wounded. I remember two in particular: One was Pfc. Gene Ogozalek, who was hit twice, but stood his ground. He was later medevaced to the hospital ship off Saigon. The other was Pfc. Mike Welch. I remember Danny 'Doc' Pomeroy, a corpsman, using buttons off his shirt and wire through the button holes to hold Welch's left arm together. Doc Pomeroy is still alive today.

When it was evening, on January 26th each company was on a hill, by the Cam Lo River. India Co. spent the night on a low rise, at the west end of this valley overlooking Highway 9 and the valley. Mike Co. was on a small hill at the east end of the valley near the wide creek bed that fed into the Cam Lo River, and Kilo and Lima Companies were north and west of Mike. Each company set up a defensive perimeter around its position. We were set up like a triangle on three separate hills overlooking Highway 9 that lay between the hills. We were 2 km north of Camp Carroll, at that point.

Between Mike and India was a creek that fed into the Cam Lo River, which was just west of India Co., and north and slightly west of Mike was a bridge over the creek. Between the bridge and India Co. was an open field with only grass and some bushes. Highway 9 ran east to west through this open field and valley.

My platoon was ordered to watch and control this bridge: to provide security for it. It was the only bridge in the valley, and, if it was destroyed, we couldn't get more convoys up to Khe Sahn.

In the next couple of days, North Vietnamese soldiers crossed the river. Most crossed at night, but we saw them coming across. They had a rope across the river and were holding on as they crossed to keep their footing. There were hundreds of 'em, and once they came over they got into this creek bed. A whole NVA battalion had gotten embedded in this creek bed, just west of Mike Co., on Mike's Hill and Lima Co.

Early on January 27th, we heard small arms fire coming from Mike's Hill, when there was some light. I was a corporal and a squad leader, and I told my squad this is not going to be a good day, and to clean the M-16s. I even joked this could be our last meal. I was always making light of things and keeping moral up with jokes, but I was also hiding my own fear.

They began assaulting Mike and Lima Companies' hills. During the morning we could hear NVA mortars and 105s firing. Why we never called artillery in on 'em, I'll never know.

The NVA were out of range of India Co.'s M-16s, but some of us fired at them anyway. One of our men, Cpl. Richard Kovalski raised his M-60 machine gun and began to fire at them. He killed some and the others scattered. Col. Mike Bendell, our battalion commander, called India Co. and told Capt. Pritchard Mike's Hill was being overrun and he needed for India Co. to come and help wipe out the NVA attackers in his rear area.

Capt. Pritchard told Lt. Stewart, 3rd Platoon commander, to move his platoon east and attack the NVA from behind. We knew this was a suicide mission, when Lt. Stewart told us we were going to fan out on both sides of Highway 9 and walk towards the enemy.

I told everybody in my squad to take as many magazines as you can carry, because we're probably not comin' back. We all knew it was a suicide mission. We could not do it and survive, because there's no cover. Third Platoon, my platoon, was to the right of Capt. Pritchard and 2nd Platoon was to his left. We were in an open field and Capt. Pritchard and his staff were on the road. 1st Platoon stayed on our hill to secure it and be available if needed.

Col. Bendell was yelling over the radio for India Company to attack. Capt. Pritchard was young and aggressive, so we marched down from the hill we were on and lined up in a rank, just like in the Civil War. Capt. Pritchard was walkin', with his whole staff, down the middle of the road. Richard Kovalski was the lead M-60 and he looked like a Mexican bandit with belts of rounds over his shoulders. He was a big guy and was about five yards ahead of Capt. Pritchard's group of about five guys.

Kovalski had his M-60 on fully automatic and was sweepin' the area in front of him and knockin' off gooks. Kovalski was the only person on the road that was not killed. That was probably because he was bending down to shoot NVA in their spider holes along the hedges on the roadside and bullets flew over him. He was layin' em out. He was hit in the foot, but not seriously and kept fightin' to the end.

Second platoon was in the field on the Captain's left side, and I was in the field, on his right side, with my squad. I was about 30 feet from him. My platoon was the lead platoon. Our 2nd Squad was to my right, and 3rd Squad brought up the rear.

The NVA knew we would come down the valley to help, when they assaulted Mike's Hill, and set a trap for us to walk into. The two platoons of India Company moved east in a rank, from left to right, and just then two NVA jumped up in front of 3rd Platoon and started to run east. Third Platoon's 3rd Squad fired and killed the two NVA almost immediately, but had begun to charge forward. Then the other Marines on the field advanced screamin'. As their advance gained speed, a loud battle cry came from them.

At that time, we saw NVA jump up and run, and everybody was screamin', 'Hey, let's get 'em!' And we ran after them, but we kind of stayed in line. All of a sudden NVA over on our left opened up on us with machine guns, including a 50-cal. machine gun emplaced on top of a rise on the other side of the creek. And the NVA along the creek jumped up, from hidden positions, and killed most of the patrol. They killed Capt. Pritchard, another staff sergeant, and Gunny Mikatis. Radioman Bernard Stark and a few other grunts were also shot. Stark lived, even though he was shot twice in the chest. I turned and looked, and I saw Capt. Pritchard and four men with him hit. They were just blown apart. You could see the blood just splatterin'.

Capt. Pritchard won the Navy Cross for that action. He was from Oklahoma City, and was new in our company. The word was out Capt. Pritchard was married to a Playboy Bunny, and we had been trying to find out which issue of Playboy magazine she was in, so our parents would send it to us. Never got it.

Rounds were flyin' by us left and right with a zinging zip sound that you never forget. Guys were getting' hit. Marines were dead, wounded or dying all around us. I told my squad to put their weapons on fully automatic and lay down fire, which would enable the other half of us to crawl fast to cover in the thick brush 30- to 40- yards ahead. We had to get to that hedge grove that was by the creek and across the creek from Mike's Hill. We had to move the NVA out of the hedge grove, because that was the only security we could have.

Each of us had triple the normal amount of ammo on us that we normally carried. We had our flak jacket on and our ammo was in bandoliers across our flak jackets. All we carried was ammo, and each man also had six to eight grenades.

One man would lay down automatic fire and we would crawl 20 yards. Then another man would lay down automatic weapon' fire and we'd crawl another 20 yards. When we got to the hedge grove, Doc Ralph Wheeler, a medical corpsman, came up to help a badly wounded man ahead of me, and an NVA came out of a spider hold and shot Doc Wheeler right in the face. We didn't even know there was a spider hole there, it was so well covered with grass. Doc was about 5-ft from me, and I watched him reach for his canteen, as if to take a drink, and he fell back, as his face melted. His face didn't explode from that shot, it was like someone poured hot wax on his face. That's probably my most vivid memory of Vietnam. I dropped the gook with an automatic burst.

At this point, my only thought was how was I going to survive? I had to find a way to survive this battle, so it became all about John Blair. But when your leadership is gone and you are totally confused and alone, that's when our combat training kicks in and you react as taught. I was focused on staying alive and praying to God and even talkin' to my mother. My father was dead, and I did not want some Marines in dress blues going to tell my mother I was dead or wounded. I didn't think she could handle that news. I kept asking God to give me courage.

The screaming around me, and seein' my buddie's dead and the wounded lying in the field was something I will never forget.

I finally made it to hedge grove at the east end of the field, and I was alone. I start crawlin' in it. I had my M-16, and I noticed my rifle had jammed. Taped to its barrel was a 10- to 12 -inch part of a cleanin' rod. In case a round was defective and jammed, you'd take that cleanin' rod, and you'd slide it down your barrel and knock the round out. Jams would happen a lot when the barrel heated up, and all of us had a short cleanin' rod taped to our rifles' barrels.

I took the cleanin' rod off and was using it, and an NVA soldier raised up in front of me with his weapon pointed at me. I swung my rifle up, with the cleanin' rod still in it and pointed it at him. To my surprise, he threw up his hands and surrendered. This was observed by another Marine and documented. It was later written up in the *Marine Corps Gazette*.

I walked him about 10-yards back to where they brought in the wounded, and I put 'im there, and everybody there yelled, 'Kill the son of a bitch! Why are you bringing 'im here? Kill 'im!'

I just kicked him down and said, 'You do what you want with him.' They didn't kill him, and I received credit for the capture and was awarded a bonus R & R to Singapore for it.

For some reason, I went back toward the battle. It was just an instinct. I get to this creek leadin' up to the bridge, and it's got a horseshoe bend in it. There's a sandy bottom in this creek and not much water. I slide to the bottom and walk around this bend and here's two NVA soldiers comin' at me. I turn and run. They turn and run. I climbed up the embankment and lay there prayin'. I was worried about somebody comin' up behind me. I looked down there, and all of a sudden they come walkin' around the corner. One lays down and the other gets up in the hedge grove behind him up on the bank to set up an ambush, and one of them laid down there like he was dead.

I could easily turn around and go back, but for some reason, I slid back down the bank. When I got within 10-ft of them, I shot the guy layin' there. I shot on full automatic, and I just kept goin' up the hill and shot the guy in the bushes above the creek, and he fell into the creek bed. At that point, I was hyperventilating. I was so scared. I was talkin to God and my mother, and I started thinking, which is a bad thing to do. You don't think. You react. I could hear the firing. I could hear the action. You can never forget it.

So, I came around the corner of the hedges and there was my friend, Sgt. Bob Espinola, sneakin' around the same corner the NVA soldiers had come around. Bob was right guide of our platoon, at the time. He was from Boston, Massachusetts, but he lives in California now. I said, 'What the hell are you doin'.'

He said, 'Where in the hell are we? Man, I'm so happy to see you.'

I said, 'Do you know I just killed two NVA?'

He said, 'I saw them, heard the automatic fire, and decided to see what was going on, because I knew it was an M-16 and another Marine.'

We didn't know where we were. We decided to crawl up the bank from the creek bed, because we could hear the yelling and gun fire. When we got to the top, we looked to our left and could see Highway 9 and could also hear and see the NVA guy on a 50-cal. machine-gun open up on our Marine company. We were 50 or maybe 100 yards ahead of our company, and we looked to the left and saw dead Marines from my platoon laying on that field we had to cross. You could hear people screamin' and hollerin'. It was sad. It was sad and will always be imbedded in my memory. It doesn't go away.

The NVA's 50-cal. machine gun and some of their men were in a position across the open area between us and the other side of the road. They were firing at Marines that was still laying in the field. Lt. Stewart, our 3rd Platoon leader, was sittin' and in pain from a wound in his left leg. Cpl. Bob Harriman, his radioman, was by his side. Cpl. Harriman told me later Col. Bendell was on the radio screaming why India Co. wasn't pushin' forward. Harriman said he yelled back 'Sir, it's because the officers and the gunny are either dead or wounded. We're doin' the best we can against superior fire power.' India Co. was no longer an organized unit.

Bob and I knew what we had to do. We decided we were going to go take out the NVA 50-cal. machine gun, before we lose everybody. We actually sort of hugged each other and said our goodbyes. We knew we'd never see each other again. We had to crawl 50 yards in the open to get to where the 50-cal. was, cause our men were tryin' to get the 50-cal., and they couldn't get it.

I suddenly realized I had left my rifle back at the creek bed, where I met Espinola. We were half way to the NVA 50 cal, and I told Bob I left my rifle at the creek bed. He said 'Screw you, I'm gettin' to the hedge grove along Highway 9. Go get your rifle.' So, I crawled back and got my rifle and we went back toward the 50-cal. NVA were shootin' at us. I feel they knew we were there, but they couldn't see us and communicate with the 50-cal. Small arms fire was zinging by us.

We got to the road and there was real big brush. The machine gun was on the other side on a little knoll, and you could see the barrel. The NVA were dug in there, and you could hear them talkin'.

At that time, a chopper gunship was hovering over us and pointin' to the NVA's 50-caliber's position ahead of us, and waving to us to go get 'em. They were shootin' the helicopter's 50-cal gun at the NVA, and the NVA shot the gunner and the co-pilot, and the pilot banked and left, and the chopper sputtered out of there.

I had four grenades and Bob had three. The first grenade I threw hit my helmet and rolled back, and Bob and I looked at each other and said holy shit! God was with us. I tell you, if you didn't pray over there, you didn't believe in God. That grenade would normally blow up and send scrap-metal into us, but most of it blew the opposite way. So, when it blew, we threw two grenades across the road. The dirt road was wide enough for two semi-trucks or two tanks to go side by side.

We threw more grenades, at the 50-caliber's position. As soon as we threw them, I don't know how many NVA jumped up and came towards us, and we killed all of them. We were in such thick cover the NVA had to come out in the open to get to us. Why they just didn't shoot at the hedge grove we were in I will never know. They charged us and we had our weapons on automatic and we laid them out there. The M-16's magazine had 16 or 20 rounds, but what we did was we taped two magazines together with one up and one down, and switched magazines when one was empty. We could switch magazines in two seconds. Most of us always tape out magazines like that because it was quick to reload.

We were tucked in the brush, but we could see out. In order to throw the grenades, we had to move out of the brush, and throw, and then get back in. We threw two more grenades, and they kept firing. We were out of grenades, and three more NVA came at us from our right side, and almost blindsided us, except I saw 'em coming and we laid them out.

We continued to fire at them, to keep pressure on them. Bob and I took turns rising up to fire. Once the shooting slowed and stopped, we knew NVA were retreating and leaving their dead. We only had a few magazines left, but were in a good spot and stayed there until the evening. When we could see reinforcements coming in by helicopter and the gunships circling the area and not being fired on, we knew it was over.

We got up and ran across Highway 9 to see the destroyed 50-cal. position. Most NVA in it were already dead, except for two or three that were badly wounded, and we emptied our magazines on them.

While Bob and I attacked toward the road and the 50-cal., Lt. White led his men east and south, under heavy fire, and reached the creek bed and the bottom of Mike's Hill and relieved Mike Co.

Bob and I had a few scratches on us, but that was all. Then we helped stack the NVA bodies near the bridge and placed dead Marines by each other in body bags, and waited for the choppers to remove the wounded and dead. That battle went on from early morning until it was dark. It was reported the Marines lost over 100 guys killed there and many wounded. We thought we killed 200 to 300 NVA. They say the Battle for Mike's Hill was one of the longest battles in Vietnam. It felt like it would never end.

We walked slowly back to the India Co. hill, and I notice I was bleedin' through my pants, because of scrap-metal fragments and rough terrain. The wounds were only surface ones and I refused to let a corpsman write up my wound. Because my mother was alone, I felt she would be a basket case, if Marines came to her door and said I was wounded, plus I felt only if I got shot would I deserve a purple heart. A surface scratch was nothing compare to what I saw, and I did not want to temp the devil at that time by being written up for a purple heart. Never talked about it.

*Author's note: John David Blair and Robert Espinola were each awarded a Silver Star Medal for their gallantry. The Marine Corps' award citation for John David Blair reads as follows:*

*'For conspicuous gallantry and intrepidity in action while serving as a Squad Leader with Company I, Third Battalion, Fourth Marines, Third Marine Division in connection with operations against the enemy in the Republic of Vietnam. On the afternoon of 27 January 1968, while conducting a search-and-destroy operation north of Camp J. J. Carroll, Corporal Blair's platoon came under a heavy volume of automatic weapons and recoilless rifle fire from a large North Vietnamese Army force and was pinned down. Reacting instantly, he skillfully maneuvered his squad forward and boldly led a determined assault on the enemy positions, personally killing five enemy soldiers and capturing two. As the platoon resumed its advance, it again became pinned down by accurate enemy fire. Quickly*

*maneuvering his squad to an advantageous position, Corporal Blair immediately directed his men to deliver a heavy volume of suppressive fire on the enemy and, accompanied by another Marine, crawled toward the hostile force. Completely disregarding his own safety, he courageously moved across the hazardous area and destroyed the hostile positions with hand grenades, thereby enabling his unit to continue its mission. His heroic actions and aggressive fighting spirit inspired all who observed him and were instrumental in the accomplishment of his unit's mission. By his courage, bold initiative and unwavering devotion to duty in the face of great personal danger, Corporal Blair upheld the highest traditions of the Marine Corps and of the United States Naval Service.'*

When we reached India Company's hill, there wasn't hardly anybody left out of 2nd Platoon. That night, we all just went off to our own quiet places, because we were exhausted and really wanted to be alone and sleep. I wasn't even hungry and didn't eat, which is unusual for me. It was an emotional night for me. I can't speak for anyone else and didn't ask how anyone else felt.

The next day we open up with guys remaining and discussed the things we did during the battle. We laugh about some things and prayed for the guys that didn't make it and the ones that were wounded. I hit my knees several times, behind a bush on the hill, and told God I was his to do what he wanted with, because he spared me with only minor wounds.

India Co. was so low on men that they were probably going to put us with another company. They didn't do that. In fact, they made Bob Espinola platoon sergeant and David Turnage a sergeant and made me platoon right guide. I got promoted to sergeant not too long after that. We didn't get a Lieutenant till July, so we kind of ran our platoon for three or four months.

Each company was hit badly, but Mike Co. was hit the worst, because they were closer to the creek bed and were hit by a surprise attack by NVA that came up at them from there, when the battle began.

We went back to Camp Carroll and replacements joined India Co. We ran patrols, around Camp Carroll, for a few weeks and then marched to Khe Sahn to reinforce it. While we were at Khe Sahn, we went into the nearby mountains and to different hills around it. On patrol, we did some major hill climbing and hiking near the DMZ and stayed close to Laos. We set up camp, on some hills, and engaged the NVA in small skirmishes that lasted 30 minutes to two hours.

We were at Khe Sahn in March and part of April. The runway was still down. It was cut up by artillery. The only way they could re-supply was for the C-130s to drop stuff on the runway. No choppers could come in, because of the artillery and small arms fire. We took artillery almost every other day, for a while, except for one day when we received over 100 rounds of artillery.

Khe Sahn was a mess, because of the siege. It was a red-dirt shit hole and the rats were everywhere, and the NVA had left several of their dead outside the Khe Sahn perimeter, and their bodies were rotting.

Some time, in February, after Mike's Hill, I think we were in some place in the area of Khe Sahn, and we were being hit by snipers. They were pickin' us off one by one, and we couldn't take the sniper out. We had fired mortars to get him, but we couldn't get him. So, the Captain told me Blair you take a squad and go get that sniper. We knew where he was firing from, and we had to get there before he fired. He always opened up at us in the mornin', so we had to leave at 12 o'clock at night and go across three or four rice paddies, in the valley to reach the area where he fired from.

I think I was only a corporal then and just promoted to squad leader. We got to one part of a rice paddy, and we were sittin' there. Kovalski was with us, and morning started comin' up and the sniper was firin' again. He was

30-yards away, and we could hear him firin', but we couldn't see him.

We had to go through another rice paddy to get to him. My Captain was on the radio yellin' at me, 'He just shot another man. Blair, get that guy.' He was raisin' hell, but we were scared to death to go over there. It was early Sunday mornin', and we had to cross this rice paddy to get to the sniper. We thought we were leavin' ourselves wide open. If there was a sniper there, there was someone there protectin' him, and we were only six guys, and we were going to get killed.

So, we crawled up through the rice paddy to the raised side of it, and he's still firin'. We put all our weapons on fully automatic, and Ski did that with the M60 machine gun, and we just opened up and shot everything in front of us that we could shoot down. We fired low and high. We emptied everything we had, knocking down small trees and bushes. It sounded like a war zone.

He didn't fire any more, and we went up to where he had fired from, but we couldn't find him. We looked everywhere, but could not locate a body. We probably scared the shit out of him, and he took off. The Captain was on the radio sayin', 'Did you get him? Did you get him?' I said we're tryin' to verify, and he said, 'What do you mean you're tryin' to verify?'

We were afraid there were other NVA there, but we slowly crawled up there, and we couldn't find his body. We couldn't find anything, and, when the Captain asked again if we got the sniper, I lied. I told the Captain, 'Yes sir, we got him.'

And the men in my squad looked at me and said, 'What the hell are you doin' sayin' we got him?'

I just said it off the cuff, and I was prayin' don't let him shoot any more.

When we came back, we were like heroes. We know we're movin' out the next day and all six of us were sittin' there thinkin' please don't shoot. We decided if a sniper shot again, we'd just tell 'em it was a new sniper, but there were no more sniper shots while we were there. I was promoted to sergeant, shortly after this incident.

I caught malaria in the rice paddies. That next night, I had malaria real bad. They choppered me out to Dong Ha, and I got a shot and was takin' the orange pills when I got back.

Bob Henderson, who was my assistant squad leader, he walked up the hill, the same way we walked up for company meetings. Your assistant squad leader took your place, if you were sick. That morning after I had been medevaced for Malaria, Bob Henderson was on his way to the meeting and stepped on an old mine that had been there for years. It blew him to bits. Paul Harris and Bill Waldrup got shrapnel in them, because they were walkin' with him. We all had been walkin' that same trail for three days. If I had been there, that wouldn't have happened. They had to pick his parts up with a shovel. That really upset me. You know, you think back and think maybe that was the reason why I caught malaria. Incidents like that bother. That's why a lot of people get PTSD.

When I went to Vietnam, I broke up with my girlfriend. I was single. I didn't have any debt. I was wide open to the training. I just wanted to survive the war. Being single was one of the best things to be. While I was over there, one guy got a letter from his wife that she wrote to one of her lovers and put into an envelope addressed to him by mistake. That kind of thing really did happen to guys that were married or had girlfriends in the States.

I was one of the only ones in my company that went on three R & Rs while I was there. I went to Singapore once and Australia twice, because I was single, and I could afford to do it. It didn't cost a lot to go on R & R over there. If you spent two or three hundred dollars, you spent a lot of money.

The next big battle India Co. fought was Foxtrot Ridge. At the time, I didn't know the date when it happened, but I learned since it was the first week of July

1968, and that the ridge is about 4 Km south of Khe Sahn and just south of Highway 9.

We would always set up a perimeter defense, with a single strand of barbed wire, if we had it, around the ridge's top. A young Marine with a flamethrower burned off vegetation where we wanted to place the wire. His flamethrower jammed, and he got down on one knee to fix the problem. He began to unscrew something on top of it, and I asked him if what he was doing was safe. He said it was, but I told my squad to get far back. A few seconds after we moved back, the flammable liquid in damned thing blew out of the place he had opened, and he was instantly covered in flames. He started to run along the ridge screaming. Another Marine and I ran after him, and I was able to catch up and hit him in the back and knock him down. Then we rolled him in the dirt and put out the flames. His clothing was burned off and his whole body was burned and even his privates were burned off. He was screaming in pain and asking us to do something to stop the pain. He was carried out on a chopper, but he died.

Another incident, during 1968, happened in the A Shau Valley. We were supposed to be a blocking force, but they inserted us into the wrong co-ordinates, and began to extract us, on CH-47 Chinook helicopters, to insert us into the right co-ordinates.

The extraction did not go smoothly, because there was really tall elephant grass on the landing zone. When the Chinooks' landed, the jet engines under their rear rotors started grass fires. We were in a defense perimeter around the landing zone, and, as more Marines were extracted, we tightened the perimeter. The fire spread and started to cook off small arms rounds that had been dropped. That made the men nervous and there was radio chatter about snipers and incoming small arms fire. That was when a red smoke that had dropped from some Marine's pack was ignited by the spreading fire.

We were comin' up this hill. I remember like it was yesterday. There was supposedly some NVA on the other side of the saddle in this hill. There was grass and bomb craters there. As we were approaching the top, somebody had popped the wrong smoke.

Two Sky Hawks, from a carrier-based Marine air wing were in the air over us and heard the radio chatter and saw a group of 50 to 70 troops on the ground where none of our men were supposed to be, they thought we were NVA. When they saw the red smoke plume, the first one rolled in and dropped his 250-lb bombs on us. The explosions were tremendous. It wounded or killed a lot of Marines.

The men fired at the Sky Hawk, as it tried to gain altitude, and a sergeant was screaming into the radio for the second pilot not to bomb us, and trying to get the Marines to stop firing at the first Sky Hawk. The Sky Hawks were dropping bombs on the lower part of the other side of the hill.

I was comin' up the hill, with my platoon, and some Marines had reached the top of the hill. I could see the bombs comin' out, and all of a sudden, bombs hit the top of the hill. About 18 Marines were killed and others were wounded.

When the bomb hit, it was so powerful it threw me at least 30 feet, and I landed down below the base of the hill. My ears were ringin', and I thought I had lost my legs, 'cause I couldn't feel my legs. I didn't even want to look down. When I did, they were there, and I didn't even have any blood on me. After a while, I got up and walked up on the hill.

The first Marine I came upon was pinned against a tree by a big piece of metal. Bomb shrapnel had severed the leg of another Marine from the calf up and cauterized it. He was still alive, and we were tryin' to talk to him. Another Marine had been hit in the head. We carried our dead to where CH-47s were landing and taking off. We had them lined up to go out on one of the last choppers to leave.

While we were there, a civilian news photographer was taking photos of the dead Marines. It's documented that I moved in front of him and took my rifle off safety, and chambered a round, and put the muzzle in his face, and told him to drop the camera. He wouldn't, till he realized that a dead civilian photographer, especially one that was taking pictures of dead Marines, was no big deal to me or any other Marine there. Then he dropped his camera, and we opened it and took out the film. We gave him back his camera and sent him back with the dead. A few minutes later, we lifted out.

That Sky Hawk pilot, from what I understand, got a chopper ride to our company. He knew what happened, and he thought he was to blame for it. Capt. Sexton told me the pilot stopped flyin' after that. I met someone, at a Marine Corps reunion that was one of the pilots in that attack.

We were inserted in another place, on the ridge, and prepared our positions very well. We dug foxholes and had one man to a foxhole, but near each other and strung barbed wire around our perimeter.

Before dawn, on July 5th, we were attacked by two companies of NVA. They used automatic shoulder weapons, machine guns, and grenades as they attacked. We used all our weapons, including mortars, against them and our company commander, Capt. M. A. Sexton, called in Marine artillery on them.

At one time, they breached our defense, but I saw them and crawled under our own barbed wire and moved my men to higher ground. I was a sergeant then. We couldn't see the NVA well enough to fire accurately at them, so we all jumped on top of our bunker and opened fire on them. They started to throw grenades at us, but we kept firing and some of my men even threw some of their Chinese-communist grenades back at them. We beat them back, and they left 12 of their men dead, at our wire.

The heaviest NVA attack hit our 3rd Platoon. A staff sergeant was leading us. We beat back that attack, and the NVA left 63 of their dead in front of 3rd Platoon's position. We lost two dead and several wounded.

We were lucky to beat them back, because, when our Captain called for help, he was told the choppers couldn't come in, because there was too much ground fire. We were told Broken Arrow, which meant no reinforcements would come to help us. India Co. was not expected to survive this attack.

For two hours, the NVA tried to overrun our positions. Then they broke off the battle and withdrew. I did not know it when we were fighting, but learned a long time after that the battle lasted for nine hours. It happened, during the night and early morning.

The next morning, we searched outside our perimeter and found 107 dead NVA. We also picked up 75 NVA automatic weapons, two heavy machine guns, a lot of Chinese-communist-made hand grenades, anti-tank projectiles, and many documents. I learned years later that altogether the Marines lost 13 men dead and 44 wounded in that battle.

Early on June 15th, my battalion, the 3rd Battalion, 4th Marines, was in a defensive position about 12 km southeast of Khe Sahn, during Operation Scotland II, when units of the NVA 325th Division attacked. We were greatly outnumbered, but repulsed them, after hard fighting. We lost 17 men dead and 61 wounded and killed 219 and captured 11. We recovered a lot of enemy weapons from the battle area, after fighting ended. Those included 23 crew-served weapons and 55 small arms.

When we went into Laos, for the first time, we were going to go in and take over. It was during the summer, in '68, and it was hot, but I don't remember just when that was. We came up on a canteen truck, on the side of a road. It was camouflaged, and we took the camouflage off it. In it, they had Coca Cola cans, no ice, American potato chips, and a lot of other American snack food. We took it over, but you say to yourself how in the hell did they get this stuff.

We came upon a dead elephant. The NVA used elephants to carry supplies on the Ho Chi Mihn Trail, and they'd shoot 'em when the elephants weren't able to carry for them anymore.

We found out how they would infiltrate at night to get by us and get supplies into the south to the black pajama people. They would have one person run with comm wire, curing the day, and, at night, the people carryin' the supplies would hold on to that wire with one hand and follow the trail. They did this from place to place, along the trail they were on.

During B-52 attacks, they would go into a tunnel and on each side of the tunnel they had beds stacked up five and six high. They would go into those prepared places in a mountain and sleep, until the attack was over.

We had other skirmishes, but nothing else major. A battle could last three minutes or two hours. In one of the battles that was more like a skirmish, the Army had flew into this hill to take it, and the hill got overrun. The Army left their dead up there. Two days after that, we were sent up there to get the bodies. Marines don't do that. We don't care if it costs us another life, we go get our dead.

We make sure everybody's accounted for. That's why it took us so long, when we did the bodies. We had to make sure that the dog tags fit the person that was there. If they didn't have dog tags, we had to find out who they were.

The body bags were the saddest part, but you just had to go through it. We had a sayin' over there, better him than me. That's just how you lived, when you were over there.

I remember one time our company got stranded on a hill for three days without food or water. The monsoons came, so we had to buckle down. They couldn't get any supplies in, and it rained so bad that two guys would put large, flat rocks together and lay a poncho on it. Then they'd take sticks and raise up another poncho over the one on the rocks. It was a canopy. They lay on the bottom poncho, and the water would flow under it and downhill around the rocks. We lived like that for two, three days. When they finally dropped in food, it was melted ice cream in Dixie Cups. Capt. Sexton was so pissed off, he called headquarters and asked what the hell was this? He said this must be for the Army guys: we need real food. We want C-Rations!

One time, I was told to take some of my men and set the Claymore mines up. I said 'we can't set 'em up sir, 'cause there's no C-4 in 'em.' That was because we would take the Claymores, open the backs up, take out the C-4 and cut it in sections. Everyone carried a little C-4. When you light it, it would boil water in seconds, instead of using those tablets that take forever to heat.

We were sittin' together another time, and I remembered we had been told we could take roots and squish 'em and put 'em in the water and heat'en up. So, I took the roots and I mixed them in there, and I boiled the roots, and it was like broth. The other men said, 'I'm not going to drink it. Let's see you drink it, Blair.' I drank it and my lips swelled up real big. It looked like bee stings and felt numb. These things scare you more than a bullet. Eventually the swelling subsided.

I remember when I got an insect bite on my belly. It was just the size of a quarter. I woke up the next mornin' and it was the size of a big red plate. I went to the corpsman and he put some salve on it and it eventually went away. When I was over there, I always wore white crew socks my mother sent me. And she always sent me a wash cloth, tooth paste, and a new tooth brush. That's what I wanted her to send me. I wanted to keep my teeth clean and my genitals clean. My brother asked me what I wanted him to send me and I had him send me half a pint of liquor. If you sent cookies, they'd be hard as a rock, by the time they got there.

Another time, we were coming into a hot LZ, and the pilot landed ahead of our Marine company in the middle of a field surrounded by NVA. We were flown in on a Chinook. The NVA killed the pilot and the two 50-cal. door gunners on our chopper. We always landed with the back door down, and I had my squad put our weapons on automatic and we ran out the back-door firing on fully automatic towards our unit. We had gun ship support or we would have never made it. Shit like that happened sometimes. We were Blessed and lucky. It wasn't our time.

When a man had about a month left, they put him in down time. They would put him in Dong Ha and you worked out of there. When my turn came, I was there for about two weeks, and they called me back out to the bush. Lt. Dick Bartolomea, 3rd Platoon commander said, 'Blair, what the hell are you doin' here?' I said they told me you needed some people, so they sent me back out.

We had a lull then. You didn't fight all the time. When there was no fightin', we had some great fun. You were gambling, talkin', playin' cards, and reading mail from home, or writin' letters, but you were always out in the bush. What kept everybody sane is that you were with most of the same guys for 13 months, although replacements came and went individually and not as units, and Vietnam was a beautiful place.

Lt. Bartolomea had them send a chopper to get me out of there. I said, 'Where is he going to land? We're down in the valley.'

He said they were going to drop a rope down with a harness on its end, and haul me up in. I said, 'I'm not doin' that. If there's a sniper here, I'm a dead man.' I said, 'I don't want to be shot in a harness hangin' from a chopper.'

He said, 'You've got to go.' So, he sent some guys around to watch for snipers. When I was being pulled up, that was the scaredest I've ever been. I just knew someone was goin' to pick me off, but they didn't.

I didn't have time to change clothes, before they flew me from Dong Ha to Da Nang in a chopper. When I got on to the commercial airliner, I was funky. They put me in first class and we flew to Okinawa. I finished my tour in Vietnam in November 1968.

We were on Okinawa for two or three days, and, because I was a sergeant, an E-5, you could go out the gate into town: especially being a combat veteran and havin' a Silver Star, because they knew who was there. I had a great time on Okinawa. There was only one guy there that I had gone to Vietnam with, and he and I talked, and it got a little emotional at times.

I came, from Okinawa, to L.A., on an Eastern Airlines' commercial flight, and was sittin' in a bar, at the airport, havin' a drink with a Marine named Woody that came back on the same flight and was also headed for Atlanta. Two long-haired hippie guys and two long-haired hippie girls came by, and one of the hippie guys takes a beer off the counter and pours it over my leg and says, 'You kill any more babies lately?' I looked at Woody and said what's this all about. He said, 'Blair, let it go. Let's just get home and forget about all this crap.'

We were over in Vietnam for 13 months and we didn't know what was goin' on in the U.S. You didn't have e-mail or a TV. You didn't know what was goin' on. Even when I went on R & R, I didn't look at a TV. We had no idea that protests against the Vietnam War were goin' on.

With the Silver Star, the Corps' gave me a choice of three duties: Kaneohe Bay, Hawaii; Vegas, and recruiting duty, and then they sent me to DI school, at Parris Island. I was so pissed off. I went through all the training to become a DI. It was twice as hard as recruit training. If recruits had to run three miles, you had to run six; if they had to climb the rope in 30 seconds, you had to climb it in 25; and you had to go through the obstacle course quicker than anybody else, because the DI had to show them everything they had to do.

At the DI school, one instructor is the senior DI and the other is junior DI. The senior DI is mostly a weapons expert and the junior DI is a physical training type. I was a physical training type and was assigned to 2nd Platoon. When I would not extend my duty station at Paris Island for another 2 years, they had me re-assigned. Before I was re-assigned, the commanding officer asked me, if I'd be his driver till he reassigned me. Then he sent me to Washington, DC, to a high-security, de-coding center, where they break codes from other countries. I wore modified dress blues there, and I was platoon sergeant. It was right across from American University. It was really good duty: one day on and two days off. I took some classes, at American University, while I was there.

When I got my Navy Achievement Medal, in 1969, up in Washington, D.C., they made a big deal about it. The medal was presented at a ceremony.

They offered me seventy-one hundred dollars to stay in. I was seated with the Colonel and he said, 'You've got the Star. We need leaders like you to go to Vietnam.'

I said, 'If you can promise me I won't go back to Vietnam, I'll stay in.' My father always told me, you either stay in as an officer or get the hell out, but if he was still alive then he'd probably made me stay in, because not too many people make E-6, Staff Sergeant, in four years.

In Vietnam, I was in three major battles and many skirmishes. The major battles were at Mike's Hill, Foxtrot Ridge, and The Saddle. Skirmishes included Camp Carroll; Khe Sahn; Alpha 3; Cam Lo Hill; C-2; Hill 689; Con Thien; Dong Ha; Hill 552; Phui Nui; Firebase Shepherd; and LZ Stud, at Vandegrift.

In addition to the Silver Star Medal, I received the Combat Action Ribbon; Navy Achievement Medal with Combat V; Vietnamese Service Medal with four stars; Meritorious Unit Citation; Good Conduct Medal; National Defense Medal; and Vietnamese Campaign Medal with device.

Before I joined the Marines, I had no guidance, after my father died. I worked for the Coca Cola Company part time. My next-door neighbor was a supervisor, at Coca Cola, and he took me under his wings and tried to make sure I stayed out of trouble, but I was in and out of trouble. But in those days, in a town like Columbus, you'd always get a second chance. They knew my mother's situation and had known my father, so I was getting second chances. But sooner or later, I was probably going to get in a lot of trouble. What the Marines taught me was responsibility and hard work. I matured in the Marines.

When I got home, I didn't have to explain anything to my buddies. The Silver Star had been written up in the paper. All my friends knew about it, and I didn't have to explain. My mother's friends made a big deal out of it, but I put away all that Vietnam stuff. Reports of a lot of my actions in Vietnam were sent to my mother, without my knowledge. There were articles in the *Marine Corps Gazette*, and *Sea Tiger*. My mother saved them and also every letter I wrote to her. I cherished those letters. My mother passed away of cancer in 1993.

When I came home to Columbus, Georgia, my mother had moved, and I didn't even know where I lived. I had to call my buddy to tell me where I lived. Then I started workin', for a company called Broyhill Furniture Rentals. I worked for them for about nine years and worked my way up.

On June 6, 1970, I married Diane Andre. She was from St. Petersburg, Florida, but was working in Atlanta, when I met her. We make our home in Canton, Georgia. We've been married for 45 years. Our daughter is April Self and our sons are John David Blair, Jr. and Michael Andre Blair. We also have a grandson and a granddaughter.

Then I became Executive Director of the Trib Group, the rental industry buying group, and was there for almost 15 years. In 2008, I went into sales, as Vice President of Sales for PTS Financial Group. My boss Tony Farrell, is owner and CEO, and was a Marine, so I'm sure that as long as my health's good, I'll continue workin'.

A few years ago, I joined Marine Corps League Detachment 1311, in Woodstock, Georgia. It has been very rewarding to talk and meet with other fellow Marines.

In 2005, we were able to contact at least fifteen of my Marine buddies from India Co. that I served with in Vietnam in 1967-1968. We had our first reunion in 2006 in Atlanta and have been meeting once a year since, in different states. After my first reunion, I began to put up these photos and medals here in my den.

In September 2012, Richard Kovalsky, an M60 machine gunner and squad leader, in India Co., attended a Marine Corps League reunion, in San Diego. It was the first time in over 45 years he met and discussed Vietnam with us. Rich and I had been very close, and I spent time, at his house, in Haverstraw, New York, after getting out of the Corps. After that reunion, he took his own life.

I talked with him two days before he shot himself, and he was depressed then. I told my wife I might need to go see him. I even asked Ski if he needed me to come, and he said, 'I will get through this.'

Nina, his fiancé, said being with us brought too many memories back and Rich was more emotional than ever before. Then his mother died suddenly, and it caused him to snap. Rich had PTSD before the reunion, and the reunion just brought to the surface all that he kept inside so long.

We just had one India Company reunion out in Prescott, Arizona, and have another planned this year for October 7th to 9th, in Pensacola, Florida. There are about 17 of us guys, from India Company, that try to stay together. All our families and friend are really close. We all have a special wooden plaque that says 'India Company 3/4, Brothers Forever! Once A Marine Always a Marine. Semper Fi!'

Richard Kovalski (left) and John Blair, in a bunker, at Con Thien, before Christmas, in December 1967

During a respite from combat, at Con Thien, in November 1967, men of India Company, 3rd Battalion, 4th Marines enjoy sunshine and relaxation between skirmishes. John Blair is the Marine in the middle who leans on his elbow while another Marine rests his arm on his shoulder.

John Blair stands watch, on a hill, at Khe Sahn, in March 1968.

A Protestant religious service is held, during a lull in fighting, at Khe Sahn. John Blair is seated on the far side of the front row and faces towards the chaplain.

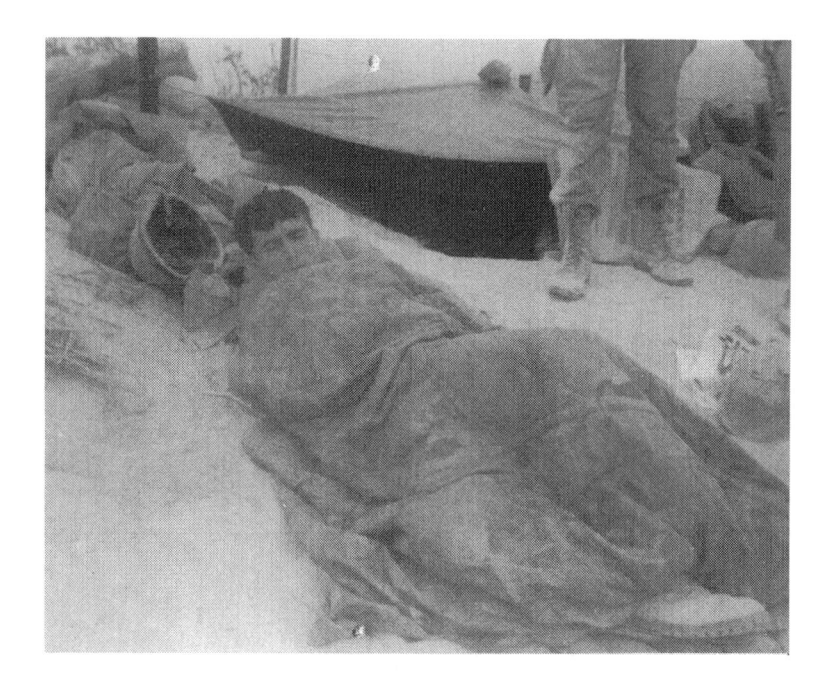

John Blair sleeps between watches. During the 77-day-long siege at Khe Sahn; men slept when and where they could.

This group of India Company survivors was photographed on September. This group photo of India Company survivors was taken on September 2013, at Pensacola Naval Air Station, Pensacola, Florida. Kneeling, front row, left to right, are Gene Ogozalek (wounded Jan 25, 1968), Pfc, Scranton, Pennsylvania; "Wild" Bill Waldrop, Corporal, wounded twice, Hanceville, Alabama; Bob Ayers, Corporal, Prescott, Arizona; Layne Hefner, retired Sergeant Major, Pensacola, Florida; Kevin Hawkins, Bethel, Maine, Corporal, severely wounded, major hearing loss.

Standing, back row, are Bob Espinola, Sergeant, Fremont, California (won a Silver Star, at Mike's Hill) with John Blair, Sergeant, David Turnage, Sergeant, Pensacola, Florida; James "Smokey" Wittmeyer, Corporal, Round Rock, TX (died of heart attack last year).

# Cary Stuart King
interview of October 6, 2016

My name is Cary S. King. The S is for Stuart. I was born in Atlanta, Georgia, on June 18th, 1941.

My dad was Hyman Meyer King. He was born in Cape Town, South Africa, and was a year and a half when he came to the U.S. His father Isaac King and those relatives migrated to South Africa from Russia and Riga, Latvia.

My dad started off basically as a salesman. He was a child of the Depression, so he worked. My grandfather had a produce business, at the old Farmers Market, on Lee Street, out in southwest Atlanta. He worked for him for a while and ultimately, he ended up becoming President of a big food distributorship called Capital Fish and later Capital Food Company.

My mother's maiden name was Swerdlin. Her first name was Nelle. She was born in Atlanta. After marriage, she did a variety of things. When they first got married she worked at Sears Roebuck, as a secretary. Later on, my parents owned a jewelry store, near the old Farmers Market. It ultimately went under, probably from bad management. Then she went to work for the Veterans Administration, and worked there till she retired.

I have one brother. His name is Dennis Harvey King, and he just turned 70 years old. He lives here, in Stone Mountain.

We moved around a lot, when I was in elementary school, and I went to several. I went to Grady High School and graduated in June, 1959. Then I went to Georgia State College and graduated in August, 1963. I also did a lot of course work at Georgia Tech.

I had been in the ROTC program, in high school and at Georgia State, and was commissioned as a Second Lieutenant, on August 22nd, 1963. I'd been accepted to Emory Law School, and I started and then decided I needed a break from school. So, I quit Emory Law School, before getting very far, and went on active duty, in October, and went to the Field Artillery Officers Basic Course, at Ft. Sill, Oklahoma. It was about a two-month course.

I was engaged to this girl, in Atlanta, and I was very much in love. The day the course ended, in December 1959, I got 30 days leave and orders to go to Germany. She was upset. I was upset, 'cause we weren't married yet, and I drove home, in a raging snow storm. I drove straight through, from Ft. Sill, until I hit Greenwood, Mississippi, and my car spun off the road. Luckily, I didn't get hurt and the car wasn't damaged. I spent the night in Greenwood and got back to Atlanta, and I explained to her: maybe I would go to Germany and we would wait about a year and then I would come back and we'd get married. It didn't exactly work out that way.

I was home on 30-days leave and went to Germany to an artillery unit called the 2nd Battalion, 83rd Artillery. The unit had 8-inch, self-propelled artillery pieces, on tracked vehicles. I flew out of Charleston Air Force Base into Frankfurt am Main military airport and was met by a Lieutenant that was my sponsor and took me to a little town called Büdingen. The 3rd squadron, 12th Cavalry Regiment was also there.

I basically was there from late December '63 or early January '64, until about the spring or summer of 1966. The Vietnam War started to heat up, and we started to hear about it, in Germany. They started pulling troops out of Germany, in '65, and deploying them back to the States for units that were obviously getting ready to go to Vietnam. There was no secret about it.

I was sent to the 3rd Armored Division's Aerial Observer School, in '64, to become a trained aerial observer, which meant I would adjust artillery and air strikes from helicopters and light aircraft. L-19s mostly is what we were flyin' in. I did quite a few things in Germany. I started as a Second Lieutenant. Besides being a forward observer and later an aerial observer, I also had been a fire direction officer for one of the firing batteries. I had been a recon and survey officer, at battalion. I took the recon and survey platoon out and identified our gun emplacement positions. I was also the assistant operations officer, at battalion headquarters, and right before I came home, I became a battery commander. There were four guns in an 8-inch unit. Germany was good command time.

In July '65, I got married. I was a first 1st Lieutenant by then. The girl I married was not the girl I was engaged to earlier, but to another girl I met on leave back here in Atlanta. It was a kind of a fix-up thing. Her name was Linda Cohen, and I'd taken her back to Germany. She was originally from Lewistown, Pennsylvania, and was working in Atlanta as an X-ray technician.

I came back to the States, in '66. Not long after that, it was obvious that the war in Vietnam was really heatin' up. I'd already been to Aerial Observer School and was flying missions with the 83rd Artillery, in our training exercises, in Germany, and adjusting artillery fire. Sometime around March of '66, I think, I was promoted to Captain. They were accelerating promotions to Captain, because they knew what was gettin' ready to happen. At that point, I had three years' experience, so I was, in relative terms more seasoned than the young Lieutenant, although I was fairly young myself. I turned 25, in June of '66.

As soon as I heard Vietnam was heatin' up, I volunteered to go, and the Army sent me orders to Ft. Leonard Wood, Missouri. I'm going to guess it was in about September '66. I was one of the few combat arms officers that was there. They had a lot of engineers, ordnance, and other specialties, but not a lot of artillery, or infantry, or armor. I volunteered for Vietnam again, shortly after I got there. My wife was pregnant with my first child, my daughter, and that child was born on April 5th, 1967. Her name is Kimberly Ann. I didn't really tell my wife or may parents that I'd volunteered for Vietnam either time, because I just didn't feel they would receive it real well.

But I felt like I was, at that point, a career soldier, and I had a regular Army commission, so I felt like that's what is involved. I felt like I had a duty to do.

At Ft. Leonard Wood, because I was artillery, I was given command of the Special Troops Company, which is like 600 people that you never see: they're all headquarters people. So, the colonel that I was workin' for put me in charge of the rifle range and the infiltration course, and I ran them and the Company. I had a couple of company formations, during that year, and I was glad I didn't have more than that, because they were all these headquarters people that needed haircuts and their uniforms looked like hell and they looked like hell mostly.

The first sergeant and I were the only combat arms people there, and we were like cringing when we saw these guys show up. Ft. Leonard Wood was also good command time, because I got to experience some different kinds of troops and non-artillery troops.

In August or September '67, I got my orders to go to Vietnam to report to the 1st Infantry Division. I took leave, got my wife and child settled in Pennsylvania, where she was from, with her parents. In October, I flew to Oakland Army Terminal, in California, and just missed my plane. So, they put me up in the Fairmont Hotel, in San Francisco, for three days or so. Then I think I went over on Flying Tiger Airlines. I think I arrived there October 28th, 1967.

We were supposed to land at Tan Son Nhut air field, in Saigon, and as we were comin' in they got rocketed. So, they diverted us to Bien Hoa air field. I was told at that time that Bien Hoa air field was the second busiest air field in the world, countin' helicopters and fixed wing aircraft. As we started to land at Bien Hoa, they got mortared. At that point, the reality of all that sort of gets yeh, and you realize, oh, shit! I knew I signed up for this, but I didn't realize I was not going to have time to get oriented, before I hit the ground.

We got in okay, and they sent us over to Long Binh, and that was a huge base camp. I would guess it had tens of thousands of acres. It was in III Corps, where the 1st Infantry Division was. They issued the uniforms and all that good stuff. The next morning a 2-1/2-ton truck came and picked up myself and a dozen other people, and we drove over to Di An, which I found out later was the headquarters for 2nd Brigade of the 1st Infantry Division.

A brigade consisted of three battalions of infantry, a battalion of artillery, and some other elements like some engineers, quartermasters, transportation, aviation assets, and other support elements. The division, which was headquartered Lai Khe, was organized with three brigades.

I reported in to what was, in effect, the personnel section of 2nd Brigade. The guy I ran into there had gone to Georgia State, so he knew me. He was a Major in the Adjutant General Corps there. He welcomed me and then sent me to 2nd Brigade headquarters. He said they're short some officers. He said it was in the S2 shop. I said, 'I'm not an intel guy and I'm not an infantryman', and he branch transferred me to the infantry. I said I hadn't been in infantry since college ROTC, and he said I'd figure it out.

I started off as the Assistant S2, for the brigade. About three days after I got to Vietnam, there was a huge battle, up at Loc Ninh. I later found out it was an area where the 1st Infantry was always getting into it with the enemy. We had an air field, at Loc Ninh. It wasn't a base camp. It was almost like what was called a fire base up north. We just called them night defensive positions, but they were fire support bases with artillery and infantry in them.

I got sent to Loc Ninh three days after I got in country, because they got hit the night before. There was a 105 unit in there and at least two companies of infantry in there protectin' the air field. I was tryin' to get oriented the day I got up there. I was up there to get intel, and, if they captured any prisoners, to get information from the prisoners. That night, they got hit again. When I say they got hit, I mean there were VC in the wire. They were almost on top of us. The artillery lowered the tubes down to zero level and were firing straight over the head of the infantry.

I was there and callin' in air strikes, and doin' whatever I could, because I didn't really have an official position in there. I was almost there like an observer. That was my first taste of real action, in Vietnam. That battle started about 10 o'clock at night and lasted pretty much into 7:30, 8:30 the next morning. I was terrified, but made it through. Then I got called back to brigade, so I caught a chopper back.

We would start about six o'clock in the mornin'. We'd have breakfast and get started with whatever our day was goin' to be. I was runnin' courier runs up to Phu Loi: one of our other base camps and picking up intel there from those guys and bringing it back or takin' intel that I had up there and meetin' with them and seein' what they had. The 1st Aviation Brigade was at Phu Loi.

I had three regular jobs and worked for two different brigade commanders, during the first six months I was there. My first job was order of battle. Second Brigade was responsible for certain villages, and I was responsible for intel reports and radio relocation and monitoring. Prisoner interrogation was my second area, and with the information we gathered, we were creating an infrastructure of who were the VC leaders in each of these villages. I had a prisoner interrogation team that involved interpreters and military intelligence people. When we captured a prisoner, we would do the interrogation at brigade level: usually in the field. We would bring them back, but the interrogation started in the field.

A lot of time, the VC leaders in these villages would go by aliases. We would send in an infantry platoon or a company, depending on the size of the village, and try to get the villagers to rat out who were the VC leaders. Sometimes they would and sometimes they wouldn't. Sometimes they would say that they're dead, that they were killed. And sometimes, when you would catch the leader, he would say he wasn't the leader. So, we would take him into custody anyway. We would do our interrogation, and usually we would get the information sooner or later.

If we took into custody somebody who was really a heavy-duty Viet Cong intel source: for example, a ranking person who may have been a Major or Lieutenant Colonel, we might turn 'em over to the J2, in Saigon. Occasionally we would send them to the Koreans, who would interrogate 'em too. They didn't always come back from those visits. We were told they escaped or tried to escape. I had my own theories, about that.

There were three battalions of infantry in the brigade, and, if any of them took prisoners or captured documents, I would go out there to the field with my team and do the interrogation.

My third job was to be with the infantry on Search and Seal Operations. The brigade would take a company or re-enforced company and they'd circle a village, in the middle of the night. It would be a village that they suspected the VC were comin' in and out of and using for food and refuge or wine or women or were storing ammunition. Helicopters would fly over after we sealed it, and broadcast, in Vietnamese, 'Don't try to leave the village. It is sealed. Anybody trying to leave will be shot. If you are VC, put down your weapon and surrender. In daylight, the village will be searched house to house. When daylight came, I would go in, in behalf of the brigade, with the infantry company.

My job was to advise the brigade commander as to where, from intel reports, we believed there was enemy activity. He would then order the battalion to send a company out to seal off this village and a search to be done. Usually Lt. Col. Edwards, the brigade executive officer, the XO, would go with me. We would interrogate people and check their papers, at a central place in the village. I remember Chanh Luu, a village where we did this. We sealed that village, and as we started to go in, we started to take fire, from one of the huts. One of the guys with me just took a LAW rocket and took the hut out. A LAW rocket was like a bazooka, except the tube was disposable. That took care of that.

We would go in and sometimes find, in cellars, under huts, they would hide people, they would hide weapons, they would hide VC. They would hide all kinds of stuff in there. We would go house to house. I would be further up the road, in the village, and I would hear somethin' blow up, and you would know what was goin' on is one of the infantry platoons found somethin' and they were blowin' it up to make sure the enemy couldn't use it. Or you'd hear somebody shooting, a hundred meters behind you: you knew what happened was they looked in the cellar and there was a VC down there, and either the VC was shootin' at them or vice versa: usually both. That was a routine thing. We did a lot of those Search and Seal operations, in 2nd Brigade.

I got to Vietnam the end of October '67. November was pretty active. We had that one heavy contact up north. It was 3rd Brigade's contact, and I was in Loc Ninh. Around the first part of December or maybe it was mid-December of '67, things got very quiet. We went from havin' fairly major contacts throughout the division area of operation to, all of a sudden, hardly able to find a VC.

I was goin' to my intel sources: prisoner interrogation, and documents that were comin' in, and villagers that were givin' us information. We had a lot of moles out there that were feedin' us information: some of it dependable and some not so dependable. We started to get these reports, in late December of '67, that the VC were planning some kind of big operation. I had to make a briefing every night to the Old Man: Col. Tidwell, the brigade commander. He used to get very irritated at the intel reports, because he didn't think, all the time, that we were getting' accurate information. He would say he couldn't send his people out there, if we weren't gettin' him the accurate stuff. And I would say, 'This is what we got.'

When I started to tell him that the VC were plannin' some kind of a big operation in January of '68, he kind of said, 'Where are you getting' this information?'

And I said, 'The usual sources: interrogation of prisoners captured in the field, talkin' to some of the villagers, and some intercepted radio transmissions where there's a lot of discussion of stuff like this.' He wanted to know if I had verified my information with Division. I said, 'We're sharin' information with the other brigades, and that's what I got right now.' He didn't believe me, and he probably didn't think I was on top of it, because I'd moved up to the S2 position, because the S2 got killed, and S2 was a position for a Major: somebody senior to me and somebody that had more experience.

To tell you the truth, because he had that skepticism, I wasn't so sure of myself sometimes. A lot of these intel sources will mislead you on purpose, because they're really workin' for the enemy, and they just want to give you bad information to get you all hyped up. It's no different today. I listen to these terrorist reports, and it strikes me that there're probably plenty of moles out there deliberately giving them bad information.

January was a continuation of December. We had small contacts with our ambush patrols that were out in the field, where the ambush patrol would run into two VC, three VC, but we could not find a big Viet Cong unit or find anything indicating big movement of troops. The Colonel kept saying to me, and logically so, if there's all these big plans, and all these big units are movin', why aren't we actually pickin' up troop movements.

Sometime around mid-December, the Old Man called me in, and he said: 'King, you're an aerial observer, right?'

And I said, 'Yes, sir.'

And he said, 'On nights when nothin's goin' on, I want you to fly with the brigade aviation assets in the no-fire zones and the free-fire zones. They'll teach you how to use this thing we call "Bloodhound". I want you to add that information to your intel reports every night.'

"Bloodhound" is a box that looks like a polygraph machine. It had hoses that you hooked to the skids of the helicopter, and it would detect carbon dioxide concentrations. It doesn't distinguish between human carbon dioxide and animal, so it could be a herd of water buffaloes as easily as it could have been troops moving. Any time we got heavy concentrations of carbon dioxide, I would call out hot spots. I was in the back of the chopper watchin' the machine, and a guy next to me with a map would mark them on the map. He was a navigator. He had to stay constantly on top of where we were. If we had heavy concentrations of carbon dioxide we'd put artillery in there or maybe we'd even put troops in there.

I was flying these missions three, four nights a week, and we started getting heavy concentrations of carbon dioxide in strange places. We'd fire artillery in there sometimes. Sometimes we'd send an ambush patrol out there to see what was goin' on, and it was just quiet. We couldn't figure out why we were getting' these heavy sightings. I'm getting' debriefed every time I come back, at the TOC, the Tactical Operations Center, at Brigade Headquarters, by the S3, the operations officer: my buddy Maj. Bob Duker.

He kept sayin' the carbon dioxide concentrations could be water buffalo. I said, They could be. I can't tell you what they are. If you want to send some troops in there, that's the Old Man's job, not mine.' They would occasionally send troops to a hot spot, and it wouldn't' always result in anything. We couldn't figure out what was goin' on.

I figured it out, after the Tet Offensive. That these units were moving at night, and then they were dressing as civilians and infiltrating into the villages, so that, if you sent a patrol out there the next day you wouldn't find them. They'd be merged in with the farming population, in a particular village or they'd be sleeping and hiding in the cellars. But there were heavy movements at night, and that got all those people down there around these various big cities, before the Tet Offensive, by movin' them only at night without making contact with us, and then hiding in the daylight.

January goes on and we're getting little contacts here and little contacts there, but nothin' significant. Around January 25th, I'm out flyin' a mission on this Bloodhound thing and came back in about 10 o'clock. I'm getting' debriefed at the TOC, and one of the guys says, 'There's some civilian, with long sideburns, back in your hooch.'

I said, 'Yeah, right!' I thought they were jerking me around. I said, 'What civilian would come out here to Vietnam to visit somebody?' He said he was not crapping me around. So, I go back to my hooch and my lifetime best friend, a guy named Larry Taylor, is asleep in my bed. So, I wake him up and he say he got a hop from U-dorn and do I think I can get two, three days off and we can take a little R & R.

Larry had served four years in the Marine Corps, as an aviator, a helicopter pilot; got out and signed up for Air America; and was based in U-dorn. He later went back in the Marine Corps and is now a Marine retired two-star general.

We went up to the Officers Club. It was a tent, where you could get liquor, and we had a few drinks and we had dinner, in the mess hall. The next mornin' I went to Col. Thebaut, and I said, sir, this guy's been friend, since we were 121-years old. Any chance I can get a three-day R & R, in our area, down on the South China Sea called Vung Tau. He said, we were getting' ready for the Tet holiday, so we'll be on stand-down anyway, so go ahead: take a couple of days. This was like January 29th or 30th of 1968.

I threw a few civilian clothes in a bag and got a hop in a helicopter down to Bien Hua. From Bien Hua, I think we picked up a ride on a C-130 and got to Vung Tau, about five o'clock that evenin', and now it's January 30th. We get to this hotel, and we checked in and there's a Captain in fatigues that's clearly never been in any combat situation, and he's the manager of the hotel. He says, 'There's some enemy activity around here. You guys have a good time, but be careful.'

I said, 'Where's the enemy activity?'

He said, 'It's 18 miles up the beach', and I laughed. He wanted to know what I was laughin' at, and I said, '18 miles up the beach! They might as well be back in the States, as far as I'm concerned. I just left a situation where enemy activity was a hundred yards away. I'm not worried about something goin' on 18 miles up the beach.'

We checked in and my buddy said he was going down stairs for a beer. I said I would go to the room and sack out for a while. You can sleep standin' up, when you're in combat. You get 15-minutes off and you sleep. I went up and fell asleep and slept for a couple of hours. Then Taylor came up to the room and said, 'Let's go somewhere.'

So, I put on a pair of Bermuda shorts and a shirt, and somebody knocked on the door, and it was the hotel manager. He had a flack vest over his fatigues. He says, 'Nobody's allowed to leave the hotel. There's enemy activity eight miles up the road.'

I said, 'I already told you I don't give a you-know-what, about enemy activity miles up the road. I don't care.'

He said, 'The MPs could arrest yuh.'

I said, 'Good. Let 'em arrest me. I don't care. What are they going to do, send me to Vietnam?'

We went downstairs. We had a couple of beers, and when we went to leave the hotel, MPs wouldn't let us leave. They said they believed there's going to be enemy activity downtown, and the VC were stirring things up a little bit, knowin' that we're all on stand down.

We used to joke that the U.S. and the Viet Cong used to take their R & R down in Vung Tau. They didn't bother each other. It was unwritten that you don't mess with each other down at this R & R area.

Well, it turned out that that was the beginning of the Tet Offensive. We didn't know it.

I had a buddy, Richard Allen, from Montgomery, Alabama, who was in command with an ordnance company, in Vung Tau. Allen and I had been in Germany together, in the 2nd Battalion, 83rd Artillery, and when he finished his artillery stint, they transferred him to ordnance.

The next day, January 31st, I got a jeep from somewhere, and Taylor and I headed out to see Allen. We get over there, and he says, 'Man this stuffs goin' ta hit the fan.'

I said, 'What are you talkin' about?'

He said, 'There's all kinds of little spot reports all down here.'

And again, I laughed and said, 'Listen, I'm not worried about little spot reports down here. I just came from War Zone D. I'm not worried about something goin' on five miles from here.'

He said, 'No, there's somethin' goin' on.'

I go back to the hotel, there's a note at the desk, from 2nd Brigade headquarters: 'You are to get back to your unit, as soon as possible. Heavy enemy activity has been reported in your area. Somethin's goin' on and you have been directed to get back to your unit any way you can get there.'

I leave my buddy, Taylor, in Vung Tau, and get a hop from Vung Tau to Bien Hua. As soon as I land, I'm walking across the airfield and there's one of the 2nd Brigade choppers. I asked he could get me to Dagger Pad. Dagger Pad was our call sign. He said to get in, and I asked him what was goin' on. He said, 'All hell's breakin' loose, but we don't know what's goin' on. We just know there's a lot of enemy activity reports and stuff goin' on.'

So, I get back to brigade headquarters and report in. I was really gone about a day and a half. Don't know where Taylor is, at this point. They said Old Man wants to see you right away. I report to the Old Man, he says, 'Those reports that you were gettin', evidently there's something to it.' I'm sittin' there thinkin' to myself, which was really wrong, now that I look back, I'm thinkin', 'Good! Somebody's finally believin' what I'm sayin'.'

He said he wanted me to go down to Saigon that night. There's going to be a briefing for the big guys Gen. Abrams and Gen. Westmorland. He told me I was briefing the intel I knew for 2nd Brigade and to get up to speed on what they got since I left. Abrams had not taken over. Westmorland was very much in charge, at that point.

I said, 'Who else is gonna be there?', and he said, 'we're part of the umbrella defense of Saigon. First Division's got the north side east of the Dong Nai River. Twenty-Fifth Division's got west of the Dong Nai. Either the 25th or us are gonna be sendin' troops down into Saigon.' He said, 'There's good intel they have infiltrated government buildings.' By this time, we already knew they were in the Phu Tho Race Track.

I said, 'What am I briefing about?'

He said, 'They're goin' to want to know what areas we have pacified, what areas are vulnerable, what areas are protected in the 2nd Brigade area, because we're the brigade closest to Saigon. Man, I went into a panic thinkin' I've got to brief two four-star generals one of whom is the commander of all the troops in Vietnam.'

Then I thought, 'That's what you signed up for, Pal.' So, I got ready.

I flew to Saigon on a H-13 helicopter, which is one of those little bubble helicopters. It looked like in MASH, in the TV show. The pilot was a crazy guy. That helicopter does not have night instruments that light up at night and you can navigate with. So, he handed me a Zippo lighter and said keep lighting it so he could fly to Saigon. So, we landed in some little building in Saigon: me with the cigarette lighter shining to the horizon and the air speed instruments and all that stuff.

The next morning, first thing, we do a briefing. I do the briefing for the brigade, and my division commander Gen. John Hay, is sittin' in the back, and I'm thinkin' don't screw this up King. So, I briefed Gen. Westmorland, and he didn't ask me anything. He said, Thank you, Captain', and Gen. Abrams, who had been sittin' in a chair with his helmet kind of down on his nose, said, 'Captain, have you been out in the field in combat?'

And I said, 'Yes, sir.'

And he said, 'How long?'

And I said, 'Three, four months now.'

And he said, 'What's the matter with these "Ruff Puff" compounds?'

"Ruff Puff" were what they called RFPF, the Regional Force Popular Force. They were the local Vietnamese: kind of a militia. I'm thinkin', 'Do I tell the truth?' I'm lookin' at the brigade commander and he's lookin' at me like answer the man's question. So, I said, 'Well, Sir, a lot of those people are fightin' with '03 Springfields and antiquated weapons. They need better weapons to hold those little compounds.'

Apparently, they were worried that the Viet Cong were gonna overrun these little compounds. He said, 'How many in your area?'

I said, 'I don't actually know the answer to that, sir, but I'm guessin' 200, 300.'

He turns to some colonel sittin' there and says, 'How many we got in the warehouse, in Okinawa?'

The Colonel said, 'M16s?

And Gen. Abrams says, 'Yeah! Thank you, Captain, you can sit down now.' Sure enough, about two weeks later, the Ruff Puffs got all these weapons.

That was the start of the Tet Offensive. By February 1st or 2nd, it was clear that the VC were all over Saigon; that they were hittin' Bien Hua and Long Binh; they were hitting every major city in our area of operations. We didn't know, at that time, that there were some North Vietnamese units involved, in our area. There were more NVA regulars up in I Corps and II Corps, but there were some NVA that were advisors working with the local VC, in our area.

The intel was beginnin' to come in, 'cause they were capturin' people with helmets, and uniforms, and things the VC didn't have. We knew there were some NVA in Saigon and in the Phu Tho Race Track.

Our primary concern and our biggest enemy in our area was the 273rd VC Regiment, which was a unit of several hundred people in the 2nd Brigade area. They moved between 2nd Brigade, 1st Brigade, and 3rd Brigade areas, but almost exclusively in the 1st Infantry Division area.

We're told no mails goin' out; no mail's comin' in, and that may go on for a prolonged period of time. We were in 100% general alert condition. The Old Man sent me to the water plant, in a village called Thu Duc, with a reinforced company, and a sergeant and a radio with a 292 antenna, which is a big radio. He said, 'We think the water plant is gon get hit tonight and overrun.'

I moved in to the Thu Duc water plant. The first night, we got hit, and they came across a soccer field. There were gooks that got to the wire and were killed there. We held off the attack. Their plan was to blow up the water purification plant, so we would not be able to get fresh water out to everybody, and we would be in trouble.

Then I went down to Saigon, to Tan Son Nhut air field and consulted with a couple of our units down there and some units from the 25th Division. Gave 'em the intel we had. Was there one night, when the VC launched a major assault between the Vietnamese Armed Forces compound and Tan Son Nhut air field. The VC got caught in a cross fire. We killed more than 600 VC that night. I spent the night mostly callin' in artillery; talkin' to the aviators, bringin' air strikes in.

I remember this: I remember aircraft takin' off from Tan Son Nhut air field, pullin' up like this, at maybe 60 or 70-degree angles, and droppin' their ordnance right on the other side of the air field. I'll never forget that. And I also will never forget how many bodies there were. I'd seen plenty of dead, at that point, but I'd not seen that many in one place and one time.

I also remember driving down from the water plant across the Newport Bridge over the Saigon River. I don't know why it was called the Newport Bridge, but the road over it was the only really major road that was paved, in Vietnam, when I was there. It was between Saigon and Bien Hua and Long Binh. It went over the Newport Bridge, and we called that Highway 1. I remember coming over that bridge and seeing a whole lane that was blown away, by a barge that the VC had floated under there. I remember seeing bodies lying literally everywhere.

Americans policed up our dead. We didn't leave dead on the battlefield, except maybe for the moment. There were a lot of Vietnamese bodies there that could have been Viet Cong or they could have been South Vietnamese. We stepped over bodies. I've never seen so many bodies in my life. I've never seen so many wounded in my life.

Somehow, we got through the next three or four weeks. I was the S2 from brigade headquarters for Task Force Ware, which was a task force put together, after the Tet Offensive. I provided the intel for them as to where the VC were goin', because they were runnin', they were tryin' to get away. I went to a major contact out along Highway 13, which we called Thunder Road. In our division it connected all of our base camps all the way to the Cambodian border. That's where all of our road convoys would go. That's where we sent our re-supply for the 3rd Brigade, which was up by Cambodia.

In one of the last big contacts I was involved in, one of our units got in contact with the VC, in a cemetery, by the side of Highway 13. The last remnants of the 273rd VC Regiment, we later found out, were in that cemetery and the U.S. unit literally annihilated them. For all practical purposes they eliminated the 273rd VC Regiment.

That's kind of how it went—one fight after another. They were tryin' to get back out into the jungle and get away from the major population areas, and we're blockin' 'em, we're catchin' 'em, we're killin' 'em, as they're retreating.

I was awarded two Bronze Stars with V devices and three Bronze Stars for meritorious service. One of the meritorious service awards was to do with Operation Lam Son 67, from February 7 to March 31st, 1968. It involved the 1st Infantry's 2nd and 3rd Brigades and Vietnamese troops and was kind of involved with the Tet Offensive. I was one of the 2nd Brigade's key components. Two of the Bronze Stars were just thanks a lot for don' a good job.

Around the end of March, we had gotten a new brigade commander, a Colonel named Allen. This guy was a full Colonel. Had been a World War II tank commander, under Patton and was a great guy. He'd take me out in his helicopter, and we'd go flying.

I was getting close to six months in that assignment, and the way it worked over there was that after six months an officer could ask for a different assignment or they would move you to a different assignment. Col. Allen said to me, 'What would you like to do?' I said I'd like to go back to artillery. So, he gave me command of a 105 battery whose battery commander was goin' home. It was Charlie Battery, 1st Battalion, 7th Artillery. I took over that unit, in April, I think.

Some of the heaviest contacts I was involved in were with this 105 artillery unit: from the Tet counter-offensive, which we started in April or May, all the way through August, when I left there and went to Headquarters Battery, Division Artillery.

We had a contact, in War Zone D, where they'd moved us out in this jungle position, with the 28th Infantry, where I lost three dead in about five minutes, from a RPG, a rocket propelled grenade. The enemy tried to overrun us. We had infantry with us, and they took a lot of casualties that night too. That was in late June '68 or early July '68. I was with the 105 unit, at that time.

One of the Bronze Stars with a V device was for that night. What happened was that one of my gun sections got hit with this RPG. People think that you have a clear memory of everything that happened, but you don't. It started so fast and was total chaos. It always amazes me when somebody does have a clear memory of what exactly happened. I was up at the command post, and I was asleep. The first thing I remember was a huge explosion. I saw the flash and I could hear people yellin', and I could hear machine gun fire and mortars goin' off. And I jumped out of the CP. It was about 11 o'clock at night.

My gun section was maybe 75 meters away from me. I had my guns kind of around a bomb crater. There were six guns in my battery and two guns in each platoon. They were shooting by platoons, because it's too hard for the fire direction center to keep track of which platoon is firing where, if more than one platoon fires at a time. This particular platoon was shooting north, in support of an infantry unit.

The VC were walkin' the mortar fire through the perimeter towards us. When I saw the flash, I saw that it was down in my gun, so I took off for the gun. When I got down there, the assistant gunner and the gunner were laid out, and I could see the breech block on the gun was blown open. My gun chief, an African-American guy, was screamin', 'I'm hit! I'm hit!'

I looked at Philip Law, the gunner, and he was just blown wide open. Myself and one other guy kind of put his entrails back inside; took a shirt and tied it around him; took a couple of rifles and made a kind of a stretcher. The assistant gunner was Chambers. He was just chewed up. I tried to rouse him and I couldn't rouse him. He was dead.

The other boy was a kid named Zboyovski. It was a Polish name. Please don't ask me to spell it, but he was from Pittsburgh and was about 19-years old. I said what about Z, and they said he's awake, sir. I said get Law and

Chambers up to the aid station, and myself and another guy carried Z up there. We got up to the aid station, and mortars are comin' through the position. You could feel them comin' your way.

I saw a little blood on the front of Z's uniform, and he said, 'Am I gonna die?'

I said, 'No, you're okay, I think.' I heard the mortars comin' in, so I laid on top of him. I didn't have on a flack vest, but I didn't want him to get hit again. The next mortar round, lucky for us, exploded just beyond us, and I think that's when I got light shrapnel in my butt and the back of my head. It might not have been shrapnel. It could have been rocks. Zboyovski died that night.

I didn't even know anybody had noticed anything I had done. When you get a decoration, somebody else recommends you, and they write it up. So, they wrote me up, for goin' down there, evacuating the casualties, and protecting this guy. The first Bronze Star with V was awarded for that.

That same night I got shot in the right calf, by a 30-cal., like a carbine, fired from somewhere in the perimeter. The bullet came in here and went out back here. I got patched up by the medic. The Purple Heart Medal was awarded for that.

The second Bronze Start with V device was much later: maybe September. I'd taken over Headquarters Battery, Division Artillery. We were flying from Phu Loi up to the Lai Khe, the 1st Infantry Division headquarters. We were over kind of a large, open area, and I felt the chopper bounce, and I looked out the side of the chopper, and the pilot said to me, 'I think one of our armored vehicles down there just hit a land mine.'

I had the division artillery commander, who was a Colonel, and the executive officer of the division artillery with us, and I said to the pilot, can we go down and check it out? He said he was not sure, because we had the division artillery commander with us. I said ask him and he said, 'How about if I just do it?' So, he circles around and it's clear that there are some casualties. One of the tank's treads is blown off, and they're by themselves out there.

I said, 'Land. Put me off, I'll stay there with them, in case there's a ground attack, until you get some other support.' He put me down there, and I tried to treat the casualties. Just about everybody inside was either dead or seriously wounded. I think there were four men in that tank. The driver was dead, the gunner was dead. I tried to get the back door open, but I couldn't. I stayed there, until they were able to get the place secured, and somebody recommended me for a Bronze Star with V. I don't know that it was a big deal. I never got shot at.

There were a lot of contacts involved in that unit. We moved from one position to another position, always by helicopter. We were moved six or seven times. We'd go from a jungle position to a position on Highway 13, on the road. We were always firin' in support of infantry units and armor units. The Black Horse unit, the 11th Armored Cavalry, was in our area. Plus, we had what we called "Quarter Cav", the 1st Squadron, 4th Cav.

While I was in Vietnam, I also earned the Combat Infantry Badge, five Air Medals, the Vietnam Campaign Medal with 60 devices, and two Army Commendation Medals, one of which was for valor, Air Crewman Wings, and three-unit citations.

I came home in November '68. Then I went to Redstone Arsenal, Huntsville, Alabama, and was in the Army until January 1970, and then got out and off and on stayed active in the Reserves. I retired from the Reserves, in 1987, as a major or a Lieutenant Colonel. Guard rank is not the same as active duty rank, so I'm not sure.

By the time I came home, I had a second child: a son, Scott Richard, who is now a law partner with me. He was born in 1969. We separated in '79 and got divorced in '80 or '81. I remember that. Then I got remarried December 30th, 1984 to a girl I grew up with: Sherry Adelman, and we've been married ever since, and reside in Brookhaven, Georgia.

I now have six grandchildren: four boys and two girls, and three step-daughters.

I went to work for my father, in the food business, when I came out of the Army. We sold food wholesale to restaurants, hotels, country clubs, schools, and other businesses. He passed away four months after I got out, from a heart attack, at 57. I didn't care for it, with my father gone, but I had to feed my family, so I stayed in the food business for a while. I finally decided, in my mid-to-late 30s that I was going to go back to law school. So, I worked all day long, went to John Marshall Law School at night, graduated in '83. I couldn't go back to Emory, because I couldn't afford it and they didn't have a night program.

I graduated from law school in '83; was sworn in in February of '84; and I've been practicing ever since. I actually practiced for a couple of years, while I was in law school, with a couple of different firms. I'm a partner of Jacobs & King and practice law here in Georgia and am admitted to practice in the U.S. District Court for the Northern District of Georgia, the 11th U.S. Circuit Court of Appeals, and the U.S. Supreme Court.

I'm very involved in the Georgia State Bar and I'm the chairman of the Military and Veterans Law Section. I'm a member of the Military Legal Assistance Program for the State Bar and a founding member of the Fulton County Veterans Court, and a founding member of the Atlanta VA Medical Center's *pro bono* Legal Clinic, since '98. We provide lawyers, every Tuesday and Thursday that work for free with veterans that can come in to discuss legal problems and get help to try to resolve their problems. That's at the VA Medical Center, on Clairmont Road, in Decatur, Georgia. We also have another clinic that has two lawyers every Friday, at old Ft. McPherson. The State Bar and the Augusta Bar also have a clinic, in Augusta.

We have a clinic at Emery Law School where law school students meet with Army veterans and help them with VA benefits, VA claims. I sit on the advisory board there. We also just re-opened one at the Georgia State

University Law School that's chaired by Patty Shewmaker and her husband. They're both veterans.

I'm a board member and past president and chairman of the Atlanta Vietnam Veterans Business Association. And I am a member of Vietnam Veterans of America, the Vietnam Memorial Foundation, and a volunteer with the Georgia USO at Atlanta's airport. I interview for oral history for the Atlanta History Center, for the Library of Congress and was a member of DeKalb County's Veterans Advisory Committee. I'm also very involved in helping open up Veterans Courts throughout the state to work with veterans that have got off track: helping them set up mentor programs.

I'm a board member of Emma's Emmbassadors Autism Fund, a former board member of Georgia Crohn's and Colitis Foundation, the Atlanta and U.S. Humane Societies, the World Wildlife Foundation, and on the Alumni Board of Directors of John Marshall Law School. I'm a member of Jewish War Veterans.

In 2013, I received the Marshall-Tuttle Award from the Military and Veterans Affairs Section of the State Bar of Georgia and the United States Department of Veterans' Affairs, as the Outstanding Lawyer for 2012, for my years of legal service to veterans.

I never really filed for any disability, after I got out. It was always on the record, but I never did anything. In 2012, I was shaving one day and I felt a knot in my neck. So, I went to an ear, nose, and throat doctor, and they, eventually, took it out. It turned out it was follicular lymphoma—non-Hodgkin lymphoma--that my oncologist told me, immediately, was Agent Orange-related, when he found out that I'd been in Vietnam.

That's another little tidbit I walked away with from Vietnam. I went through about four weeks of radiation treatments in January 2013. Luckily for me, I have not had to go through chemotherapy. There is always the possibility that I will. I am now in remission. I was having to have PET scans every three months. I'm now down to every six months. If everything goes well they're going to move me to PET scans once a year. The VA did award me a hundred percent disability on my cancer. I've told them many times they can keep the money, if they'll take the cancer.

'This photo was taken during in late March or early April 1968, after the Tet Offensive. We are on a Search-and-Seal Operation, in a village, I think, was named Chanh Luu. On the left is Lt. Col. Edwards, the 2nd Brigade executive officer. I'm on the right probably chewing tobacco and holding a village boy up for a photo.'

63

'This photo was taken of a formation, on the day before I went home from active Army duty. The guy in the front of the formation is me, but I cannot remember the names of the other individuals in the photo.'

# Marcus Gary Monk
interview of August 23, 2013

My full name is Marcus Gary Monk, and I use the name Gary Monk for most purposes. I was born March the 13th 1942, in Birmingham, Alabama. My parents were both from there. I have a younger brother, who is now an attorney, in Birmingham.

I went to grammar school and high school, in Birmingham, and then went to Auburn University. I got a degree in forestry, in 1965. The Vietnam War was really mushrooming then, and, towards the end of '65, it became obvious that I was going to get drafted, if I didn't get into something quick. I wanted to be an aviator, and I passed all the tests for the air force and the navy, both of which had a backlog, and they said it was going to be about six months before I could start OCS, and they could not give me a draft deferment until then. So, I was pretty concerned.

I went to see the Marine recruiter, and the same story about backlog, except he said, 'We can keep you from being drafted,' and I said, 'how is that?'

Well, they swore me in as a Private, and he said, 'Now, if you don't show up for OCS, you're AWOL. I don't care if you get married, and you have 10 children.' Back then, if you got married or had children, you were exempt from the draft.

I went home and waited, and was called to go to OCS five months later. When I finished OCS, in late '65 and got my commission as a Marine Second Lieutenant, I also got an honorable discharge as a private, on the same day. And from there I went straight to Pensacola and went into flight school. I trained in fixed wing aircraft and then to helicopter training and was designated a Naval Aviator. It took almost a year and a half, and from there I was assigned to Santa Ana, which was a Marine air base, at the time. Now it's John Wayne Airport, in Orange County, California.

While I was in training, at Pensacola, I got married to a college sweetheart. Her name was Alice Marie Venable. She is deceased.

I checked in, and they had a number of assignments, and my wife happened to be pregnant. They said, 'We're forming a new squadron: HMM 364 and it could be nine months before they are ready to deploy.'

I said, 'I'll do that', so I would be there when my child was born.

We started forming this squadron. There were very few of us to start with. I was probably one of the first two dozen officers. Eventually, it grew, and we had about 50 officers and 150 enlisted men. Because we were a brand-new squadron, we were also getting brand new helicopters. It was a brand-new model of the CH-46B, which had bigger engines and a little better avionics than the CH-46A. Our nickname for it was 'the frog', because it kind of looked like a frog. We had to pick our helicopters up at the factory: at the Boeing Vertol Plant, just outside of Philadelphia; fly the across the United States and at the same time get trained.

Then my daughter was born, and two weeks later I was on my way to Vietnam. And we went by ship, aboard a small aircraft carrier. We stopped in Hawaii and Okinawa, just for a day. We got to Vietnam and off loaded from the South China Sea right into our base, which was Phu Bai, and that was about a mile south of the imperial capital of Hue. Our base had been a French airport.

Now, here's the interesting part about that: at least interesting to me. An advanced party of our unit left about three weeks before we did. They got to Vietnam. They went to Da Nang and checked in with the First Marine Air Wing, and the First Marine Air Wing said, 'Who are you?' Typical Marine efficiency!

And they said, 'We're HMM 364.' They were at a complete loss. They had no idea that we were coming.

Our men waited around for a week or so, and finally the air wing said, 'Why don't you go up to Hue Phu Bai, and you can be based there?'

They did, and of course, there was no living facility there. So they installed tents, showers and other facilities. The First Marine Air Wing said, 'We will build you a permanent facility across the runway from the tents.' Well, it took about six or eight months.

We had all our gear on board the aircraft carrier, and we started off-loading, on November 29th 1967. It was raining. The monsoon season was beginning. We had tents with wooden pallets for the floors and nothing else. We had nothing else, except tents and the stuff we'd brought with us. It was pretty primitive. A lot of mud! Lots of mud!

Things were changing rapidly in the Marine Corps, as far as commissioning new pilots. I was a first S, as were all of the others, except for men that had been Marcads. They were young men that had no college degree, but had passed a test that qualified them to take flight training. If they completed it, they were designated as Naval Aviators. They had been trained at Pensacola, as Marine Aviation Cadets. When they got their wings, they were commissioned. We had a few of them. They were Second Lieutenants and may have been commissioned for six months, when they joined us.

We had been in Vietnam for about a month, and one night we had an all-pilots meeting, in the tent. I was still a 1st Lieutenant. The commanding officer called me and said, 'Monk and Demaria come up here.'

And I thought, 'Oh, boy, what have I done wrong?'

And he said, 'I want to congratulate you. You've been promoted to a Captain. I thought he was joking. I didn't have any bars. I had to borrow some bars. I was a Captain with just three years or so in the Marine Corps; I was about the first senior guy in the squadron. That was in December of '67.

It had nothing to do with me being better than anyone else. It was just the paperwork chain. Within a short time, all of the other guys that were senior first Lieutenants became Captains.

We had a Lieutenant Colonel as CO, the EO was a major, and then a major that was operations officer, and another that was maintenance officer, and that was it for months. We were carrying the load. I'm not saying that to be self-serving.

Our senior Captains, who were soon to be promoted to major and Lieutenant Colonels, had already been in Vietnam once. And most of the senior Captains who had already been selected for Major, but hadn't been promoted yet, had been our instructors, in Pensacola. They were the plane commanders and we were the co-pilots. These guys, with a few exceptions, had seen enough, and as soon as they could, they got themselves a desk job, at wing or group, and did all sorts of things, such as safety officer. They wanted to be career Marines, but they wanted to get a check, on their record, that said that they had had combat administration experience.

They were really pushing us to become plane commanders. In helicopter talk it's called "HAC", for helicopter aircraft commander. You had to have, I think it was, 300 or 500 flying hours, in aircraft type, if this was your first aircraft command. So pretty soon you had very junior Captains who were carrying the load: flying the flight time.

We did a variety of missions. We would go out with a bunch of helicopters and insert troops. We could carry 12 to 18 combat troops. The number we could carry depended on their equipment, the temperature and the humidity. Sometimes, not often, they would be South Vietnamese army troops. A troop insertion would involve every one of our helicopters that we could get up. We got to Vietnam with 35 helicopters. The Tet offensive began in late January 1968 and ended in late February. By the end of it, we were down to 17 helicopters.

Then there were medevacs, which were probably the most dangerous missions. In the Marine Corps, we did not have specified helicopters with a red cross on them. Whenever you got the call to be a medevac, you would have a gunship that would go as your wing, and that was a UH1E, a Huey, as our people called it. You would fly out and pick up the guy and bring him back.

The medevac missions were interesting. The Marine Corps had three classifications of medevac. On a routine medevac, you flew out to get a man that generally had been either injured or possibly wounded, but was not in a hot zone. It was just a routine pickup and being him back to the medical center.

The middle classification was a priority medevac. That was when there was a little more urgency; maybe a little more danger. The worst was an emergency medevac, and that was when it was life threatening and or the zone was hot. And the absolute worst of the worst was a night emergency medevac.

We also did a mission which could be routine, and that was just carrying supplies around. We would carry either internal or external slings with everything from water, to ammunition, to food.

The other mission we did, which again could again be routine or be frightening, was recon unit inserts. The Marine Corps has a group called Force Recon. These are young men who do reconnaissance, and they would go out for extended periods: anything from seven to 13 days out in the boonies, and they would have reconnaissance missions to count the enemy, count trucks, count whatever.

There's no way to silently slip in a helicopter. We would go in, and we would land in a predetermined zone. We would sit there for one or two minutes. Then we would drop the ramp. Two or three men would run off. If they didn't take any fire, the rest of them would get off, and we would leave. And then they would, I guess, leave the area. And a lot of time the pickups were just exactly the same: routine. If they made contact, that was when it got really dangerous. Really dangerous!

Sometime in '68, after the Tet offensive, we got called out, and we had an emergency extraction. By this time, I was a plane commander and a pretty senior plane commander. A Marine Corps reconnaissance team was in contact and being fired upon, and they wanted to be extracted. So we fly out, we have a wingman and two gunships: two Hueys with guns and rockets. A wingman was another member of our squadron, and his job was, if you went down, he was supposed to come in and get you and your crew and the men you were sent to extract. In a case like that, the pilot of one of the Hueys assumes command, because we also called in fixed wing aircraft, and they would come in and they would drop napalm and various types of ordnance.

So, the Huey pilot in command is talking to the recon leader, on the radio. It was an FM radio, and we were listening. He was talking to the guy, and you could tell the guy was running. And the pilot said, 'Where is the enemy? Where are the bad guys?'

The recon leader said, 'Right behind us.'

The pilot said, 'How far behind you?'

And the recon leader said, 'I don't know. Maybe 50 meters.' That's about 150 ft.

The pilot said, 'Do you want us to put some fire on them?'

And the recon man said 'Yes!'

The pilot said, 'Drop a smoke and keep running, and we'll put fire on them, meaning napalm and other ordnance.'

So, they popped a smoke, and are running down this ridgeline. By this time, it's getting close to getting dark, and I'm thinking, 'Oh! Oh! This is not good.'

The pilot said, 'Have they stopped?'

The recon leader said, 'Yes.'

I asked, 'Are we clear to come in?'

He said, 'You're cleared in.'

We come in and could not land. It was in a forest or jungle. So, I had to hoist each one of them out. All we have is a horse collar for each one to put over his head and shoulders and hold on to. I'm talking to them now myself. I said, OK, we're going to hover. We had two 50 cal. machine guns and one on each side, and I said to my gunners, start shooting, but save enough ammunition for when we come out. So, we were down in the trees. This sounds like John Wayne stuff, but remember, I was young and still stupid.

So, I say to the guy on the ground, 'I want the radio man to be the last man up the wire.'

He said, 'Yes, sir.'

The crew chief is running the hoist and talking to me on the inter-com, and says, 'OK, the first one is on the wire. He's got the radio.' So now, the rest of them are on the ground, and I can't talk to 'em.

So, I'm screaming out, 'Get 'em on! Get 'em on! Get 'em on!'

The crew chief says to me, 'Skipper, there's a man coming up standing in the horse collar. That hoist comes up through a hole in the floor and goes up to a set of pulleys. And the crew chief says, 'Skipper, he just cut off two of his fingers, in the pulley.'

I told him, 'We're coming out.'

And the gunners and the gunships start firing. It is now dark and the gunships are shooting tracers. It was reassuring to see those red dots. And the gunships say, 'We can't see you.'

So, I say, 'Ok, I'm going to turn on my lights.' I don't know why I did that.

I turned on my lights, and they said, 'OK, we gotcha', so they could come in on either side, and we got out of there.

Now here's another thing about this "pop a smoke" thing. We learned fairly early on that if we were picking up troops out in the field, if we said, 'Pop a yellow smoke', there may be two or three yellow smokes popped, and it wasn't all our guys' smoke. So we would say, 'Pop a smoke, and identify it.'

And they would say, 'Popping a green or red.'

And a pilot would say, 'I've got it in sight.' And that way, we wouldn't get fooled.

We called the electronic line dividing North and South Viet Nam the McNamara Line. It was an electronic infiltration barrier designed to stretch across Laos and the demilitarized zone in Vietnam and we spent days and days hauling stuff to build it. It probably cost millions and was never finished and never worked. The Vietnam section was begun in 1967, but much of the equipment for it was used for the defense of Khe Sanh, in January, 1967, and the section planned for Vietnam was cancelled.

The NVA, the North Vietnamese Army, went around the demilitarized zone and came into South Viet Nam, at Khe Sahn. They also attacked Con Thien, from February 1967 through February 1968. I once carried out 18 dead Marines in my helicopter. The Marines had run out of body bags and most of the dead had been dead for a couple of days. The corpses were bloated, and the arms were tied with commo wire. You can imagine the smell.

Two of our aircraft were shot down at Con Thien. Both were CH-46D Sea Knights. One was shot down about 5 miles south of the landing zone, and the crew tried to walk south. During the first night, a "Puff the Magic Dragon", an AV-47 gunship, that was supposed to keep them surrounded with suppression fire ended up shooting the co-pilot. He survived and later became a Delta pilot. It took three days to get both crews out.

I was in a hot spot three times. The first time, my squadron was involved in the resupply of Khe Sahn, in 1968, during the siege. The battle for Khe Sahn happened just before the Tet offensive. Khe Sahn was an air base, up until that time. It was in an old French coffee plantation, and there was a beautiful waterfall and this little village. It was very close to the Laotian border. It was on a main road, if you want to call it a road. The main road going north and south was Route 1. Then there's Route 9 going east to west, across the north of South Viet Nam, about one click, one kilometer from the Laotian border.

It became very obvious from reconnaissance and what have you that the NVA, were putting in an enormous number of troops around this airbase. Marines had occupied most of the hilltops. This runway, which could accommodate C-130s, was kind of in a valley, by a waterfall, with Marines on these hilltops. When the siege began, they were bringing in B-52 strikes every day. Lyndon Johnson had a sand model of this built, in the White House basement, and he kept saying, 'This is not going to be another Dien Bien Phu.' He did not want a political disaster of us being overrun, and it was very close.

The C-130s could come in and land at the air base. But after a while, the enemy had the runway all targeted, so they would fly down over the runway, throw out parachutes, and the parachutes would jerk the pallets off. That's how the Air Force and Marines re-supplied the combat base. But the little outposts on these hills several kilometers from the air base that were manned by Marines had to be re-supplied by helicopter.

The Marine Corps had blasted all the vegetation. I mean, there was no cover around those hills. So when we came in with six or eight helicopters there was no question that you were going in to some hillside. I went into a hillside once and we got shot in the transmission. We were taking fire most of the time, but this particular time, we got shot in the transmission, and that's a bad thing. We had twin rotors. Not the Chinook, but it looks like the Chinook. It was a Sea Stallion.

I looked around, and I could see this fluid just gushing out of the transmission in the back. We were pretty far north. We were maybe five minutes from the air base itself. I pulled off there and said we're going back to Khe Sahn. My co-pilot, who was also a Captain like me, but was not a plane commander yet, he was very concerned. And he said, 'Put it down. Put it down.' I said, I'm not going to put it down, because if we land in the valleys, that's where the bad guys were. So, we're flying along and this transmission is now completely empty. We did make it to Khe Sahn. I got just inside the concertina wire and landed in a bomb crater. I said to the crew, ya'all get out. I'll shut it down. And so, I'm sitting in the cockpit, and I shut it down. It only takes a few minutes, but I was the last one out.

All of the crews of helicopters wear a thing called bullet bouncers. It was not a flack vest. It was a solid plate, kind of like a plate of armor. You had a front piece and a back piece. Now the pilots did not use the back plates, 'cause we had armor plate seats, so we put that down under our feet. I had this armor-plate vest on, and as I jumped out the thing came up and hit my lip and bloodied it. I jumped into the bomb crater, beside these other guys. These guys at Khe Sahn had it really bad, and one of the grunts crawls over to me and said, 'Sir, you're going to have to move that helicopter.'

I said, but not this nicely, 'If you want that helicopter moved, then you move it.'

He said, 'They'll blow it up.'

I said, 'Then we need to get out of here, don't we?'

Another time, I was inserting a recon team, in 1968, and the weather was good, we landed, we dropped the ramp. The thing what was bothering me was, in a lot of these places we were using the same landing sites, not every week, but often. We waited a moment, and nothing happened. And again, the crew chief's talking to me. He says we're taking fire. Contrary to what most people say, a helicopter is so noisy you really can't tell, unless someone shooting at you is real close. You can see the holes, but you don't hear sounds. You can hear, your own 50 calibers, because they're real noisy. Well, we weren't firing.

The crew chief says the first two guys are out and they're down. So, I'm screaming, not kindly, 'Get 'em on! Get 'em on!'

And he said, 'The Lieutenant's out there. He's got one on board and he's going back to get the other one.' By now, our gunners are firing. They don't know what they're firing at: they're just shooting. And my crew chief said, 'The VC threw a grenade at him, and he jumped on it. It didn't go off. He picked it up and threw it back. He's got the other guy.'

I said, We're out of here. Raise the ramp!'

The grenade didn't go off either time. That Lieutenant was a 1st Lieutenant. He was younger than me, and probably weighed 130 lbs. I called him up, when we got back.

The third time, we were inserting some troops. This helicopter had two jet engines, and because the engines were susceptible to foreign-object damage, such as dust and dirt, twigs and leaves, they had a big fiber-glass thing, about this big around, stuck on the front of the engine. It was foam-rubber over a fiber-glass shell. And if you took a hit on one of those, it would break off a little piece that would go into the engine and ruin it. And that was what happened. The helicopter flew on one engine, but not well. I kept the troops aboard and made it back to a safe base.

I had a medevac once, which was kind of bad. This was probably in the summer of '68. We had a Marine outpost kind of on the edge of a cliff that dropped off pretty significantly. We were told, on the first day, that we've got a routine medevac. So, we flew out there, and the clouds were low enough so you couldn't get in. So, the next day they said it's significant. Still couldn't get in. At the end of the day, they said, It's an emergency! You've got to come in.'

My philosophy was, I'll do anything I can to get these guys out, but I've also got to weigh the fact that I've got five people on this helicopter. I don't want to kill five to save one. So, we flew out there, and the clouds were low again, and the only way I could get in was, I could fly to the side of the cliff and back in and put my back wheels on the edge, and I did. The front wheels were hanging off. We dropped the ramp, and I was hovering there. We weren't taking fire.

I looked back from the helicopter, and this young Marine walks up. He has a big Ace bandage around his head and a big smile on his face: probably from the effect of morphine. I thought, 'We risked our ass to get this guy.'

The crew chief said, 'He's on', and I said, 'raise her up. We're out of here.' Once we were up, I had the co-pilot fly and said, send that guy up here. I was really going to give it to him. And he came up, and I said, 'What's wrong with you?'

He raised the Ace bandage, and his eye was hanging out. I felt about this small. I went, 'OK! OK! Go back!'

I don't want to disparage anyone. It was horrible for the grunts out in the field. When it was raining, there was mud. When it was hot, it was dusty and miserable. It was horrible, and occasionally these guys would want to get out, and they would go on R & R, or they would say they were sick. So, we had to be very careful about flying along and them seeing us up in the air and saying come help us.

Right about that same time, one of those people at a desk someplace said there's way too much profanity on the radio. There was a lot, and this is the kind thing someone at a desk could think of. And so, a big order, 'No more profanity on the radio. Everybody observe proper radio discipline.'

We're flying along one day, and they knew our helicopters, 'cause we had a purple fox painted on the tail. If they could reach us on the radio, they did. So, I'm flying along and this guy comes up on the radio, and he says, 'Purple Fox. Sir! Sir! We've got a medevac down here.'

I said, 'How serious is it?'

And he said, 'Oh, sir, it's bad.' They usually don't make the most intelligent guy in the world the radio guy.

I said, 'Say the nature of your injury.'

A lot of times, when they put these guys out in the field, they would send in a fixed wing and just bomb the fool out of the area. And in the bomb crater there was nothing. But as it got further away from the blast the tree stumps got taller and taller. And he said, 'Oh, sir, he fell down and stuck a stick right up his alpha sierra sierra.'

I was laughing so hard, but I said, 'We're coming to get him.' Sure enough, he was injured.

Two weeks later, when the Tet offensive really erupted, the city of Hue was captured by the NVA, and we could stand on our bunkers and see a mile away, down the road, on the top of their citadel, an NVA flag flying. They kept Hue, for two weeks.

The Tet offensive was a big turning point. We had been told we're winning. We had been told we've got 'em. We didn't have them. They had us. The NVA took an enormous beating, during the Tet offensive, but at the same time it became obvious they were able to make these enormous strikes all over South Viet Nam. I mean, all over—all the way from the north to the south. Although they lost thousands of soldiers, it became obvious that these guys are not whipped. To me that was an eye opener that really concerned me.

We got to go on R & R. I met my wife once, in Hawaii, and I went to Hong Kong twice. When I was in Hong Kong, at the end of March '68, I decided to stake myself to a real nice dinner, at a place called the Peninsula Hotel, which is really nice. I was sitting at a table along a wall, and about one or two tables down was this older woman. She later told me she was an American ex-patriot living in the hotel. She and her husband had lived there for years and years and years, and her husband had recently died.

I was enjoying my meal, and she leaned over and she said, 'Are you a serviceman?'

I was in civilian clothes. I said, 'Yes mam, I am.'

And she said, 'What do you think about the news?'

And I said, 'I don't know what you're talking about.'

And she said, 'Lyndon Johnson, the American president, announced he's not going to run for president again.'

I was absolutely thrilled. I thought, 'The war is over.' I thought, 'I probably won't even go back to Vietnam. They'll just let me go right home.' Well, as you now, the war was not over.

She said, 'Come down and have dessert.' And we talked.

I was exuberant. I thought, 'It's over!' My personal feeling about Vietnam, then and now, was we wasted a lot of young men. But it didn't take long to realize we were not winning. We would put these massive troop strikes in; they would sweep through an area; and then we would pull out. Khe Sahn was such a long and hard battle. Once the battle was over and the enemy did not take it, within a month, we pulled out and left it. I mean, we just left it. They would go back periodically and do reconnaissance missions out of there.

The Marine Corps' tour of duty in Vietnam was 13 months. Everybody else was 12. I left on November the 23th, 1968. During my time there, I was awarded two Distinguished Flying Crosses, 38 Air Medals, a Navy Commendation Medal, a Bronze Star, and campaign ribbons with two or three battle stars.

When I left Vietnam, I had orders to the Naval Air Station, Pensacola, where I was assigned to be a flight instructor. I instructed in T-28s which is a single-engine, propeller driven airplane, teaching students how to fly instruments. I was there for approximately two years.

While I was in Vietnam, I occasionally heard Project Phoenix mentioned, but not with any specific information about it: just rumors that it was a secret operation. My understanding now is that Project Phoenix started out to be an effort to change the feeling of the Vietnamese people in the small villages, to encourage them to not support the Communist insurgency, but rather to support the Vietnamese government and what they were trying to do. I think that eventually it evolved into a program where, when South Vietnamese people were identified out in the field as Communists or Communist sympathizers, they started arresting them. I think eventually it evolved into assassinations, by Americans and by Vietnamese. I think initially the Vietnamese involvement was governmental and later on the Vietnamese army was involved.

They had a multitude of agencies and police forces, which I read about in the book *The Phoenix Program*. That, to me is symptomatic of what went wrong, which is that the program became so involved in paper work and reporting that it lost sight of its mission, which was to change the hearts and minds of the Vietnamese people. I think that was the failure. I think it evolved into an evil program that I would be ashamed to be a part of, and I think most Americans would be ashamed to be a part of.

The stories about the guys that were out there that began having second thoughts; seeking legal help, because of what they were doing. I think all of that is symptomatic of people doing things that they know are wrong.

I had no contact with Project Phoenix, while I was in Vietnam. I did do some work with the CIA through their aviation arm called Air America. Their helicopters were white and blue. In some cases, when we would insert South Vietnamese troops, and sometimes Marines, the CIA guy or the Air America guys would be there, in their Huey, and they would be responsible for carrying the province chiefs and the important people, by their definition, into or out of the zone. They were pretty quiet. They did not take over anything, and most of the time, they were flying in civilian clothes. Most of them had 38 cal., snub-nosed revolvers on them, which I always thought was kind of useless. If they were shot down, they were going to be killed, and a revolver was not going to do much to save them: unless they were going to use it on themselves.

I don't know if Operation Phoenix harmed our war effort. What concerns me is whether that sort of thing carried on in U.S. conflicts after Vietnam, such as Central America, Iraq, and Afghanistan. Was that same type of mindset prevalent among some of our military and our CIA and other, associated, secret organizations? That bothers me.

I certainly had no great insight, but it didn't take long, after I got to Vietnam, to realize that we were not going to win the war. We would do a sweep of an area and put in Marines, and most of the time the guys who were on their second tour had already done that area two or three years before. We would do these sweeps and bring our guys back, and of course the Communist forces would just move back in. There was no permanent, positive result from what we did.

It dawned on me, that we were hoping that by some miracle the Communists would give up. They weren't going to give up, because the war was like a football game in which my team can't go beyond the 50-yard line and their team can go wherever it wants, including out of bounds. And our cheer leaders were in Washington and their cheer leaders were right there with them. Their coaches were right there with them. Our guys were ensconced in Da Nang, and Saigon, and MAC V, and I often wondered, if they really knew what was goin' on.

About a week before the Tet offensive, we took a truck and we went into Hue on a day off. Our squadron was stationed just a mile south of the city of Hue, which is a big deal to Indochina. In their history, it's where the emperor had been; they had a citadel, and all sorts of stuff there. We walked around the city. We ate at the local stands, along the way. We drank beer, had a good time, and came back.

Within a week, Hue was under total control of the Communists, and they were flying their flag over the Citadel. There are a lot of people who are reluctant to say we lost the war in Vietnam. They will say that Tet was a defeat for the Communists. It may have been a defeat, but I'm tellin' you that they shook the roots of our confidence, because we were told we were winning, yet they hit us everywhere in Vietnam at the same time.

I think there was a real disconnect between what was really happening and what the perception was among the leaders.

I know that there was some false reporting going on. I was in a flight that went to a place called Con Thien, by the DMZ, and it was a really bad place. When we finally could get in, after the Tet offensive, we were carrying in water, food, and ammunition, and we were bringing out wounded and dead. And our squadron alone brought out more KIAs, from Con Thien, than the military reported to the press was reported killed in the entire I Corps. Something was wrong there.

Khe Sahn is another example of something wrong. We knew it had very high priority. The Marine Corps and, I think, the government, was determined not to lose Khe Sahn. They put an enormous amount of support into saving Khe Sahn from the North Vietnamese Army: B-52 strikes; fixed wing strikes of all kinds.

Every day during the siege we would take a flight of eight to either Dong Ha or Quang Tri and wait until the fog cleared at Khe Sahn. Then we loaded up with externals, such as food, water and ammo, and flew to Khe Sahn. We would orbit while Air Force and Marine fixed-wing aircraft bombed and strafed the valleys near every hill we were to resupply, on that mission. We would then hover over the hill and release our loads. Then we would land and drop off any replacements and pick up any dead and wounded. We could only land for a short time, usually about 20 seconds, before the NVA would begin firing mortars, and they had every hill bracketed. The worst was Hills 881 North and South. I piloted the last helicopter in, each time, because I was the first pilot in our squadron to become a plane commander, so I was tail-end Charlie. We usually did three hills a day, weather permitting and always took fire. I was shot down there.

The leader of that effort to take Khe Sahn, for the NVA, was Gen. Giap, and he was evidentially the guy that had defeated the French at Dien Bien Phu. We killed hundreds, if not thousands of their troops there, but within a month of when Giap pulled the NVA troops out of there, we abandoned the base and bulldozed it. If Khe Sahn was so important that we put all that effort and blood into holding it, why did we pull out and leave it?

I think the answer is that the U.S. government decided to let all that American blood be shed just to show Giap we were tougher than the French. I think it was also part of a public relations effort of Pres. Johnson to show we were winning.

If you say to a lot of my contemporaries that we lost the war in Vietnam, they will get very angry, and they will say the politicians made bad decisions or the generals made bad decisions. But the fact is that, if you go into a limited war, expect limited results. And we were in a limited war. If you say we didn't lose that war: when we pulled out of Vietnam, whose flag was left standing? It was not the South Vietnamese and it was not ours. It was the North Vietnamese.

My opinion now is I'm not sure we should ever have gone into Vietnam. The South Vietnamese government was a corrupt government. South Viet Nam was a corrupt society. It was corrupt from the git-go, and we were trying to reform them, at the same time we were fighting a war against the Communists. There were rumors, when I was there, about the big generals Ky and Thieu both being involved in drug trafficking.

I don't think we could have won that war, unless we were willing to stay there for decades and decades. The American people certainly wanted us out. That was clear.

By the time we got around to deciding what size the peace-negotiating table was going to be and whether it was going to be round or oblong, I think the North Vietnamese could see that the U.S. wanted out at any price. I think, in the negotiations in Paris, we were primarily trying to get out and save face, and I don't think we did. If we had stayed there another 10 years operating under the same rules we were operating under when I was there, I don't think we'd have won.

Strategic bombing does not win wars. It did not deter the British when they were bombed by the Nazis. It did not deter the Germans, even though we bombed them into oblivion. While I thought that the bombing of North Vietnam was necessary, it was very restricted, as to what they were actually allowed to bomb. They couldn't bomb certain places near Hanoi, and so forth, but I just don't think that the bombing would have forced the North Vietnamese to their knees.

The only way to have won was to invade and conquer North Viet Nam and replace the governments of North and South Viet Nam with governments of our choosing, and that was politically impossible.

After I left the Marines, I got hired by Delta Airlines and went to work there, in March of 1970. Once I completed training, I was assigned to the base at Dallas. I stayed there two years and then moved to Atlanta. I flew for Delta for 32 years. It was a very good career. I enjoyed myself. I was a Captain, for about half of that time, and the last six or seven years of my career, I flew international: primarily to Europe, but sometimes to South America.

My first wife and I moved to Atlanta, from Dallas, and she unexpectedly passed away, in '76. We had an eight-year old daughter and twin daughters that were six months old. I was single for a couple of years, and through a blind date, arranged by my first wife's sister, met my present wife, whose name is Penny. And we've been married 35 years, and together we had a son. She raised all of the children, and they refer to her as mom.

Penny had never been married, and, of course, never had children. And so, this was a big thing for her: going with some guy who had babies still in diapers. So, we got married, and the babies were about two-and-a-half. Went on our honeymoon; came home; and I had to go fly. I said Cathi the older daughter, has soccer tomorrow. You have to take the Gatorade, for Cathi's team, and Cathi, and carry her to the game. I had a big station wagon.

So, I go off flying. I call that night and get this report: She loaded the twins, Cathi, and the Gatorade and got to the soccer match, where one of the twins fell in a mud hole, and was covered in mud and started screaming. So, Penny arranged with one of the other mothers to bring Cathi home, and drives home with the twins to clean them up. She pulled up to the driveway, and they're still screaming, and she realized I have not given her a house key. A good start, right? She pried off one of the screens, and all the time the babies were in the car, screaming. She said she got a screen loose and started to climb in to the house through the dining room window, and looked back, and the babies were now howling with laughter. That was a not too auspicious a start to our home life.

During 17 years of the 32 years I worked for Delta, I also had a construction company. I built a total of 117 houses, in North Fulton and Cobb Counties, here in Georgia. And I was generally building in the higher end, mostly in golf course communities. I finished my building career in Country Club of the South, in 2001, and retired from Delta, in 2002. Penny and I live in Cobb County.

I have some hobbies. I like to do bonsai trees: miniature trees, and I do a lot of volunteer work, primarily in two areas. I do trail work on the Appalachian Trail, in the Georgia Mountains. And I usually do that once a week: cleaning up, cutting leaves, cutting blowdowns, occasionally build or repair shelters and privies, and what have you.

I am also an instructor in chain saws and cross-cut saws, and I instruct both volunteers and Forest Service people. I do that as a volunteer, because the Forest Service can't afford to pay their own guys to do it.

And I'm involved in a charity called "Family Promise", which provides homeless families with housing. And we have 13 congregations in this area that are involved in that.

Right now, I'm doing a lot of memorization work for the first degree of Freemasonry. I am scheduled to be examined in my proficiency in it next month, in Roswell Masonic Lodge. My father was a Mason. I wish I had done this 30 years ago.

Gary Monk said, 'This was the "hooch" or tent we used as living quarters before we moved to our newly-built quarters, right before the Tet offensive of 1968. This picture was taken in late December 1967 or January 1968.'

Gary Monk said, 'This is a photo of me in front of the remains of my Sea Knight helo. It was taken, on the day after we crashed at Khe Sahn. There was a temporary lull in battle, in this area, at this time.'

Capt. Gary Monk (right) plays acey-deucy with Capt. Trev Sarles (background), in their quarters, at Phu Bai, early in 1968, while Capt. Jake Spohn watches the game's progression.

# Jonathan Tobias "Toby" Mack
interview of November 20, 2015

My name is Toby Mack. I have a longer name that my mamma assigned. My real given name is Jonathan Tobias Mack, but I am known in the working world as Toby Mack. I was born in December of 1944, in Cornwells Heights, a northeastern suburb of Philadelphia, Pennsylvania.

My father's name was Henry Stauffer Mack. He was a sales executive with a number of companies. He was not in the service, during World War II, because he was older than service age. He was a purchasing executive with Fleetwings, a company that made fighter aircraft and aircraft wings. My mother's maiden name was Jane Euretta Kerr. She was from Philadelphia.

I have an older brother Bill and a younger brother Rick. My younger brother was at home, but my older brother was at war, in the Air Force's 8th Tactical Fighter Wing, flying F-4 Phantom fighter-bomber jets out of Ubon, Thailand into North Vietnam. He flew 100 bombing missions over North Vietnam.

I went to primary and secondary schools in Pennsylvania. I went to primary school in New Hope and began high school there. I finished high school at Council Rock High School, in Newtown, in June 1962. I went on to college, at Penn State University, and got a Liberal Arts degree, in June 1966. I had gone through the Naval ROTC program, at Penn State, and was commissioned as an ensign, when I graduated. I went into active duty with the Navy, right after graduation.

I had orders to a destroyer, the *Johnston*, DD-821. The ship was home-ported in Charleston, South Carolina, but I didn't report directly to the *Johnston*. Instead, I went through three training programs to be a nuclear submarine warfare officer, so I would have the proper qualifications when I came aboard. Each school lasted six to eight weeks.

The first one was Anti-Submarine Warfare School, in Key West. I learned about sonar and other then current weapons, one of which was ASW torpedoes; ASROC rockets; and submarine warfare tactics.

From there I went to DASH School or Drone Anti-Submarine Helicopter School, in Dam Neck, Virginia, to learn about a weapons system that involved a large, pilotless helicopter. It was one of the first drones in operational use. It was controlled from a pedestal on the destroyer and flew from the destroyer's flight deck. Underneath its skids, it could carry one or two ant-submarine, homing torpedoes. It could also carry a nuclear depth charge.

If there was a submarine contact, you would take it off and control its direction, altitude, and speed with a joy stick. When the helicopter was in the air, you would transfer control of it to the ship's combat information control center. The CIC. The ship's radar showed where the drone was, and the CIC could vector the drone out to the submarine contact, which could be a few miles from the ship. When the drone was in position, an electronic command would release the homing torpedoes or bomb, and an acoustic, sonar-based homing system in the torpedo would spiral down and search for the submarine. When the torpedo found the submarine, it would home in on the submarine and kill it.

Then I was assigned to a school, in Norfolk, Virginia, which was basically nuclear weapons school, because the destroyer carried a couple of nuclear depth charges. As anti-submarine warfare officer, I was in charge of maintenance and operation of those weapons.

Those schools lasted from June to sometime in November 1966. Then I was flown to Naples, Italy, where I joined the ship, which had departed on a deployment to the Middle East. During the next three or four weeks, the anti-submarine officer went through a turn-over check list with me, and I then relieved him as nuclear submarine warfare officer.

We stopped in Beirut, Lebanon, and went through the Suez Canal; stopped in Ethiopia; Saudi Arabia; two Red Sea ports; and in what is now known as Yemen, which was then the British protectorate of Aden; and then around the tip of the Arabian Peninsula and into the Persian Gulf. We spent the next couple of months operating in the Persian Gulf. We were assigned to the U.S. Navy's Middle East fleet, which is a small fleet of ships, more or less permanently stationed in the Persian Gulf. We did exercises with most allied navies, in the Persian Gulf. We stopped in Iran, which was then a friendly country, and in Bahrain, where we still have a naval base.

Then we came back through the Straits of Hormuz, around the Arabian Peninsula, through the Red Sea, through the Suez Canal, and into the Mediterranean. We operated with the Sixth Fleet, in the Mediterranean for several weeks. I remember celebrating New Year, at a big New Year's Eve party, in the U.S. embassy, in Beirut, Lebanon. We got extended, because the ship that was relieving us was late crossing the ocean. We stopped at Majorca and then Rota, in Spain and then made our way back to Charleston, South Carolina, our home port, in January 1967.

Then we made several deployments to the Caribbean, mostly for training exercises. The mission was readiness, so we were continuously conducting training exercises both for anti-submarine and anti-air warfare.

By 1967, the destroyer's 5-in. guns, which had been so effective in World War II, against much slower, propeller-driven aircraft, weren't very effective against a very fast-moving jet aircraft. But we still tried. The guns were still useful for surface to surface and surface to land warfare. We trained to hit targets on the beach and fired at long sleeves towed behind aircraft.

We also conducted anti-submarine exercises operating with a U.S. sub, which was put in the role of an enemy sub. We had to find it and attack with practice torpedoes, which if successful, would just bounce off the submarine. Each time we went down, we'd call at several ports in the Caribbean and come back to Charleston.

By then, the war in Vietnam was really starting to heat up, so we got orders to deploy to Vietnam with Destroyer Squadron 4, which was based in Charleston. The *Johnston* went by itself to support our combatant forces there, and we did not operate as a squadron in Vietnam.

We steamed through the Panama Canal and stopped in Pearl Harbor, for supplies, refueling, etc. On our way westward, we steamed into a severe typhoon with winds well over 100-miles an hour and 50-ft waves. In those days, they had no satellite weather capability, so nobody knew the typhoon was there, and we just steamed right into the middle of it and were in it for three days.

We were all by ourselves, and spent the three days fighting to stay afloat, in mountainous seas and high winds. You really had to batten everything down, and we suffered some topside damage, but we made it to Midway, and made temporary repairs. We went on to Guam and from there to the U.S. Naval Base, at Subic Bay, in the Philippines. Subic Bay was the main operating and maintenance facility for the U.S. Navy, in the western Pacific. I wasn't aware of that history, at that time. It probably was good that I wasn't.

We did well to come out of that storm in condition to steam to Vietnam. In mid-December 1944, a typhoon with winds of 100-miles an hour hit a U.S. task force east of the Philippines and sank the U.S. destroyers *Hull*, *Monaghan*, and *Spence* and took 790 sailors with it.

On our way to the Philippines, we stopped for a ceremony, where the *USS* Johnston, DD-557, was lost, in 1944. We had a ceremony there and threw a wreath over the side, to honor the sacrifice made by the crew of that *USS Johnston,* and 186 crew members that were lost.

The *USS Johnston, DD-821* that I served aboard was named for *USS Johnston, DD557* that was sunk by the Japanese in the Battle off Samar, during the Battle of Leyte

Gulf, in late October of 1944, in World War II. Before it sank, *USS Johnston, DD-557,* accounted for many 5-in. gunfire hits and also torpedo hits, on ships of a far larger and more powerful Japanese task force. The Battle of Samar enabled U.S. and Australian warships to protect the U.S. landing force, on Leyte, and destroy part of other Japanese naval forces moving from the west.

We celebrated Christmas at sea, and got to Subic, on the 27th of December 1967. At Subic, we got ready for our deployment to Vietnam. They removed the two nuclear weapons, because we were headed for the Tonkin Gulf, which was too shallow for submarines, and we didn't want to subject them to fire from the coast of Vietnam. They also outfitted us with a couple of 50-cal. machine gun mounts amidships, on each side of the ASROC deck. The 50-calibers were for any kind of close-in engagements we might have.

After maintenance, re-fitting, and repairs, we left for the Tonkin Gulf, on the 5th of January 1968. Our assigned operating area was off I Corps, just south if the Demilitarized Zone. We were assigned plane-guard duty, and that was to rescue carrier air crews that went down into Tonkin Gulf and to escort the aircraft carrier *USS Ranger, CV-61,* that was launching air strikes into Vietnam. We had that duty through January and then came back to Subic Bay, on January 31.

We had suspected that we might have had some rudder damage from the typhoon, and that one of the ship's two rudders had worked itself loose, inside the packing that maintained water-tight integrity where it went through the ship and into the sea. So they put us into dry dock and found damage, but not enough to take us out of service.

We were then sent to the gun line off I Corps, on the northern coast of South Viet Nam. Our operating zone was between the Demilitarized Zone and the port of Da Nang. On gun-line duty you were operating from one to 4,000-yards from the beach. Our job was to provide artillery support, when requested, if the requesting unit was within range of our guns. I believe the 1st and 3rd Marine Divisions and the U.S. Army Air Cavalry were there at that time. The spotter operating with the combat unit ashore would give us a grid co-ordinate and tell us what kind of 5-in. ordnance to fire and how many. The observer would see the fall of our shot and give us corrections.

On a couple of occasions, we came under fire, from enemy artillery emplacements on the beach. They were probably North Vietnamese regular units, because they had heavy artillery. The first time was on February 9th.

The more frequent part of our mission was what they called H and I, or Harassment and Interdiction Fire. Sometime around dusk, operatives ashore would give us 25 or 30 target co-ordinates that were typically along the Ho Chi Minh Trail. Our job was to drop one round of 5-inch on each target per hour. That was the typical night mission. We would just go up and down very slowly, maybe 2000 yards from the beach, and drop a round on each target, until about four o'clock in the morning. The idea was to harass and interdict the enemy movement of materials.

We arrived on the gun line, late the evening of February 6th. The Tet offensive was under way as we arrived, and we were sent to a spot right off the South Vietnamese coast, on the same latitude as Hue, which is somewhat inland. Our guns had a 5-mile range, and we were at their extreme range to hit targets in Hue, so we had to go in as close to the beach as we could. I think we got in to about 1000 yards.

We were in the thick of that battle for quite a number of hours. We were getting calls for fire, from Marine Corps units in the battle for the Citadel, in Hue. We were firing; trying to hit enemy targets in and around the Citadel where our Marines were engaged in intense combat. After we fired quite a number of rounds, the cruiser *USS Providence* arrived and took over. It had a triple, 6-inch-gun turret and longer range, so we moved aside for it.

Each destroyer division had a chaplain; a preacher, basically. The chaplain that rode circuit with my destroyer division was aboard the *Johnston* most often, while I was on the *Johnston*, so we got to know him. His name was Eli Takesian, and he was a Lieutenant Commander. He had been a Marine, in the Korean War, and then became a Presbyterian minister. Then he became a Navy chaplain. After his duty aboard destroyers, he requested duty in Vietnam with Marine infantry, and the Navy Department transferred him to serve with the 1st Marine Corps Division.

As a result, he was there, on the ground, during the battle for Hue, and distinguished himself serving the Marines. He told me later that, during the Tet offensive, his Marine unit had suffered many casualties and was in the Citadel, in Hue, surrounded by North Vietnamese soldiers. A South Vietnamese army unit that was supposed to cover their flank did not show up, and additional North Vietnamese soldiers were arriving. The Marines, who had been pursuers, were becoming the pursued. When newly arrived North Vietnamese troops began to climb the Citadel's walls the Marines radioed to U.S. Navy ships and requested fire support.

He remembered that the *Johnston* and a cruiser assisted. He said that during that whole night he heard, 'boom! boom! boom!' all around the Citadel, as *Johnston,* and then the cruiser, placed rounds accurately and gave the Marines protection they needed. The North Vietnamese were beaten back. He said he was so proud, because *Johnston* was his old ship. He went on to become chief chaplain of the Marine Corps and a Navy Captain.

After we were relieved from our Hue City gun-fire support duty, we went back to general call-for-fire support and operated close in. During that time, we came under fire a couple of times, from North Vietnamese artillery ashore. They almost hit us once, but we didn't suffer any damage. I was on the bridge, as officer of the deck, for my section, because there was not much call for an anti-submarine officer. We were on port and starboard watch sections, in the combat zone: one section on every six hours and relieved by the other, which was then on for six hours.

On the 12th of February, I was officer of the deck and in charge of the ship, as the Captain's representative, on the bridge. We were engaged in a gun fire support mission, and all of a sudden, this great big, fat geyser of water plumed up, from right off the bow of the ship. It missed us by about 60 yards. That was the first time we'd seen enemy fire incoming, and it got everybody's attention. As near misses go, that's a pretty-near miss. So, we decided to exit the area, because we thought the North Vietnamese trained their artillery on a point, in the water, and fired when a ship came to that point.

We entered the combat zone on February 7th and remained in a gun fire support mode until late in the month of February, and were called back into gun fire support for the Hue battle on the 27th.

One of the things that happens, because you're expending a lot of ammunition, is that you have to go out and take on more 5-inch ammo. So, between missions we'd do that under way and also re-fuel and re-supply with food and other stores. We would steam out into the Gulf of Tonkin a good ways and link up with an ammunition ship, or a fleet oiler, or a stores ship to re-supply. Then we'd head back for the beach.

We finally left the gun line on the 10th of March '68, and went to Kaohsiung, Taiwan, to rest, re-supply and do repairs that you couldn't do under way. We were there for about 10 days, and left for the Tonkin Gulf, were we were again assigned plane-guard duty, for the *USS Ranger*, for a few days. Then we were sent to the gun line for further gun fire support operations.

At the end of March, we went out to join *Ranger*, doing screening and plane-guard duty, until the 12th or 13th of April, when we were detached and sent back to Subic Bay. Then, to our great delight, we were sent to Hong Kong, for R & R, for a little less than a week. All of us loaded up on Japanese Hi-Fi electronics and so forth, and stowed them aboard the ship.

We went back to the Tonkin Gulf, on the 20th of April, and operated with *Ranger* again, until the 7th of May, when we entered port, in Subic Bay again, in preparation for our return to the States. After a couple of days, we headed to Okinawa, where we arrived on May 11th. Then dry dock time became available in Yokosuka, Japan, and were sent there to get our rudder fixed. We were in dry dock for seven or eight days, and on the 16th of May, we headed back east across the Pacific. We stopped at Midway, for re-fuel; then stopped at Pearl Harbor, for more fuel and provisions, on the 31st of May. Then we headed for San Diego, where we arrived on June 6th.

The ship had to go through the Panama Canal and back to Charleston, but I was granted leave, so I flew home to my family, in Pennsylvania. I came back from leave and joined the ship, in Charleston. I was at the end of my two-year tour of duty, on *Johnston.* I took some more leave and reported aboard the cruiser *USS Springfield*, in September of 1968.

They sent me to a guided missile fire-control school, in Norfolk, because the *Springfield* was primarily an anti-air, guided missile ship. Then I was assigned as the guided missile fire control officer on the *Springfield.*

I spent my first year, in the Navy, as an ensign. In June of 1967, before leaving for Vietnam, I made Lieutenant junior grade. I made Lieutenant, after my duty on the Springfield.

I was on the *Springfield,* for less than a year, because I was selected to become an admiral's aide. The *Springfield* was home ported at Norfolk, which was also the home port for the Atlantic Fleet. I was selected to be the aide and executive assistant to the deputy commander-in-chief of the Atlantic Fleet. So, I spent two years as aide to a three-star Admiral: until March of '71. Then I resigned my commission and left the Navy.

While I was in the Navy, I received two Navy Achievement Medals, each with a combat "V"; a Combat Action Ribbon; a Vietnam Service Medal, with three campaign stars; and a Republic of Vietnam Meritorious Unit Citation.

I never had PTSD or any problems, after I came home. Compared with men on the ground, we had it pretty easy, on the destroyer. You know, we were getting served hot meals three times a day. We were taking hot showers. We were in pretty comfortable surroundings. It was rigorous to stand watch six hours on and six hours off, but there was no comparison with combat troops on the ground.

After the Navy, I went to work as vice president of the Electronic Industries Association, in Washington, D.C., and then moved to Chicago, in 1977, to be president of the Electronic Distributors Association. In 1989, I became the president of Associated Equipment Distributors, which represented construction equipment dealers in the United States and Canada. In 2013, I became CEO of the Energy Equipment Infrastructure Alliance. Now I'm back in Washington, with it. I lead a team of lobbyists that try to get the members of Congress to do the right thing.

I met my beautiful, wonderful bride, in Chicago, in 1981. Her maiden name was Marti de Graaf. She was from Illinois. We have no children. It was pretty much a conscious decision on our part.

I belong to many professional, civic, and military organizations. I'm a member of the board of the Chamber of Commerce Foundation. I'm vice president of the board of the United States Navy Memorial Foundation, which is here in Washington. I belong to the reunion group, for my ship and occasionally make reunions that they hold.

*Author's Note: For more information about* USS Johnston DD-821, *including Chaplain Takesian's valorous action, during the Battle of Hue City, in the Vietnam War, and a firsthand account of* USS Johnston DD-557 *in the Battle off Samar see* The Real Story of the USS Johnston DD-821:

As Told by the Officers and Sailors Who Served Aboard Her, *George Sites, editor.*

Toby Mack (in the foreground) is on duty, on the bridge of the *USS Johnston*, DD-821, as it steams across the Pacific towards a station off Vietnam.

On the ship's voyage west, from Pearl Harbor, 'we steamed into a severe typhoon with winds of 100-miles an hour and 50-ft waves... I'm standing on the *USS Johnston's* bridge, which is 35-ft above the water line, and we're lookin' up at this wave towering over us and coming at the bow of the ship.'

Tody Mack takes a compass reading on the ship's binnacle, while the *USS Johnston DD-821* comes alongside a fleet oiler to re-fuel.

# Donald Terrance Dowd
## interview of January 30, 2017

My full name is Donald Terrance Dowd. I was born at Key West, Florida, on August 8, 1948.

My father was David Donald Dowd. He was a milkman in Key West, and later worked, as a policeman, in a Miami suburb. My mother's name was Josephine Hernandez. Her whole family was born in Key West. She was a housewife for long time and then she took a job waiting tables, in Miami. I have one older sister. Her name is Cynthia Ann.

I went to public schools in Hialeah, Florida, and left, after my third year of high school, to join the Army, in July 1967. I was 17. I earned my high school GED, in the Army.

I went to basic training, in Ft. Benning, Georgia. Then I went to 10-weeks of medical corpsman training, in Ft. Sam Houston, in San Antonio, Texas. After that, I went back to Ft. Benning to jump school. I liked that. It was a four-week course. I finished it in October '67.

At the very end of December '67, I was sent to Vietnam. I went over assigned to the 173rd Airborne Brigade Combat Team. When my plane landed at Bien Hoa there had just been a big battle and there were dead gooks hanging in the perimeter wire. Half the airport was blown up, man, and it was a wonder we landed.

When I processed in, I was sent down south of Saigon to the 506th Paratroop Infantry Regiment of the 101st Airborne Division. The change to the 506th was made just like them saying everybody on the left go to the 101st, everybody on the right go to the 173rd. I went to a place called Phuc Vin and joined the 506th, 2nd Battalion, Headquarters Company at first.

In January 1968, I went to C Company. The enemy's Tet offensive happened when I got there, and we went on search-and-destroy patrols and major operations. We were near Saigon.

We went into the deep, dark jungles. Our company was movin' through the bush, one time, and before we come out of the jungle they told our platoon to stay in the bush. So, everybody in the platoon sat down to take a brake and the others left. We were supposed to come out, after dark, and set up an ambush. So we come out after dark, and on our way to set up the ambush we got ambushed. We walked into an L-shaped ambush. We had our rally area picked out, which was up on mounds in a cemetery, and we made our stand there. None of our men got killed. There was a lot of bullet holes in canteens and rucksacks, but none of us got hurt that night. We had to laugh about it.

After that, we went to several places. We went to Cu Chi, a district in Saigon, in summer '68, and fought a big, two-day battle there. It was a big operation. The 1st Battalion of the 506 was with us too. Then we went to the A Shau Valley and did search-and-destroy patrols. A lot of guys got killed in those places.

I went to the LRRPs and was with them, for three months, from October through December '68, on long range reconnaissance patrols. They roved around: just a squad of about nine or 10 of us. When I went out with the LRRPs, I was a medic and a rifleman. I was a good medic. I carried a lot of ammo, man.

We went on up to Dak Tek, in September or October '68, which was on the other side of a hill overlooking Dak To, where Special Forces had their camp. There was a big battle going on there, for a while, and we were in a couple of skirmishes. That was a two-day battle.

Then we went up to a higher peak, in western South Viet Nam, on the border with Laos. We dug trenches there that overlooked a Ho Chi Minh trail and the village of Dao Tec. We were trying to protect that village, which is where Montagnard's were. It was very primitive.

We'd go out on patrols, from there, and there was action down the mountain. There was pretty big opposition, and many, many men were wounded or killed. Most battles don't last too long, but, when they go two days, the loss is just great. I've been in a couple of two-days.

In November 1968, I transferred from the infantry to an aviation outfit. I was a dust-off crewman, with Eagle Dustoff. It was an air ambulance platoon with the 326th Medical Battalion. We flew on large helicopters marked with red crosses. I learned how to help out as a crewman and pick up the wounded. I used to work on 'em on the ground and put 'em on the Dustoff. Then I got on the Dustoff and worked on 'em to the hospital or the hospital ship: whatever was necessary. It was my call. If a man needed real medical care, I had him taken to the hospital ship. Otherwise, he was taken to the evac hospital, in country. Sometimes it was to whichever was closer.

I had a lot of missions: a lot of missions, man. I got so many hours in that I got 13 Air Medals.

Dustoff on Hamburger Hill was devastating. The battle there went on from May 10th to May 20th, 1969. The hill is at the west end of the A Shau Valley, very near Laos. It is 937 meters high and very steep. We lost two ships, during it, man. One was a little helicopter. I think it was a Bell helicopter. The other was a Huey; a UH-1. I flew in and out of there so many times, man. That went on for a couple of days.

We would circle in the air, stacked about 1000-ft. above each other, and one helicopter would go in. When he came out, we went down and landed. We got our ass fired on, but nobody on my helicopter was hit.

We did a lot of hoist missions and combat pick-ups. A hoist mission is a dangerous mission, but it's beautiful though, in a way. When we'd go in to a hoist mission, we'd get two snakes to go with us: two Cobra helicopter gunships. They would hover around us, and we'd be in the center, and while we were hoisting our wounded aboard in individual hoist baskets we'd be shot at. I'd just point to where the shots came from, and a Cobra would destroy that real estate. If we were able to land, our wounded would be taken aboard on litters and in ponchos.

We'd get back to our landing place; I'd take that 100-mile-an-hour tape and go around the helicopter patchin' all the bullet holes. The tape was duct tape, but back then we called it 100-mile-an-hour tape. An enemy rocket shot a chunk out of a blade on our helicopter once, and there was only about four inches width of blade left where the chunk was shot out. So, Phil Gibson of Annapolis, Maryland, our crew chief, took some Styrofoam and cut it to shape to fit the missing chunk and taped it to the blade, with 100-mile-an-hour tape, and we were back in the air.

I left Vietnam in early '70 and got out February 7, 1970. I was a Specialist 5. I was in Vietnam for 23 months and 10 days, because my time there was extended when I went from river-rat grunt to crewman medic on Eagle Dustoff.

In addition to the Air Medals, the medals and badges I earned, in Vietnam are a Combat Medic Badge, Parachute Badge, Air Crewman Badge, Bronze Star Medal, Vietnam Campaign Medal, Vietnam Service Medal with one silver and two bronze service stars, National Defense Service Medal, Good Conduct Medal, Air Medal, Army Commendation Medal, Meritorious Unit Citation, Four Overseas Bars, Expert with the M-16, Marksman with the M-14, Republic of Vietnam Gallantry Cross Unit Citation with Palm, and Republic of Vietnam Civil Action Unit Citation.

When I got out, I didn't want to do nothin', but lay back. So, I took a year off. Then my mother nagged me to go to work, so I went to work. I got a job in a factory, in Miami, Florida, making awnings for windows and lean-to awnings.

Then I worked construction, for about four years, diggin' holes; buildin' churches. Building churches was the neatest thing. There are no two churches alike in architecture.

Then I got a real job in the post office, in Miami, and I had to quit construction work.

In about '76, I got married, had three kids—two girls and one boy. The eldest is Anastasia Theresa Adams. My son is Donald Terrence Dowd II. My youngest is Heather Ann Dowd. Then I was divorced 28-years later, in 2002. I have no grandchildren.

After I got divorced, I was roaming around a lot, man. I kind of got lost. She took my house; took my cars; took my kids. I didn't have no home no more. I was on the street; already had three heart attacks; heart surgery and other surgery. I had nothin' but the clothes on my back.

In 2008, the VA gave me a 100% PTSD rating.

On November 9, 2013, Linda and I were married. She's from Oklahoma. I met her on line. I had a computer, at that time, but I lost it. I was homeless. Linda retired, in October 2014, and we moved to Cantonment, a suburb of Pensacola, Florida.

I'm a lifetime member of American Legion; Veterans of Foreign Wars; 101st Airborne Association; the 2nd Battalion, 506th Parachute Infantry Regiment Association; and Dustoff Association. I'm a member of Wounded Warriors, but I was never wounded by a bullet.

Donald Terrance Dowd, in 1967, while in Basic Training

Donald Terrance Dowd, in 2016

# Thomas Joseph "Tom" Flaherty
interview of July 14, 2017

My full name is Thomas Joseph Flaherty. Friends call me "Tom". I was born in Berwick, Pennsylvania on 1 October 1943.

My dad was Edward Flaherty. He was an electrician. My mom's name was Lucy, and she was a housewife. Her maiden name was Simon. She was from Berwick, Pennsylvania, and my dad was from St. Louis, Missouri.

I have two younger brothers. My mom and dad moved us to Florissant, Missouri, which is about 15-miles north of St. Louis. My grade school was Our Lady of Fatima, in Florissant, and then to St. Vincent's High School-Pre-seminary, in Cape Girardeau, Missouri. I finished high school in 1961, and then I was in St. Mary's Seminary, for three years, studying to be a priest in the Vincentian Order. I left there in September of 1964, with about 2-1/2 years of college completed.

I attended one semester of night school at St. Louis University while I worked during the day for the St. Louis City Police Department, September to December 1964. I took one semester of calculus and one semester of physics. I started as a full time, day student at St. Louis University, in January 1965, majoring in chemistry and minoring in physics and mathematics. I took 12-credit hours each semester, until I graduated, in June 1967, with a Bachelor of Science degree, with a major in chemistry and a minor in physics and mathematics.

When I dropped out of seminary, in September 1964, I lost my college-student deferment and received a draft notice in January or February 1965. I had started full time night school, at St. Louis University.

My dad was in the Navy, during the Second World War, so I went down to the Navy recruiter, in St. Louis, and took numerous tests. I did pretty well in all of them, and qualified to go to flight school, at Pensacola. The recruiter told me that, if I wanted flight school, I had to join the Navy and would be leaving in a couple of weeks to start flight school. I told him I wanted to finish college first, and he sent me down the hall to the Marine Corps.

I walked into the Marine recruiter's office and was so impressed by the Marine Corps and the people there. I took more tests, and they told me I qualified for the Marine Corps Platoon Leader Class program, and, if I joined the Marine Corps, on that day, they would tell the Draft Board that I joined the PLC program, and they would make me a corporal that day, and my job for the Marine Corps would be to finish college, maintain a good grade point average, and take 12 credit hours a semester. My major was chemistry, and I minored in physics and math, and I would have to go through PLC training for six weeks in each of two summers or 10 weeks in one summer.

I took 12 hours each semester, until I graduated on June 2, 1967, 2-1/2-years later, with a Bachelor of Science degree with a major in chemistry and a minor in physics and mathematics. I went through the PLC program, in the summer of 1966, at Quantico. When I graduated from college, I was commissioned a Second Lieutenant in the Marine Corps Reserve, and I had orders to The Basic School, at Quantico, starting July 15, 1967. We were at Camp Upshur for a couple of weeks, and then they moved us to Camp Barrett, both at Quantico. There were guys there from all over the country and from every university you could think of.

My roommates, at The Basic School, were Mark Fibelkorn, from Durango, Colorado, who had been on the ski team there and graduated in only three years, and John Ferrigno, who had played tackle on the University of South Carolina's football team and on the Marine Corps' football team, at Quantico. The quality of people I was with was impressive. There were All American athletes, a Rhodes Scholar, and a large group of Naval Academy graduates. We were in The Basic School Class 2-68 and graduated on January 3, 1968.

Mark and I and a bunch of other guys had orders to 5th Marine Division, at Camp Pendleton, so we determined we were going to drive to Camp Pendleton, and start our lives on the beach in southern California. I drove to my parents' home and spent a couple of days with my mom and dad and my middle brother. My youngest brother, Charles, was already in the Army and in Vietnam.

My middle brother, Dan Flaherty, was the third baseman for St. Louis University's baseball team. He went to college on a full baseball scholarship, and, in 1967 or 1968, St. Louis University went to the NCAA semi-finals. He was an All Missouri Valley Conference player for two years. He eventually became a Secret Service agent and guarded most of the recent presidents and secretaries of state.

After the visit, at home, I drove to Camp Pendleton. Mark, his wife, and child drove there in their own car, and when we got there, he and I checked in. He got assigned to the 3rd Battalion, 27th Marine Regiment, India Company, and I got assigned to Golf Company, 2nd Battalion, 27th Regiment. We were both at Camp Margarita, at Camp Pendleton. I got a room at the Camp Delmar BOQ, right on the beach.

I reported there towards the middle of January 1968, and I was assigned a platoon. We went out in the field on training exercises right away. The only other Lieutenant in the company was Charlie Neil, who was an All-American diver from the University of Indiana. He had quit law school, in Chicago, to join the Marine Corps. Our company commander was an Air Force Academy graduate. He had just gotten back from Vietnam.

I think I was there for two weeks, and one morning, at about 2 o'clock, I got a phone call to get into battalion right away and bring all my uniforms, except my dress whites, my dress blues, and my sword. I drove in right away and got there at three or four o'clock in the morning, in my new car. When I reported in, the company commander told me that the regiment got orders to go to Vietnam, and they were leaving. He was not going, because he just got back from Vietnam, and we were going to get a new company commander and Lieutenants for the other platoons. No one was allowed to leave the base.

We had a meeting of all the officers in the battalion and were told everyone was going to be issued weapons, flak jackets, helmets, packs. We were taking our 81mm mortars, with our 106mm recoilless rifles, and our 50-cal. machine guns. Those men that had been back in the States for less than a year weren't going, unless they volunteered. Those that had been back more than a year were going whether they wanted to or not.

After that meeting, a Marine handed me thousands of dollars and told me that I was the pay officer for the battalion, and I was to pay everyone that wasn't going to Vietnam.

We got a new company commander, new Lieutenants, in addition to Charlie Neil and myself, and I got a complete new platoon. We were trucked up to El Toro to the Marine Corps Air Station, which is about 20-miles north of Camp Pendleton. We were formed in company formation, in a hangar there, and C-141s started coming in. Every Marine was supposed to have a sea bag. Officers were required to carry a sea bag and a Valpack, which is a hand-carried travel bag.

Someone ran up to Charlie Neil and me, as we were loading, and gave him a roster that was supposed to be a roster of Marines on the airplane. He was senior to me by two months. My platoon and Charlie Neil's platoon were on one of the first planes to be loaded. There were 95 Marines in each aircraft. We took off, toward the evening. It got dark. We had no idea where we were going, other than the general area of Vietnam.

The planes landed in the dark, and we figured out we were in Hawaii, because it was real humid and hot. It just smelled like a tropical island. The plane Captain told us we were going to be there for a couple of hours, while the plane was re-fueled, so we mustered everybody and check to see if everybody on the roster was on the airplane. We had been given the wrong aircraft roster.

We took off after a couple of hours. It was still dark. And we flew over the Pacific. There was only one window in the airplane. Charlie Neil and I sat in the back next to a jeep that was loaded with a 106-recoilless rifle and a lot of wooden boxes and C-Ration boxes.

The next place we landed was Wake Island. We knew it was Wake Island, because we found a Wake Island memorial there. We were there for a couple of hours, and the planes took off again. It was daylight. The next place we landed was Okinawa. We knew we were on Okinawa, because the whole two hours we were there, B-52s were taking off from Kadena Air Force Base. They were loaded with bombs under their wings and in their holds. They were all painted black.

We were there for a couple of hours, while the plane re-fueled. It was now probably February 14, 1968. We had no idea what was going on or where in Vietnam we were going. We took off, and, a couple of hours later, we started circling and descending. I looked out the window, and I could look down and see tracers going back and forth and explosions. All of a sudden, the planes landed; they dropped the rear gates, the jeeps and all the boxes and C-Rations were pulled out.

It was hot, and the smell of JP-4 jet fuel was overpowering. There were explosions going off, and we were told to run for the ditches by the runways, which we did. We stayed in the ditches for half an hour to an hour. I found out that we were on the Air Force side of the air base at Da Nang. Then trucks pulled up and we loaded on them. It was dark and there was a lot of firing going on all over the place. Trucks took us to another place. We found out we were at 1st Recon Battalion, 1st Marine Division Headquarters. We were told to get off the trucks and go into old wooden shacks and get some sleep. We spent the night there. There was firing going on all night long: artillery and machine guns, and nobody could sleep.

We boarded trucks the next morning and they drove for maybe an hour, and we pulled into this big fire base. We found out later we had traveled on Highway 1. The company commander told us we're at the 3rd Battalion, 5th Marines' fire base south of Da Nang and to get snapped in, because 3rd Battalion, 5th Marines were leaving in a few days to help take Hue City back. We were gonna replace them.

Me and the other Lieutenants from Golf Company were assigned a tent, and we met the Captain and Lieutenants from India Company, 3rd Battalion, 5th Marines. They had just fought two large battles with the NVA and had trapped a VC battalion up against a river that we had just crossed over. They told us they had wiped them out and stripped the enemy of all their gear and weapons. They were all walking around with NVA gear and weapons on. It was kind of bizarre to see. A couple of months later, around July or August 1968, a mortar round killed all of them except one Lieutenant.

A couple of days later, they boarded helicopters and left. We started running what they called Rocket Belt patrols south of Da Nang—our battalion and the 3rd Battalion, 27th Marines, which was east of us by a couple of miles, on the other side of Highway 1. We were five to eight miles south of Da Nang and guarding the two main approaches to it from the south. Our tactical area of responsibility was east of Hill 55 and west of Highway 1, and north of a river called Song La Tho. Hill 55 was the regimental command post for the 7th Marines.

That was our responsibility for two and a half or three months, in the Duc Ky area. We ran patrols from south of our fire base to the river. South of the river was the 7th Marines' tactical area of responsibility. We also ran one platoon size patrol each day, but we did most of our work at night, because the NVA and VC moved at night. The first fire-fight I was in was on February 20, 1968, while on a three-day patrol, at an outpost in Thanh Quit 1.

Every patrol we went on we ran into VC or NVA. I'm not quite sure who they were, but they were running patrols in the same area. We went on patrol for three days at a time. We would set up a platoon patrol base each night and run two squad-size night ambushes and one, squad-size patrol in the area we were patrolling. We didn't have very many casualties.

We had to watch out for booby traps. It was quite obvious to me and my squad leaders and sergeant that, as long as we stayed off the paths, trails, and rice paddy dikes, and went where the enemy wouldn't expect us to go, we wouldn't trip booby traps. And, as long as we moved the platoon patrol base at least once every night, at various times, we could avoid mortar attacks. You really had to think of what you were doing.

There were times that you did have to go on trails, but they were very rare. I told my squad leaders only to go on trails that I authorize. I told my platoon that, if I caught them walking on trails, my platoon sergeant was going to beat the living hell out of you, and I'm going to prefer charges against you for disobedience of a lawful order. They obeyed, and, as a result, only one Marine in the platoon tripped a booby trap, and that was on a trail. We got involved in one ambush, because a squad leader got malaria, and the corporal that took his place disobeyed my order.

As for contact with the NVA, what you had to do was go after them very aggressively. We went on platoon-sized patrols, but we were re-enforced by two machine gun teams, one mortar team, and a rocket team. The machine guns, the mortar and rocket teams would be dispersed with the squads, which is what the Marine Corps teaches you when you go through patrolling, at Quantico. The more you maintain this tactical efficiency, the less the NVA fool around with you.

We were at the outer limits of the North Vietnamese Army's 122mm rockets' range to the Da Nang Air Base, and our job was to keep the NVA a bay, so they couldn't rocket the air base. The more we kept up aggressive patrols in our area of responsibility, the fewer rockets the NVA and VC sent toward the air base.

On April 4th, Lt. Charlie Neil got killed crossing the old railroad tracks on a path, and 1st Platoon lost their commander. The man in front of Neil tripped a spring-loaded booby trap that popped up in the air and blew up in his face. The corpsman tried to save him, by doing a tracheotomy, but he died there on that path. That just re-enforced my rules, about paths and trails, for my platoon.

First Platoon got a new commander. He was a warrant officer from the Air Wing that had volunteered to go to the infantry and become a platoon commander. We were really short of Lieutenants. We lost them to booby traps and rifle grenades.

We were out on a three-day patrol, on May 2nd, and we figured it was around May Day, and the NVA were going to attack Da Nang. We were especially watchful, and, as we came through the village of La Tho Bac 2, the last village on our patrol, on May 4th, on the way back to our base camp, we spotted fresh trenches that had been dug by the enemy or the villagers. We knew something was up and we reported this to our battalion intelligence officer, our battalion S-2. Most of the three-day patrol was done at night.

When we got back to the battalion, we were supposed to have two days off, so we could clean up, eat, and get some sleep. That night, instead of getting sleep, two of my three squads were put on night time ambushes. One was way down in Duc Ky and La Tho Bac 3, along the old French railroad. The other squad was sent to a place called Phong Luc 3. Weapons Platoon attached a machine gun team to each squad. They took the place of the battalion's

Fox Company ambush squads, because Fox Company got pulled out to start Allen Brook the next day, and was attached to 7th Marine Regiment for the start of Operation Allen Brook.

About two o'clock in the morning, on May 5th, I was asleep, and a phone message came in from my squad that was on the French railroad tracks. They told me they had just ambushed a North Vietnamese Army scout team. They had killed one and the other two were wounded, but they got away. I told them to keep the body there and bring it in the next morning. I went back to my cot to get some sleep, and I heard mortar rounds going off, and our base camp got mortared. Most of the rounds hit in our company area. We got hit with 82mm mortar rounds, and all three of my squad tents were hit, and two tents in Weapons Platoon burned down.

A lot of firing had started, before the mortar rounds began to go off. There was machine gun and small arms fire all over the place. My platoon sergeant got the squad that was there and put them in bunkers, but they forgot to get me. Our base camp was hit by something like 96 mortar rounds.

The first round came in and detonated in the bamboo right above our tent. I was laying down on my stomach, and a piece of mortar shrapnel hit me in the back, but I was not the only one wounded. Our company executive officer, 1st Lt. John Francis was also hit by shrapnel. The company gunny and the Weapons Platoon commander, who was a sergeant were there with us, but they were not wounded. A lot of men elsewhere in the base were wounded and a couple were killed as well as men from the company Weapons Platoon. Everybody was awake, and nobody could sleep for the rest of the night. For the rest of the night, corpsmen were taking care of the wounded and the killed.

After the mortar fire had closed, Cpl. Tom Mitchell, who was a machine gun squad leader with Weapons Platoon, G Company, noticed a badly wounded Marine lying on his cot in a Weapons Platoon tent that was on fire. The wounded Marine, Lance Cpl. Schlamp, was unable to get up and out of the burning tent, which had begun to collapse. To make matters worse, the fire's heat was detonating machine gun and rifle ammunition stored in the tent.

Despite the danger, Mitchell immediately went into the burning tent and through it to Schlamp who he picked from the cot and dragged from the tent to safety. Mitchell received painful burns rescuing the Schlamp, but, despite them, continued to search for other casualties and help them to the battalion aid station.

Later that morning, 1st Platoon was out on patrol in the Duc Ky and La Tho Bac 3 areas, and, in the morning, they attacked an NVA Battalion crossing the Song La Tho River along a destroyed railroad bridge. The NVA retreated back across the river, and the 1st Platoon came down to the bridge and then pulled back into La Tho Bac 3 to fill their canteens and get out of rice paddies and in among trees. I knew all this was happening, because I was on duty in our company bunker listening to what was happening on the battalion and company radio nets.

The NVA battalion circled around and crossed the river at another point and got in behind and in front of 1st Platoon and took them under heavy fire. The 1st Platoon started calling out for help, because they were getting pinned down, and their platoon commander was wounded, and they had two dead.

I told Sgt. Richard Gonzalez, my platoon sergeant, and Sgt. Richmond, our platoon right guide, to get everybody who had just come in from the night ambush patrols ready to go out again to rescue 1st Platoon. The two squads from my platoon that were out on ambush came back in. About 15-minutes later, the battalion commander told my company commander to send my platoon and three tanks out and rescue 1st Platoon. I was re-enforced by two machine gun teams, a rocket team, and a mortar section, from Weapons Platoon.

I put a machine gun team with the two lead squads and the two lead tanks and rockets and mortars on the third tank with another squad, and the tanks took off. The Colonel in charge of the battalion told me I was in charge. Another Lieutenant was with us, in charge of the tank platoon.

We took off, at high speed, for La Tho Bac 3, which was two or three Klicks, three kilometers, away from where we were. We drove right through a group of NVA. They were as surprised as we were. We shot at them but were moving too fast, headed for La Pho Bac 3. A platoon that followed us, told me that those NVA were setting up mortars.

Before we reached La Tho Bac 3, we crossed a rice paddy that was probably 300 to 400-yards wide, and the NVA started firing rocket propelled grenades at us. They hit the first tank, and a lot of guys got sprayed with shrapnel. The tanks stopped, and we dismounted, and set up a base of fire. Obviously, there were enemy all over the place. I estimated there were two complete rifle companies of them. They were south of us; they were west, in front of us; they were north of us firing at us. Later on, we found out they were trying to get in behind us.

We could not stay in that open field, because we were going to get mortared. We were only 50-yards in front of La Tho Bac 3, where the NVA were, and I called in an air strike. We marked the target with Willy Peter, white phosphorous, rocket rounds, from our 3.5mm bazookas, and a few minutes after I called for an air strike, two U. S. Marine Corps A-4 Skyhawks came out of nowhere. I'd say they were no more than 50-ft off the ground. You couldn't see the Skyhawks coming, and you couldn't hear 'em coming, because they were so low and going so fast. They caught some of the NVA right in the open.

They came in and dropped napalm right on the NVA. They were right on target. Then they came around and dropped two 250-lb Snake Eye bombs right on target. Then they made a pass firing their 20mm canon. We had an artillery battery, at our fire base, and, after the Skyhawks left, I called in an artillery fire mission. Their first rounds were right on target. After they fired a couple of fire missions, I then called in battalion 81mm mortars. They were right on target, right from the beginning.

I was trying to gain fire superiority, because once you gain fire superiority, you can then maneuver on the enemy and attack 'em. Then I told my troops to fix bayonets. We had to get out of the open paddy field, before the NVA got their mortars set up, and we were going to attack the tree line to our front. I called the mortar attack off. They ceased fire, and we got up and attacked right into the tree line, and the NVA were caught in trenches and bunkers. Two of the tanks followed our assault into the tree line.

When we reached them, the enemy still had their heads down, from the bombardment. I know that, because I walked up to a trench line and saw probably 15 or so with their heads down, in a long trench line. We killed them all, but, before that happened, one of them looked up at me and threw a grenade at me, and another one fired at me with his rifle. My helmet was knocked off and I was hit on the head and knocked down unconscious. My head was cut. Next thing I know, my corpsman is standing above me telling me that it's my second Purple Heart of the day. One more, and I was going home, because, if you had three Purple Hearts, you could go home, if you wanted.

I got up, and my company commander walked up to me. He brought two more tanks and a platoon from Hotel Company to re-enforce us. He told me to change my east to west attack direction to north to south to attack where 1st Platoon was pinned down. We were already through La Tho Bac 3, when I told my platoon to stop their attack to the west and to head toward the south to where a well was, and 1st Platoon was pinned down.

We started attacking toward the south, and a bullet went right by my ear. I hit the deck, and there was a big explosion. A rocket propelled grenade had landed beside me. I thought my leg was blown off. A corpsman came up to me when I way layin' there, and he gave me a shot of morphine, and I was out of it until nine or 10 o'clock that night.

While I was in a morphine-induced sleep, Sgt. Gonzalez learned that I had been seriously wounded and found me lying on the ground bleeding heavily and bracketed by RPG fire. He jumped on top of me and protected me from nearby exploding RPG rounds and machine gun and small arms fire. While doing that, he suffered numerous shrapnel wounds.

When enemy fire lifted momentarily, Gonzalez, despite numerous painful, bleeding wounds, arose and distributed ammunition amongst the 3rd Platoon's survivors, reorganized them, and continued 3rd Platoon's attack toward 1st Platoon's survivors. Eventually, more battalion units reinforced the 3rd Platoon's attack and caused the enemy to retreat from the area.

Sgt. Gonzalez and the survivors of 3rd Platoon reached the remnants of 1st Platoon later that evening and Sgt. Gonzalez set up a night perimeter and landing zone, for the remnants of G Company's 3rd and 1st Platoons and the battalion reinforcements. Then he called in helicopters to evacuate the many wounded Marines.

For his aggressive, fearless leadership and extraordinary tactical judgment, Gonzalez was awarded the Navy Commendation Medal with Combat V. In 2015, I submitted, to the Marine Corps, a recommendation that Gonzalez conduct that day in 1968 be rewarded with the award of the Navy Cross.

Cpl. Mitchell was with the platoon, in spite of the burn wounds he suffered earlier that day. During the engagement, he cared for many wounded Marines, while under direct enemy mortar and RPG attack that caused numerous wounds to his chest, back, arms, and legs.

Mitchell also led his machine gun team in support of the attack upon an enemy squad, in a trench line, to the immediate front of the platoon, which his team was supporting. Without hesitation and without regard for their own safety, Mitchell and his assistant machine gunner jumped into an enemy occupied trench and killed most of them with his M-60 machine gun fire, which helped to capture the trench.

Mitchell was awarded the Bronze Star Medal with Combat V, for his actions on the morning and afternoon of May 5th. In my opinion, Mitchell's actions that day warrant award of the Medal of Honor, and, in 2015, I submitted a recommendation for the award.

The Medal of Honor recommendation for Sergeant Mitchell is presently under administrative review at the Awards Branch, Headquarters Marine Corps, Quantico, Virginia. The same is true of the 1968 awards of Navy Commendation Medals with Combat V to Sergeants Gonzalez and Mitchell, which I am trying to have upgraded to the Navy Cross Medal.

During that same battle, after 1st Platoon's commander was seriously wounded, as well as many of that platoon's members, my platoon approached their position, along with three tanks. We were hit by enemy RPG, machine gun, and small arms fire in front and dismounted from the tanks. With the tanks, we established a base of fire, and I called in an air strike and 81m mortar fire upon the enemy position.

The platoon then assaulted directly into the enemy position. Sgt. Dickie William Richmond, right guide of 3rd Platoon, took am M-60 machine gun, from a wounded machine gunner, and led the left flank in this assault. When they reached the enemy, they were confronted by enemy troops in two trench lines firing machine guns, small arms, and RPGs at them.

Despite this heavy fire, Richmond lay down a base of fire with the machine gun, for the attack's left flank. Then he joined the assault of the trench lines and killed an RPG team that was firing at 3rd Platoon. After that, he led the men in over-running two additional trench lines full of enemy troops, which eventually caused the enemy to retreat and enabling him to lead 3rd Platoon members to 1st Platoon's survivors and lead them to safety.

All this combat occurred between around 3:30 or 4:00 o'clock in the afternoon. I had looked at my watch right before I got wounded, and it was four o'clock.

When I woke up, it was dark, and you could hear this terrible screaming. I thought, man, I've died and I've gone to Hell. I was afraid to touch my leg, because I thought it was blown off. I finally realized it was Spooky, a C-47 that had been called up and was firing into the area south of us. I look up and I could see the stream of machine gun tracers coming from the aircraft's 7.62 mm rotating machine guns.

The firing stopped, and it was late at night, and the next thing I know, I heard two guys behind me, and there was Lt. Jerry Buckley, who was 2nd Platoon commander, and Staff Sgt. Mobley, who commanded Weapons Platoon. The company had been pulled back into La Tho Bac 3, and had set up a perimeter for the night, and my absence was noted. Buckley and Mobley had come out to find me.

My platoon had made it to 1st Platoon and rescued them, and brought the remnant back into the perimeter along with the two dead and the wounded. Fox Company was coming in to reinforce Golf Company, and the NVA had retreated back across the river. Lt. Buckley and Staff Sgt. Mobley picked me up and took me to the perimeter, and helicopters started coming in to take out our casualties. In addition to the two dead, there were lots of wounded, including 2nd Lt. Doug Frantz, a platoon commander of a platoon from Hotel Company.

We were medevaced to Da Nang, and I was there a day, before I got medevaced to Cam Rahn Bay. I was in agonizing pain. It really hurts, when you get hit. The doctors came by my bed and told me that I was being medevaced back to the States. I told them I'd rather be medevaced to Japan, if possible. I didn't want to go back to the States, because the Marine Corps might make me come back and do a complete tour again. I knew that, if I was in

Japan, I'd still be in the Far East and that would be part of my 13-month tour.

I was medevaced to the U.S. Naval Air Facility Atsugi, Japan. I was being medevaced with a lot of Army soldiers that had been wounded during the relief of Khe Sahn and a lot of Marines that had been wounded in a battle at Dai Do, just south of the DMZ. At Dai Do, 2nd Battalion, 4th Marines had stopped the 304th NVA Division, at that village on the Cua Viet River. The whole time I was there I heard these Army guys, from the 1st Air Cavalry Division, talking about the Marines that they saw, at Khe Sanh, when they relieved it. They could not get over how wild those Marines were, and that their uniforms were dirty, their uniforms were in tatters, and their boots were muddy and white from wear. I was in so much pain I couldn't talk.

I was loaded on the outside of a helicopter that took me from Atsugi to the U.S. Naval Hospital, in Yokosuka, Japan. That was exciting, and I forgot about my pain, while I was riding on that helicopter. When we got there, the hospital was full to bursting with Marines. I was taken to a room on the officer's ward. In the room was another U.S. Marine, 2nd Lt. Dave McAdams of Gaston, Oregon who had been wounded in the Battle of Dai Do, and Chief Warrant Officer 4 Powell.

Gunner Powell, as we called him, had joined the Marine Corps in 1940, when he was 16. He had fought at the Battle of Guadalcanal with the 2nd Raider Battalion, and had fought on Tarawa and Saipan. In the Korean War, he had landed with the 1st Marine Division, at Inchon, and had fought at the Chosin Reservoir. He was from Louisiana and made sure he told me.

Gunner Powell was tall and very handsome. He was also very charming. Everyone loved him, because of his cheerful and effervescent personality and his ability to tell an endless number of funny jokes. He was the life and center of all of the wounded US Marine officers on the ward, which included several wounded infantry Lieutenants and even two wounded Marine Majors: one an A-4 pilot and the other a CH-53 pilot, both of whom had been shot down during the Battle of Khe Sanh.

Gunner Powell was one of the most amazing men I have ever met in my life. I could not get out of my bed and walk for several weeks because of my leg wounds and Dave McAdams was in the same shape. Gunner Powell would entertain us with stories of fighting the Japanese on Guadalcanal, the North Koreans at Inchon and Seoul and the Chinese at the Chosin Reservoir.

Once I could get out of bed and walk on crutches, Gunner and I and the two Majors had many adventures and escapades together, in Yokosuka, at the 7th Fleet Officers' Club and at Lake Yamanaka, on Mount Fuji. Our escapades and adventures could fill a book.

Another guy that was in the officers' ward, at the hospital, was a guy that was wounded when a mortar round blew up right in back of him. The whole back of his head down to his feet were covered with shrapnel, except where he had his flak jacket. In order to get that shrapnel out, the doctors had cut his muscles and his skin in layers to try to get as much shrapnel out as they could. He was really in bad shape.

I got discharged from the hospital toward the end of June, 1968 and ordered to Okinawa where I was supposed to recuperate for six weeks and get my leg back in shape. I was there for a week, and I just couldn't stand Okinawa. I used to go to a briefing every morning, at Camp Schwab where there would be an S-2 briefing on everything that was going on in Vietnam. I saw my battalion had been put on Operation Allen Brook, and I just went to the doctor and said I want to go back to my unit. The doctor said I was supposed to be there at Camp Schwab for another five weeks, in order that my leg would have time to recover. I told him I wanted to leave and get back to my company. He said, 'Okay, if that's what you want.' And he gave me a medical release, and I left the next day.

I got on a C-130 to Da Nang. The 1st Marine Division knew I was coming and they had somebody there to meet me and took me to Division G-1 Personnel, where I met the division G-1, a full bird Colonel. He said he had a job for me at G-1. I said, 'Sir, I don't want to be in G-1, I want to be back with my unit.' He sent me to the 27th Marines. I went to the 27th Marines regimental headquarters and told them what I wanted. The S-1 sent me back to my battalion.

The battalion was on Operation Allen Brook at Go Noi Island, about 25-km south of Da Nang. It was a terribly bloody operation. I got in a helicopter, with my rifle, flak jacket, pack, canteens. I told my first sergeant I wanted my platoon back, and he said okay. They have no Lieutenant. We had to transfer the one that replaced you. The troops tried to kill him twice. He didn't follow my prescriptive for patrolling and got several members of my platoon killed, because of his stupidity, and then the men tried to kill him twice.

On Go Noi Island, 3rd Platoon was sent to rescue a 2nd Battalion sniper team that was being attacked by a much larger enemy unit. The platoon reached the snipers, while under heavy small arms fire. Platoon members were ordered to throw one grenade each toward the enemy and then assault. After the grenades were thrown, heavy enemy fire continued, and Sgt. Richmond stood up, on his own initiative, and charged the enemy while firing his M-16. His courage and example caused the platoon's other members to rise and charge the enemy, in the face of small arms fire. As a result, the enemy retreated and he sniper team was led to safety.

For his actions at Go Noi and his earlier actions on May 5th, when I was severely wounded, Richmond was awarded the Navy Commendation Medal with Combat V. In 2015, I submitted, to the Marine Corps, a recommendation that Richmond's conduct on May 5th and on Go Noi Island be recognized by the award of the Navy

Cross. Richmond has died since, but I know that his family would appreciate this recognition for his actions.

I re-joined my battalion, on June 27, 1968, during Operation Allen Brook. My roommate, at Basic School had been in India Company, 3rd Battalion, 20th Marines, and he'd gotten killed along with all the officers in his company except one, on May 17, 1968, during Operation Allen Brook. That operation ended late in August, and we were back to Rocket Belt patrolling.

Then the NVA attacked Da Nang, on August 19, 1968, Ho Chi Minh's birthday, and we became involved in the battles of the Cam Le and Can Do Bridges, which are the two bridges over the Can Do River into Da Nang from the south. It was a large battle, in which my platoon was sent out with three tanks again to re-enforce Fox Company that was involved in a battle with the NVA along Highway 1. I medevaced Lt. Buckley, our 1st Platoon commander, and the company commander of Fox Company, Capt. Collins, who were badly wounded.

We then chased the remnants of the NVA regiment, which had attacked the Cam Le and Can Do bridges, down toward the Que Son Mountains, and while we were chasing them about 10-miles south of Da Nang Typhoon Bess struck, so we had to carry our dead and several wounded with us for two days through the typhoon.

Finally, the typhoon ended and the Marines were pulled back to our fire base. The typhoon had blown down all of our tents, so everything was wet. Then we got word that our regiment, the 27th Marines, was being pulled out of Vietnam toward the beginning of September. I got orders, from division, to the division MP Company at division headquarters, at Da Nang. We packed everything, and then we got word that we were not leaving Vietnam, we were going into Elephant Valley on an operation. We unpacked everything, and then we got word we were not going on the operation. We were going to Camp Pendleton, in the States, and anybody that hadn't done a full 13-month tour was going to be transferred to another unit.

On September 7th, the 27th Marines left Vietnam, and I got transferred to MP Company, 1st Marine Division. I served out the rest of my tour with MP Company.

Since I did a 13-month tour, I was in Vietnam when the Tet Offensive of 1968 happened and when the Tet Offensive of 1969 happened. When the 1969 Tet Offensive took place, the NVA attacked 1st Marine Division headquarters. They took the bunker, at the top of Freedom Hill, from the division band, and killed everybody that was in the bunker.

A composite rifle company was made up of people at division headquarters, and commanded by Capt. Frank Kaveney, a Marine lawyer with the 1st Marine Division legal office, who was a graduate of St. Louis Law School. We were together at the university. Later, he was in the Platoon Leader Class-Law and I was in regular PLC. He was a lawyer, and he came to me and said, 'What do I do? How do I take that bunker back?' I told him what to do and how to do it, and that night they attacked the NVA in the bunker, and they killed them all and took the bunker back.

The NVA also attacked the gate opposite division headquarters, and I was there when they attacked. We pushed them back. There was a really funny incident, during that offensive: the NVA got into the 7th Motor Transport Battalion area, and their sappers went to the unit's mess hall, and they blew the livin' hell out of the mess hall. The Marines eventually killed them all, but the mess hall was destroyed. Why the NVA went to the mess hall and blew it up nobody knows for sure.

Things quieted down, after that, and my tour ended on March 7th, and I got orders to Camp Pendleton. At Camp Pendleton, I was in an infantry battalion of the 28th Marines. I was a platoon commander and was promoted to first Lieutenant and served as executive officer of my company. Then I was promoted to executive officer of my company and then became a company commander.

My three-year tour on active duty ended, and I applied to go to flight school. I passed all the tests, but the

Marine Corps never got back to me, and law school was my backup, in case I didn't get into flight school. I got off active duty, on July 15, 1970, but I stayed in the Reserves, and went to law school, at St. Louis University. I finished law school, in '74, and took the Bar exam in Missouri and Oregon, and passed both.

I got a job, in Oregon, with a law firm, which was run by a World War II Marine. As a matter of fact, most of the big law firms, in Portland, were run by World War II Marines or World War II naval officers. It was a very welcoming place for me. It was like being back in the Marine Corps.

I stayed in the Reserves and served with the 6th Engineers Support Battalion, in Portland, for six years, as a platoon commander, a company commander, battalion S-1, S-4, S-3, and battalion XO. I was promoted to Major, while there. The Marine Corps transferred me from there to Marine Air Group 42, at Naval Air Station Whidbey Island, Washington, where I was for three years, as site judge advocate for all Marines that were there. I was promoted to Lieutenant Colonel, while there.

After that, the Marine Corps transferred me to Judge Advocate Division, Reserve Augmentation Unit, as the Marine Reserve defense counsel for the Pacific Region. I served in that position, for three years. Then I was made the deputy chief defense counsel of the Marine Corp, and served in that position for four years. I was promoted to Colonel, during that assignment. Then I became the reserve staff judge advocate for Marine Forces Pacific, at Camp Smith, Oahu, where I served for two years. Then I didn't make brigadier general, so I had to get out, and retired from the Reserves on July 15, 1997.

The awards I received on active duty are two Purple Hearts; Combat Action Ribbon; Legion of Merit; Navy Commendation Medal with a combat V; Vietnam Campaign Medal with four stars representing the Tet Offensive, Tet Counter-offensive, May NVA and August NVA offensive; Vietnam Service Medal; Presidential Unit

Citation, as a member of the 27th Marine Regiment; National Defense Medal; and Republic of Vietnam Cross of Gallantry with Palm.

*Author's note: In a letter dated 4 September 1968, recommending 2nd Lt. Flaherty for the Navy Commendation Medal, his commanding officer wrote that 2nd Lt. Flaherty '...demonstrated exceptional leadership, dedication to duty and the highest loyalty to his men...An avid student of tactics, he provided many valuable ideas for finding, fixing and destroying the enemy. Always calm and quick thinking under fire, he was admired by seniors and juniors alike...on Operation Allen Brook, he distinguished himself several times by his forceful and decisive acts that aided materially in establishing the superiority of his unit over the enemy...'*

I was married to Margaret, October 3, 1970, when I started law school. When I was a company commander, one of my Lieutenants was a casualty assistance officer for a Margaret, whose husband had been killed. Her administrative and legal problems were complex, and he couldn't handle them, so I had to get one of the Marine lawyers from base, and together we got her problems straightened out. As it turned out, I married her.

I have one son, Thomas J. Flaherty, Jr. He's a Captain for Sky West Airlines and flies Alaska Airline routes in Sky West aircraft, which have the Alaska Airlines logo on them. My son has one daughter Brittany, and my daughter Jennifer, who is now a lawyer, in southern California, has two daughters, Ava and Mia.

I got a private, single engine pilot's license, when I was stationed at Camp Pendleton. Later on, I got an instrument rating, a commercial license, a flight instructor's rating, an instrument flight instructor's rating, a multi-engine rating, a multi-engine instructor's rating. I was a part-time instructor at Hillsboro Aviation, in Hillsboro, Oregon, for one year.

I joined the Oregon Wing of the Civil Air Patrol about a year and a half ago. I'm a Lieutenant Colonel and a mission pilot for them. I belong to the Senior Squadron, in Portland. All we do is land-rescue work. I fly a Cessna 182 G-1000. It has the G-1000 instruments in it. The gages are all digital.

I belong to the Aircraft Owners and Pilots Association and am a panel lawyer for it. I'm the secretary of the board for the Oregon Pilots' Association. I've been chairman of the Oregon State Bar Aviation Section twice. I was Scout Master for Troop 297 of the Boy Scouts, in Beaverton, Oregon. I'm also a member of the Marine Corps Association, and the 1st Marine Division Association. I am also an adjunct professor of law at Willamette University School of Law, Salem, Oregon, where another lawyer and I teach the aviation law course.

While with his platoon, at an ammunition bunker, picking up ammunition for a three-day patrol, Lt. Thomas Joseph "Tom" Flaherty shows writing on his helmet cover that says, "IMPERIALIST CAPITALIST WARMONGER CHIEFTAIN". On the other side it says "VC SUCK".

The reason for the writing, he said, was Viet Cong and NVA snipers, for whom officers were primary targets.

Flaherty said it was vital not to look like an officer when you went into the field on patrol or on operations. Enlisted men wrote various, humorous sayings on their helmet covers and mostly wore a green tee shirt, under their flak jackets, but most officers did neither. Those were ways to spot an officer.

Another way you could spot an officer in the field was by seeing a radio man or men near him. So, you had to tell your radio man to use the short PRC-25 antenna, bend the antenna into his pack when not in use, and carry the PRC-25 in his pack. The whip antenna was only used after a platoon patrol base or a company perimeter was established. Radio men were also primary targets for snipers.

So, I tried to look as much as possible like an enlisted Marine by writing humorous sayings on my helmet cover and by not wearing my jungle utility shirt until the evening when the mosquitoes came out and just wearing a green tee shirt under my flak jacket.

Of course, you never wore your rank insignia in the field and you instructed your Marines to never address you as 'Sir' or as 'Lieutenant' in the field, nor to ever salute you in the field for obvious reasons.

South of DaNang, especially on Go Noi Island, there were many old French houses of former French land owners. They were well built, but had been abandoned by their former French owners and occupants. The Viet Cong patrols wrote on the walls political statements like "American Warmongers" or "Capitalist pigs" or "Imperialist dogs". The Marine patrols would write statements like 'Charlie, I f---ed your wife last night.' or 'I f----ed Ho Chi Minh's wife last night.' Therefore, in order to look as much like an enlisted Marine as much as possible and to be humorous I wrote on my helmet cover.

Lt. Tom Flaherty and his platoon are at an ammunition bunker to be re-supplied with ammunition. Lt. Flaherty is the second man from the right.

Second Lt. Thomas J. Flaherty (left) and two of his platoon's NCOs take a break, at the main fire base of 2nd Battalion, 27th Marine Regiment, at Phong Luc 2. In the middle is Sgt. Richard Gonzalez, and on the right, is Sgt. Dick Richmond.

# Robert B. "Bob" Humphries
interview of November 3, 2013

I am Bob Humphries, and my full name is Robert Bailey Humphries. I was born in Newark, Ohio, on November 7, 1946. I have an older brother and a younger sister.

My dad was Hal Humphries, and my mother was Marge Humphries. Her maiden name was Bailey. Both were from that area.

I went to grade school in Ft. Lauderdale and to high school in Ft. Lauderdale and Jacksonville, Florida. I was graduated in 1965, from Lee High School, in Jacksonville.
Then I attended a junior college program, at Middle Georgia College, in Cochrane, Georgia. I didn't quite finish two years there. My brother and sister and I were all three in college at the same time. They were doing better than I was, so I dropped a quarter. Got out; went to work; and before I could get back to school, I got drafted. That was September 1967.

I went to basic training, at Ft. Gordon, Georgia, and from there went to Ft. Ord, California, for Advanced Infantry Training. My training company was supposed to be a replacement for either Korea or Germany, and the company commander said the last group went to Korea, so we'd be going to Germany. At the end of that tour, there were seven of us that were called out the last day, and they said, 'Bad news, for you guys, you're going to Vietnam, but you have 30 days before you leave.' The rest of the company was going to Korea, but they were leaving that afternoon.

I spent those 30 days on post detail, except for a week's leave that I used to go home. On March 23rd, 1968, I went to Vietnam, from Oakland, California. I was flown into Bien Hua. My original orders were for the 44th Aviation Group, in Pleiku. When I got there, I was assigned to the 1st Infantry Division. My specialty was 81mm mortars, and I was assigned to a special weapons company.

Our base camp was a place called Di An, north of Saigon, in III Corps. After arriving, I spent a week in 1st Infantry training. From there, I went out to the field with the 2nd Battalion of the 16th Infantry Regiment. I was in Delta Company. We worked at what we called night defensive positions. During the day, we would run search-and-destroy missions from there. And at night we had at least two companies out on ambush.

The first week I was there, I started asking people that had been there if we did anything on Friday or Saturday night, and they said no. I said, 'How about Sunday night', and they said no. We basically stayed in the field. They brought everything we needed out there. I spent my first five months in Vietnam out in the field, and during the year I spent in Vietnam, I got back to my base camp maybe three times for one night or for two nights.

Everywhere we went, we had a watch tower that was about 25 ft. high. A helicopter would carry it out to us and we would carry sand bags up to the top to protect anyone in the top. We put sand bags on the floor and the sides of it. We kind of monitored our area from it. Day and night, we would have a person on it that had an MOS to operate some kind of a radar system that picked up ground sound. He could tell you if the sound was made by two legs or four legs, and if it was walking left or right, and how far away it was.

At lot of times they would say it was so many meters at a certain azimuth. That gave a chance to the mortar platoon to see if we can't find out what it was. A couple of times we blew it away. We would send somebody out to see if there was anything out there. It worked out well.

When we moved, we'd take the sand bags down and a Chinook would come out and pick the tower up and either take it to our new location or take it somewhere else.

The first dead person I ever saw, I killed over there. I killed him with an M16. I did go out on ambushes: some at night; some company-size ambushes; and some two platoon ambushes. On ambushes I was strictly a rifleman, but I probably spent 90% of my time in a mortar section.

Very rarely could we keep a Lieutenant. They would go somewhere else. Very rarely did I have a platoon sergeant. I went over as a private and became a Pfc. when I got there. I was basically running the mortar platoon, as a Spec. 4. Then I became an E5, a sergeant. We normally had 18 to 20 men in our platoon on a good day, and three mortars.

We enjoyed counter-mortaring. If they mortared us, we could get 60 rounds at them, before their first-round hit. Normally you could hear a mortar fire. It's a "dunk-dunk" sound, anywhere from 2,000 meters to 2400 meters. A lot of times they would do it from one side of a village. We would hear "dunk-dunk", and we would have incoming in about 20 seconds. It wasn't unusual for us to fire 300 and 700 rounds, and they'd find somebody else to mortar, if we didn't kill them.

I had a couple of interesting experiences in the Iron Triangle, where vegetation was supposed to be really thick. The company commander put the mortar platoon in the back and said, 'It's so thick back here that nobody can walk through it.' We got there right at sundown and started putting out Claymore mines, and it started raining. And almost immediately you could hear somethin' walkin' towards us.

We had a break of maybe 10 ft. between us and the jungle where you couldn't see anything. It rained a little harder, and the steps got a little louder. I kept expecting something to step out. It stopped for a long time, and then it backed up. I don't know, if it was an animal or a person. I know I had my M16 pointed towards it, and a hand grenade ready, and the barrel of my M16 was moving in small circles, because I was nervous. And I knew, if it was that close, it could hear my heart beating. We spent a long night wondering if the VC were going to come back or did they set up some kind of anti-personnel mine. They never came back that night, but it felt like they were very close.

One time, we went up to a place called Loc Minh, near the Cambodian border in III Corps area, almost up to II Corps area. Our Gen. Ware was killed, when we were up there for about 10 days. I went out in a listening post, one night. It was about 150 meters outside the camp's perimeter. Three of us got out there, and there was a Viet Cong in a huge tree, and about every 15 minutes he was just shooting rounds with an AK trying to figure out where we were.

I was trying to get somebody to shoot up in the tree, and they wouldn't. I was talking to the Major, on a radio, and I said why don't you just get an M60 or a 50 cal. and just shoot up in this tree. He said, 'We may hit you.'

And I said, 'That may be the best thing to happen.'

There was a lot of movement that night. I counted over a hundred Vietnamese walked by. I was trying to get people to shoot down there; bring in artillery; do this; do that, and they wouldn't do it.

We were on a hill, and I didn't know how far it went down. And below, in front of us, there was a sling-load of 105 ammunition that a helicopter should have dropped way behind us. I didn't think anything of it. Along about three o'clock in the mornin' I was in the middle, and the guy that was on the left of me started shaking. He had a bandoleer of magazines, and if anything happened he'd get nervous and shake. His bandoleers would sound like a metallic rattlesnake. I turned perpendicular to him and laid on top of him with my chest to make him quiet. I looked over and there was about 20 or 25 North Vietnamese. They were about 25 yards from me, on my left.

So, I put my M16 up, and I told the two guys with me, 'If I start to shoot, you run.' It looked like the guy that was leading that group was an officer. He and I had eyeball-to-eyeball contact, and we just looked at each other. None of them raised their rifles, and they just kind of backed down the hill, and nothin' ever happened on that. One against 20 was not a good situation. I might get four or five, but… We left, about two days later, and the North Vietnamese probably came back and got the ammunition.

I finally got clearance for my mortar platoon to shoot. I didn't have a fire direction center. I *was* the fire direction center. In my head, I did the calculations and told them to put an illumination round in that tree down there. And sure enough, it hit the tree and here comes this little guy running down the tree, with a flare chasin' him. That was an exciting night.

I wanted to shoot him with my rifle. If I could see something, I could hit it. But I thought, if I shoot something here, I don't know what's going to come out of the jungle on the right side of me. So, I just said, 'Leave it alone.'

Another time, we were on a company-size ambush, and little did I know there was like a creek bed down beside us. I guess the VC or whoever they were had followed us and knew where we were. Two o'clock in the morning, they jumped up and started firing at us. But they were firing in front of us, where they thought we were, and not where we were. Had we been up there where they thought we were, we would have really sustained a lot of casualties. They really had a great idea where we were, but not quite. Thank gosh!

I had a great first company commander, and I really didn't get along well with my second company commander. There was nothing personal there, but when we were up at Loc Minh, he had taken over the company, and my best friend was killed there; and Gen. Ware, our division commander was killed there. Our company's losses were a result of the company commander's low competence as a field officer. We went back to our base camp at Di An for a ceremony for the ones that had passed and then for an awards ceremony. And that Captain got all kinds of awards: everything except the Medal of Honor. He had a hard problem with map reading, and his tactics weren't very good. Some men were killed or wounded, as a result.

When we went back out into the field, our whole company started shootin' at him. Why they didn't hit him, I don't know. They were mad at him. He did a bad job up there, and he got all these medals and awards that they didn't feel like he should get. You could see tracers going towards him.

When it came time for me to come home, he told me to pack up my stuff. He said, 'I want you on the first helicopter that comes in to re-supply tomorrow morning.' The next morning a helicopter comes in, and he says, 'I have a question for you.'

I said, 'Yes sir, what's that?'

He says, 'Were you one of the guys shooting at me?'

I said, 'No, sir. If I was shooting at you, I'd be the last person you'd ever see.' With that, he got extremely upset and told me to get on the helicopter and leave.

It was extremely humid in Vietnam. I grew up in south Florida: Key Biscayne; Ft. Lauderdale. When I was growing up, my mother said the humidity there was the highest in the world. In the Army, they said, 'Vietnam is so humid you won't believe it.'

I said, 'It can't be worse than Florida.' I landed in Vietnam, at about 5:30 in the morning; got outside the plane, and I thought I was going to die. At six o'clock, I was sure I was, and I said, 'If I see eight o'clock, it'll be a miracle.'

You could lay down at night, not moving, and sweat. You just sweat, sweat, sweat. It was that humid. When the monsoon came, it would be cold at night. We'd just lay down on the ground, in ambush, and wait for something to come by, at night. It felt very cold. You'd think it's freezing, but it's probably in the upper 80s or somethin'. If you could keep your face dry, you felt pretty well.

When I came home, in late March of '69, I planned to get married to Judith Henderson. I was engaged, before I left. We got married, at Lake Talmadge, Georgia, in April, two weeks after I came home. I'd go to sleep in bed with her, but she'd wake me up during the night, and I'd be sleepin' on a wood floor. I'd been sleepin' on the ground for a whole year. I finally learned that the bed's a whole lot more comfortable than the floor. I was just used to sleepin' on the ground.

That even happened in Vietnam. We'd go back to base camp and they'd have cots there. We'd wake up in the morning and, out of 20 guys, there might be three or four still sleeping on the cots. The rest of us would be sleepin' in the sand. I guess we just felt safer on the ground.

When I left Vietnam, I had five months left in the service, and they said you can pick any three posts you would like to go to. I picked Ft. Benning, Ft. Gordon, and Ft. Jackson, so they sent me to Aberdeen Proving Grounds, which made no sense. I spent five months there. When I first got there, they said there was something for me to do there, so they made an instructor out of me.

I had one class a week to give. Finally, I got it up to a total of three classes. One was a general question and answer class, one was on ambushing, and I forget what the third one was. It was good and bad. I felt like I wasn't doing enough work, but it gave me a chance to get back in the rhythm of living the way we live here. My wife was with me at that duty station, and it gave me a chance to just sit and talk to her.

I was a sergeant when I was discharged from active duty, in September '69. They put me in the Reserves and they said that since I was a Vietnam veteran to stay home, unless they called me, and I never had to report for any duty and got an Honorable Discharge, after four more years. I spent a total of two years on active duty and four in inactive, unorganized Reserves.

During my active duty time, I earned the Combat Infantry Badge, the National Service Medal, the Vietnam

Service Medal, and the Vietnam Campaign Medal, and two overseas bars.

My wife and I have been married for 44 years and have one son that's adopted. We have made our home in Roswell, Georgia, since we came back from Houston in 1988.

I went into outside sales: selling fabrics to upholstery shops, on a wholesale level. Then I kind of jumped up to a higher scale fabric company, from New York, selling fabrics, wall coverings, draperies, historical items, and similar things from all over the world to upper end interior designers. I stayed with them and retired in 2008.

I am president of the 16th Infantry Regiment Association of the 1st Infantry Division. We have five board members, and we meet once a month, by Skype. I'm vice president of the Georgia Vietnam Veterans Alliance. We started a chapter in Marietta, and I was president of that for three years, until '97, and I've been vice president of that ever since. I am also vice president of the Atlanta Veterans Day Parade.

When I came back, PTSD wasn't even a term then. I did notice that when I would go into a restaurant or other public place I would only sit with my back to a wall, so I could see what was happening. Didn't understand why I did that, but my wife knew. We lived in Houston, for a while, and had a friend that was worried about her husband and had been to the VA, and she had a small pamphlet about Post Traumatic Stress, and she wanted me to read it. I read it the next morning, in my office at home, and said, 'My gosh, this thing is talking about me.' A lot of things I would do were described in it. I made a claim with the VA and got a 30% disability rating for Post-Traumatic Stress. After four or five years, about three or four months ago, I got rated at 100% with Post Traumatic Stress.

The biggest help for any veteran is to talk to their peers: to be in a group such as the Georgia Vietnam Veterans Alliance. My chapter is Chapter One. We have a membership of about 125. About 60 people normally attend our monthly meeting.

It's just a comfort place where they can talk, and I think it cleanses the body, so to speak, that you get something out, and you talk to people that understand you. We understand each other, because we have the same experience. It didn't matter what branch of service. You were all on the same team trying to do the same thing. We all gave a lot of hours to try to make that happen. I just think it's great to be there, and it's great to see new people coming out, and it's kind of sorry that it's happening so late in life.

I've seen people come in kind of shy and unsure what they were going to get into, and they didn't really want to be there. Then they decide, well, I've really got friends there. These people are my friends, my buddies. And within a month or two they fit right in and wouldn't miss a meeting for the life of them.

I think the same is going to be true for the Iraqi veterans and the Afghan veterans: that they need to get together themselves. That's what's going to help them.

I think some psychiatrists can also be helpful. I found a great one out in Austell, from the VA, that I just think the world of. It's a lady PhD. And she's like a magnet. She can kinda look at you and just pull information out of you. That normally doesn't happen with me. I've been very impressed with her. I see her every six weeks, she's just fun to be around. It's amazing what she can pry from you that you didn't really know you had in you.

Sometimes I ask her why I do this and why I don't, and she's got a good reason why I do and why I don't. She says, you're doing fine, and I feel better after I talk to her. I'd never been to a psychiatrist, until about a year and a half ago.

Cpl. Robert Bailey "Bob" Humphries, in Vietnam, in about January 1969.

Bob Humphries (left) is beside a soldier from Mississippi that signed up for another duty tour and was killed, in Vietnam, in about 1970. I don't remember his real name. We called him "Squad". We always went by nicknames.

A portable watchtower with ground-monitoring radar, is on the right.

    Humphries said, 'Everywhere we went, we had a watch tower that was about 25 ft. high. A helicopter would carry it out to us and we would carry sand bags up to the top to protect anyone in the top. We put sand bags on the floor and the sides of it. We kind of monitored our area from it.

    Day and night, we would have a person on it that had an MOS to operate some kind of a radar system that picked up ground sound. He could tell you if the sound was made by two legs or four legs, and if it was walking left or right, and how far away it was… When we moved, we'd take the sand bags down and a Chinook would come out and pick the tower up and either take it to our new location or take it somewhere else.'

Cpl. Bob Humphries, at Bien Hoa Air Base, waiting for a flight to Ft. Dix.

# Lee Wesley Sinnickson
interview of March 1, 2017

My name is Lee Wesley Sinnickson. I was born in Brooklyn, New York, on April 25, 1948, and then my folks moved out to Center Moriches, on Long Island. I think I was three-years old when they moved out here.

My dad was Thomas Davis Sinnickson. He went to Center Moriches High School and then he went to the Army Air Forces and became a gunner, on a Douglas Dauntless, during World War II. He got the Distinguished Flying Cross. I'm actually named after his pilot: Lt. Lee. My father stayed close to him, after the war. I wish I had a talked to my father about it, but I didn't, and that's how we all are, I guess.

My grandfather, Wesley Sinnickson, was in World War I. He was in the funeral business and became a funeral director and opened a funeral home in 1940.

After World War II, my father worked for a funeral home in New York City. When his father's business grew out here, in Center Moriches, his father said to come out and work for him. While my father worked in New York, he and my mother lived in Brooklyn.

My mother was Marie Holst. Her father was a life insurance salesman. Her family may have lived in Brooklyn. All I remember was we had to walk up a lot of flights of stairs. Everyone was poor back then.

My mother's parents bought a bungalow in Mastic beach, in the late '30s. Mastic Beach is about five-miles west of Center Moriches, where I lived with my parents. My dad met my mother in Mastic Beach, when she went there, from Brooklyn, with her parents, to go to the bungalow. After they married, my parents moved to Brooklyn, where I was born. I was four, when my parents moved to Center Moriches. At that time, the whole area had a lot of duck farmers, potato farmers, commercial bottom fishermen, and fishing in the ocean, which is on the other side of the inlet. In fact, the guy that lives in front of my house dredges crabs right now, as we speak.

I went through the public-school system here and graduated from Center Moriches High School, in June 1966. Then I went to work for my father and grandfather, making sure that that's what I wanted to do for a livin', and in March 1967, I started funeral director school that my father and grandfather went to, in New York City. It was a one-year school; you attended for 12 consecutive months.

In September '67, I was washin' a car, in the driveway, and Walter Zemorski, the Mailman came by with his little push cart and he said, 'Lee, you've got greetings from the President of the United States.' For a split second I didn't know what he meant. Then I understood; I'd been drafted. I went to the draft board and asked if I could finish the school, before being drafted, and they said the funeral school was a trade school and not an accredited college, so they would not defer drafting me. So, I went into the Army.

September 18th, '67, my dad drove me to Smithtown draft board, and said good luck, and I stood under a little overhang outside in the rain, early in the morning with maybe a dozen other guys. Then we get in the bus goin' to Ft. Hamilton, in New Yok City. They told us to raise our right hand and take an oath, and some of the wise guys didn't raise their right hands. They said they had not taken the oath, so they were not in the military, and were told to go into a different room and you're in the Marines now. Then we counted off in threes, and they said when they called number one step forward, you're in the Marines too and you other guys are in the Army.

About 40 or 50 guys got in the bus, and went down to Ft. Campbell, Kentucky, and had basic training there. The food was good. You knew the war was at its height, and talkin' to your drill sergeant and other people there, you knew you didn't want to go to Ft. Polk, Louisiana. If you were sent there, you were goin' to the infantry and Vietnam. I got my orders, and I was goin' to Ft. Polk,

Louisiana, with most everybody else. That's just how it was.

Guys are cryin'; they're all upset, but hey! It is what it is. The next day, yeh get in another bus and go to Ft. Polk, Louisiana, and jungle school. We were trained there as infantrymen. I knew where I was goin', and I was okay with that. As I said, my father was in World War II, and he saw combat, and my grandfather was a forward artillery observer in World War I; my uncle was in the Korean War, and I was kind of into it. You know, I had no girlfriend, no baggage, and I was up for it.

I'm still friends to this day with the drill sergeant: Sgt. Stone. He was in Vietnam and came back, and he shared all his knowledge with us. I thought the training was good. You're trained on every infantry weapon; you're trained to kill. That's what you're there for.

We were given a month to come home, and I came home for Christmas of '67 too, for a couple of days. February 1st or 2nd, I got a plane home and was home for one month. I came home, in uniform, lean and mean, ready to kick ass and take names later. I saw my two buddies, one who has since passed away from Agent Orange. He was in college, at that time. I saw my other close friend, from funeral school, who I used to go huntin' with.

The last week of February 1968, my folks took me in to JFK airport, and I went to California a week earlier than I had to. I had to rent a car to get around, and my mother had to sign for the car, because I wasn't 21. I'm a big sports fan, and I went to a Warriors game, in uniform.

Then, on March 2nd or 3rd, I got to Vietnam, by air. We landed in Di An, a little north of Saigon. Highway 13 came through it. We were assigned to the 1st Infantry Division and went from Di An to Lai Khe base, northwest of Saigon. The 1st Infantry gave us a week of in-house jungle training to teach us what we would experience in Vietnam. At that training, I met Bruce Oates, from Pennsylvania, and Kurt Person, from New Jersey, and I still keep in contact with them. We all got assigned to 2nd

Squad, 2nd Platoon, Bravo Company, in the 1st Battalion, in the 16th Regiment.

I didn't meet my sergeant right away, because when we got to our in-country training, we were assigned to our unit, down to the squad level; they were out in the field. So, they put us in a mortar barracks, till they came in from the field. They came back, and we took all of our gear out of the mortar barracks, and we went over to our own barracks. I knew what in-coming fire was, and we just got there and in-coming, enemy-mortar fire began. You hear feeet, feeet, as the rounds leave the mortar tubes, and guys start runnin' into the bunkers.

I am semi-claustrophobic, and I remember I was waitin' outside the bunker to go in. I just can't stand dark areas. Finally, I went in there. Then the mortar rounds stopped, and we came out. And the mortar barracks that the three of us were just in, took a direct hit. That was about 10 days after I got to Vietnam, and the first part of the enemy's Tet Offensive was goin' on. We went over there, and I saw guy's wounded, and I saw guys dead. I saw guys crying, and I remember standin' there and sayin' to myself, 'I can die here. But, what are you gonna do?' After this is when I met my sergeant.

By the way, this is not called "combat". You don't get your CIB, your Combat Infantryman's Badge, until your shot at. This is just called incoming mortars. It doesn't count.

To this day, I can't take sudden, loud noises. Just the other day, I'm talkin' to somebody outside the post office. I'm a funeral director, so I'm dressed in a black suit, black tie, and white shirt, and a truck went by with stuff in the back and hit a bump in the road. It made a big noise, and I almost went down to the ground on all fours. I said, 'My knees are very bad and kind of gave out.' I didn't want to tell him why it happened.

All three of us got assigned to the 2nd Squad, because they got their ass kicked shortly before we arrived. They needed two ammo bearers and a radio operator to replace men that were wounded or killed. Bruce got the radio, and me and Kurt became ammo bearers, for the M-60 carried by Sgt. Bernardi. The sergeant of our squad was a little guy, from Connecticut. I'm a big guy. We only had seven guys in our squad. You're supposed to have a dozen, but you never have enough men. I remember my squad sergeant, a buck sergeant, had a green tie around his neck, and we were the new guys and nobody likes the new guys. He was shorter than me, and I remember him lookin' at me and he said, 'If you fall asleep on ambush, I will personally kill you.'

We never knew when we were leavin' Lai Khe. When you come back from the field, the first thing you do is you clean your weapon. They were really strict on cleaning your weapon, because back at that time, they had problems with the M-16 rifle jamming. But me personally, I never had a problem where mine jammed. You only keep 18 rounds in a magazine, because they expand. We used to tape two magazines together with black tape, and you didn't have to reach into your pouch to get another: you could just flip it around and put the second magazine into the rifle, because time was important.

All of a sudden, we'd be told to, 'Saddle up, we're goin' out.' Then you get on deuce-and-a-halves, and you go down to the helicopter pad, and you get choppered out. There were no doors, and we used to sit in the helicopter with our feet hangin' over the side, with a six to eight man squad, in a helicopter, and the two pilots and two M-60 gunners, that would sit on their flak jackets, so they didn't get shot in the ass.

You were humpin'. The guys I was with had to carry, most times, two Claymore mines; two or three hand grenades; two or three smoke grenades; and, then me and Kurt had on our backs the M-60 rounds, because we were ammo bearers. We also had to carry personal weapons, and your entrenching tool, if you had one. You took the rubber canteen out of the canteen holder, and hung it from your belt. You put the M-16 magazines in your canteen holder.

We had to carry like 30 magazines, because you never had enough ammunition. You do not know what you're gonna get into or when you're gonna get ammunition. Then, of course, you're carryin' your C-Rations. You don't know when you're gonna get food. You don't complain, because everybody's humpin'.

We got dropped off in a clearin', and the point man was from down south. It took a skill to work point, 'cause where we were the point man had a machete in one hand and an M-16 in the other hand. The vegetation was so thick you could not see the hand in front of your face; plus, you had three canopies of trees above you, so you couldn't see the sun.

Let's say you had to walk five clicks, five kilometers. The point man would have to count his steps, as he's cutting his way through the woods, an also think about getting shot at. After so many clicks, you have to turn, and by night, if you're going to spend the night there, you have to be in a clearing, so you can set up a decent perimeter, and, if you're going to be extracted, you'd better be in a clearing, so you can be picked up by helicopters.

I was always amazed this guy never got us lost. And there was another guy that walked point, and he was from down south too. He wanted a shotgun. You couldn't get shotguns, in Vietnam, in them days, and his parents mailed him a shotgun and ammo. And he walked point carryin' this shotgun.

You had to volunteer to walk point. Boy, some guys loved it. They just thrived on that shit. Behind him was another man, and there was two lines goin' through the woods. You could hear the other line, but you could not see them: the vegetation was that thick.

Now and then, you would stop in the woods and take a break, and they would send out three men, from each line, to make a circle out and come back. They went out away from the two columns and back to see if anyone was watchin' us. You can't see them. When it was your turn to go make a clover leaf, a circle, you didn't want to go, but you had to go. That was your job.

While that was goin' on, you'd be sittin' down writin' a letter home, you'd be relaxing. When the combat happens; when you get shot at, that's when you get your CIB. It was a big thing to get your CIB, because everybody had them, but the new guys. Believe it or not, you wanted to see your first combat, so you could get your CIB. You don't think about getting killed; you don't think about getting wounded. I got my CIB the first week I was there. We got shot at a lot.

The longest I was out for was six weeks. And for six weeks, every day, someone got killed or wounded. We took a beating. It was not good. This operation we were on, we were protecting Roman plows. You and I would call them bulldozers. They were large, armored, specially modified bulldozers that were made in Rome, Georgia.

One time, when we were out in the field, there was a fire fight, and you're shootin' at the enemy, and you can't really see them, because the vegetation is that thick. But, every five bullets is a tracer, and you can see them buzzin' by; and they holler, 'Machine gun, up front!' We went to the point and just got set up, and next thing you know I'm bleedin' on the hand. It was shrapnel, from whatever they were shootin' at us.

To me it was no big deal, and then I went back to the base camp, at Lia Khe, and they had six M-16s with bayonets, stuck in the ground and boots in front of them, and a helmet on top of the M-16s. You know who's dead, and you're all lined up, and the chaplain says a prayer for the guys that got killed. Then they handed out Purple Hearts, and I got one. I'm lookin' at the helmets on the M-16s there, and I'm thinkin', 'Guys got killed, and I'm getting' a Purple Heart for this?'

At our base, we were in a clearing, and to get to the chow hall, at a little rise, in the area, you were literally walking through mud up to your waist. Then you walked back to your bunker, and they always had two or three feet of water in them. You actually slept outside, in the rain, with your poncho over you. There was no tarps in this area. The area took so much of a beating we had M-50 machine guns set up on top of the bunkers.

Any time you came back from the field to Lai Khe, you got mortared continuously. Guys were getting killed and wounded continuously. And when you hear the mortar round coming; that feeeet: you just run for the bunker.

What the Army decided to do, in their wisdom, was to clear the jungle around Lai Khe, with these Roman plows. That was during the rainy season. We went out each day to protect the plows. When we went out there were maybe 50 plows. When they finished clearing, there was only five plows that were operable. The others were blown up by mines. We really got our ass kicked.

Every day when we'd come back to the base camp, from protecting the Roman plows, the Viet Cong would walk the mortar rounds in. You could hear them: feeet, feeet, and we'd be runnin' for our lives to get to our bunkers and into the mud. The rounds were hitting and the enemy was getting their range. And our guys, in the base camp, would shoot the M-50s and fire mortars.

Every day, the enemy mortars stopped, and you'd come out; do what you had to do, and the next day you went back out again. We were out with those Roman plows, for 47 days. That was the longest mission I was out on.

Other than that, we patrolled, patrolled, and patrolled. We'd go out and stop somewhere and did a fox hole. We didn't have shovels, so we used our helmets. We carried empty bags, and we'd fill them with sand and make a little protection in front of our fox hole. The next day, you would take your empty C-Ration containers and put them in the bottom of the fox hole and empty the sand bags into the hole and cover your garbage. You'd take the sand bags and empty them and roll them up and pack them in what you carried, and off you'd go again.

A normal patrol lasted from a week to two weeks. When you got into a fire fight, the machine gun would be called up front, or wherever the enemy fire was coming from, and they'd give you orders, and call for ammo bearers get up, and me and Kurt would run up to wherever the machine gun was, and you would feed the gunner the ammunition. And when it ended, some men would mutilate the dead gooks.

We only had a prisoner once. We got followed one time, and our guys in the back stopped and waited, and a half dozen enemy came through, and they caught a couple of prisoners. They brought them up to our Lieutenant. Then, when they got to a clearin', they called the helicopter and the prisoners were extracted out.

I was on patrol, and somehow, I got bit, on my left foot, by who knows what. And my foot got infected, and soon it was so swollen I was carryin' my boot. What are you gonna do? Life goes on! One night we got hot chow and mail and resupply, by helicopter, of ammunition and chow. If you got Kool-Aid, you took off your helmet and put water and Kool-Aid in it and drank out of your helmet.

Then the company medic looked at my foot, and asked how long it had been swollen, and I told him it had been swollen for a while. He said I had to get out of there or you're gonna lose your foot, if you don't get out of here. He said next time a helicopter comes with re-supply I'm out of there. Some days later, we got hot food again, and I helicoptered out.

At Lai Khe, I went to the medic every morning and night to get my foot cut and lanced and medicated. They saved my foot. Even with a bad foot, I pulled perimeter guard duty. I might not have been good enough to out in the jungle and fight, but I was good enough to pull guard duty.

I got talkin' to the people that worked there, and they asked what I did back home. I told him, and he said Graves Registration was there at Lai Khe. I did not know that. He said, put in for a transfer, and I did. Then our company took a really bad hit, and I got ordered back to it. I could have stayed back at Lai Khe shamming, but that's not what yeh do. I was well enough to get back out there, so I told the doctor, 'I'm goin' back out.'

He said I really shouldn't, and I said, 'we just got our ass kicked out there. I know what's out there.'

So, he said, 'Do what yeh gotta do.'

So, I went back out there to the field. My company was out for quite a while, at that time. I was carryin' a machine gun, and had my own ammo bearers. Then the squad sergeant says that I gotta go up and see the Captain. I'm thinkin' the only time yeh saw the Captain was when somebody passed away at home. So, I went to the Captain, and he says I hopes he never see him again.

I say, 'What do yeh mean?'

And he says, 'Yeh got transferred to Graves Registration.' He put a little humor in that, and I now know what he meant. I made my last patrol, and when the next helicopter came, the next day, I told my sergeant and left.

At Lia Khe, when a unit got into a deuce-and-a-half to go out into the field, the infantry not going would stand by the side of the road. They knew you were goin' to the helicopter pad to fight. They would holler so long sucker! Kids being kids, the men on the trucks would holler back you're nothing but a REMF. That means rear echelon mother-fucker. And they'd holler ass hole, and it went on like that. So, guess what I became?

You could hear the deuce-and-a-half comin' down the road; the dust flying. You know where they're goin'; I'd be standin' there hollerin' so long suckers or ass holes, and they'd be hollerin' at me.

When I found out when my unit would be back at the base camp, I went to go see them, and they didn't want to talk to me. I wasn't one of them. There was that dividing line. Now you're a REM; you're not one of us. And there were new guys there, and others were rotating out, and I could just feel I wasn't wanted there.

I was in infantry for seven months. When I got to Lai Khe, I was only 15 minutes from the men I fought with.

In Graves Registration, we got the GIs that were killed. We got 'em directly from the field. When I was in the field, when a person got killed, after the show was over with, they would get poncho liners and put the bodies in them, and throw them on the helicopters. The helicopters would leave, and that would be it. We didn't know what happened to them.

Well, in Graves Registration, I found out. We would be called, at all hours of the day and night, with the code word Giants: two Giants; four Giants. Two men would get in the morgue wagon, go to the helicopter pad when the helicopter would land, and we would take 'em off. They came directly from the field. Most times it was that day or the next day. We would take 'em back to the little area that we had there, and our job mainly was to ID every person that came through there if possible, from the personal effects on them. Then we would put them into body bags, and put them aboard helicopters, and transport them to Di An.

They had to be escorted to Di An, by Army personnel. At Di An, we would hand the paper work over to the Army, and with somebody from that unit, we would go through the personal effects that were on each person, and they would have to sign off that they got what we gave them. In the 1st Infantry Division, we had to make up eight copies of the effects. That leads me to believe, that before that young man's body got home to his parents, he passed through eight channels and somebody had to sign off at eight spots. That's why I had to learn how to type, and there was no mistakes.

Some of the bodies had no arms. Some had no heads, and we couldn't get those identified. Most had dog tags, but those that didn't we'd keep them there and wait till the unit came back from the field, and we'd have a sergeant come and try to identify them. They really wanted to get them identified, before they got to the embalming site, which was in Saigon.

After the bodies left, the stuff that was in their foot lockers, the unit would bring to us. We would sit with the man that brought it to us and go through the foot locker and itemize everything in it. He would sign and I would sign. That also had to be eight copies.

The 1st Infantry Division was noted for getting every single piece of personal property home that a person came with, and I believe we did the best to our ability.

Of course, we still took incoming mortar rounds in Lai Khe. When there was no bodies to take care of, we would help out. The ammunition depot was there. The food depot was there. We'd help out 'cause yeh gotta keep busy.

I always say, what we saw there, processing dead men, and everyone else in Graves Registration, in the United States Army saw, nobody should see. What we saw in the field happened so quick. Fire fights are pretty quick, and you have a total adrenaline rush. You do things you can't believe you did. You had to do those things to survive.

That one time, in the base camp, with all that mud, and that one guy with the M-79 grenade launcher ran out of ammunition. The M-79 is a very effective weapon. It fires grenade rounds through the barrel of a gun. We were in the bunkers firing out of the bunkers. He needed more ammunition, and I got up, ran through the mud, ran to where the ammunition was, picked up a crate of M-79 ammo, carried it through the mud to him, 'cause you just have to do these things.

You have to do what you have to do to survive. The guy with the M-50 machine gun, he's out there on top of a bunker firing. You just do what you have to do.

I extended, while I was in Graves Registration, 'cause the Army had a phase that, if you went home with less than five months, you got an early out. So, I extended like 55 days. My parents weren't happy, but I just didn't know if I could come home and have someone tell me to shine my shoes and get a haircut. Not after what I went through. At Lai Khe you got mortared every day and could die, but I came home.

In Graves Registration, you see people with just half a body. That's war, but what I saw there you can't comprehend. Everybody there saw it. It wasn't just me.

The medals and badges I received in the Army are the Combat Infantryman Badge, the Purple Heart Medal, the Vietnam Campaign Medal, Vietnam Service Medal, the Army Commendation Medal with one Oak Leaf Cluster, a Vietnam Gallantry Citation, National Service Medal, two Overseas Bars, and the M-14 Expert Badge.

Then I came home, and I remember going to my local pub, in town here, and people sayin', 'Hey, Lee, where the hell have you been? I haven't seen you for a while.' Your parents were happy you were home, but nobody else cared. That's why I'm glad the kids nowadays, when they come home from war, people recognize they served their country.

But the Vietnam War wasn't popular. I remember being in this bar, when the kids got killed at Kent State, and a couple of veterans are going, 'It's just as well.'

In 1969, I went to the Agricultural and Technical College at Farmingdale, Long Island, and took the mortuary science program. They were burning flags on the campus there. We formed a veterans group, but we didn't get involved with those students, because it didn't matter. But we objected to the rule that we had to take physical education. We went to the dean and told him we were veterans, and we're not takin' physical education, ping pong, or bowling, and the rule was changed, and we didn't have to.

I graduated two years later, in '71, with an Associate of Mortuary Science degree. Then I served an apprenticeship, which I did with my father and grandfather. Then I took a state mortuary test, and then a state mortuary law test, and then I was licensed. I've been at it since. I had started at the funeral home, when I was 10-years old, cuttin' the lawn, and I'll be 69 soon, and I'm still workin' there. I think I work, because it works for me.

I came home with money, because you can't spend money in Vietnam, and I bought a motorcycle, a car, and a boat. I'd come home from a bar, in the car, and I get on my motorcycle and ride off, and my mother would say to my father, 'Tom, he's been drinkin'. You can't let him go on the motorcycle.'

And my father would go, 'Marie, he's just spent 14 months in Vietnam. You can't tell him he can't go out on a motorcycle.'

I met my wife September '70, and we got married a year later. She moved out to our little town, in her sophomore year of high school, from Queens, New York. Her name was Loretta Lynn Manzella. Her father used to tell her, 'Don't forget, you're half Sicilian; you're not Italian.' I'm Swedish.

Our daughter is 42, and she's a funeral director also. Her name is Keri Lynn and she works with me. I see her every day. Keri has three daughters. She lives in the same town, and I walk my grandkids home from school every day. I'm lucky. Our son Ryan Lee is two years younger than Keri. He's not married.

I went to the VA probably six years ago, or longer. I thought if Agent Orange didn't affect you the first five years after exposure to it, you're okay. Then six, seven, or eight years ago, I buried two men three months apart. They were almost the same age, and their death certificates had down Agent Orange as cause of death. I never saw this, until then. So, I thought, 'Holy shit! I thought I was clean.' So, I went to Northport Veterans Hospital to get myself checked out. I was there for three days and they checked out every part of me. They also sent me to a psychiatrist, and I guess I lost it with this doctor. I remember I became very upset. I talked about my Vietnam experience and was moanin' and cryin'. I'd never done that before.

I remember I woke up in the middle of one night, about 20 years ago, and I was hollerin' that I believe that

American servicemen are still over there, in Vietnam, held captive. I was cryin' and screamin', 'Tthey're still over there! I'm goin' over there! I'm gonna get 'em!'

And my wife said, 'Take it easy, Darlin'. Take it easy.'

When I was with the psychiatrist, this came out, and I lost control. She recommended I go to Vietnam, but I said, 'I don't have time for that. I go to work every day, and I function well. Work is my therapy. It gives me somethin' t' do every day.'

Then my cousin Barbara and her husband Gordon Wilson came here to visit. He's a Vietnam combat vet. And me and Gordon are sittin' on the deck here talkin', and he say's I've got to go see a doctor. He say's I'm in bad shape, and I say, 'I'm fine.' He says no, I'm not, and I say, 'I'm not going to go. I function well. I don't drink, except maybe on weekends. I don't smoke. I work, and I work every single day, and that works for me.' Just sittin' on the deck tawkin' to Gordon was good, because just tawkin' to another veteran is good. There are not that many veterans in town here who want to talk, or can talk.

Could I go to the VA and get help and get a check every month? Yeah! But that's not my makeup. A lot of men need that check more than I do. That's the way I feel.

When I hear a helicopter, do I sometimes shake and cry? Yeah. When we have a funeral at the Calverton National Cemetery, the military presents the flag that covered the coffin to the widow. They fold the flag and give it to her, and then I have to speak to say a prayer or dismiss people to go to a restaurant. I have prayers for each religion, and sometimes I can't talk. Sometimes I knew the veteran being buried, and the wife, who's sittin' there cryin', and sometimes the kids. Sometimes I stand there, and they're waitin' for me to speak, and they see I'm emotional. No matter how many times I watch this, it affects me. I have to gather myself up and focus, and go, 'Lee, yeh can't stand here and cry.' I tell the people, 'I know the man who's laying here, and I know everyone standing here, and it affects me, so bear with me.'

And they say, 'Okay, Lee. We know that you know us, and we understand.'

About five years ago, a guy in town who I went to school with calls me up. He was two years ahead of me in school. He says, 'Lee, I didn't know you were in Vietnam. I was in Vietnam too.'

I said, 'Why didn't you tell me.'

He said, 'Who cares?'

I said, 'I care.'

He said for 35 years, he wouldn't admit what he saw and did in the infantry, in Vietnam. He went and got help, and now he's vice president of our Vietnam Veterans of Suffolk County, New York, and he's a total, active person.

I'm ex-president of every organization in town. When you have a business in town, you've got to show your face, and I belong to many civic organizations. I'm also a life member of the Vietnam Veterans of America; life member of local VFW Post 414; life member of the American Legion, in town; life member of the 1st Infantry Division Association. Do I attend meetings? No, but I send them checks, because it's important to support these people, because they're doin' good. I say, that if I ever retired, there's a veteran's nursing home an hour from my house, and I could see me goin' there two, three days a week and just talkin' to the men there.

Lee Wesley Sinnickson, in 1968

Lee Sinnickson inspects part of a barracks destroyed by an enemy mortar round.

Lee Sinnickson, left, and a comrade await a helicopter.

Lee Sinnickson (sitting in front, on the right, just behind the man with headphones on) and other members of his unit are on their way back to their base, after a mission.

Lee Sinnickson eats C-Rations, in the field.

Lee Sinnickson, in the field, after he became an M-60 machine gunner

# Ralph Howard Bigelow
interview of March 19, 2017

My name is Ralph Howard Bigelow. I have throat cancer, and it's a little hard for me to talk. The VA said it is probably from Agent Orange.

I was born I Catskill, New York, on July the 23rd 1948. My dad was Ralph Herbert Bigelow. He was a plant manager for National Cylinder Gas. He was born in Keeseville, New York, and moved down to Athens, New York, where we lived for quite a while.

My mother was Helen May Bigelow. Her maiden name was Russell. She was born in Catskill. She was mainly a housewife. I have a younger brother named Clinton Bigelow and a sister Anita Bigelow who is the youngest.

I went to grade school, in Stuyvesant Falls, New York. We lived there, for a bit, and I went to Ichabod Crane High School, also in Stuyvesant Falls. My dad moved quite a bit, and we ended up in Shrewsbury, Massachusetts. I made it to the 11th grade, at Shrewsbury High School, and that's when I joined the Navy, on March 22, 1966.

I went through boot camp, at Great Lakes, Illinois. After boot camp, I was assigned to be a guard at a secret project, where they were experimenting on people. It's not a secret anymore, so I can talk about it. It took place at Bethesda Navy Hospital. They had an annex set up, at the rear. There was also a diving complex back there, where Navy divers would do their stuff. In the annex various rooms were set up. When you went in, the rooms had a TV, refrigerator, and all the amenities. You got less and less amenities, in the rooms, as you went down the hall. Finally, they had rooms in total darkness: just like being in a blackout.

They were testing to see how long a person could last, without goin' bonkers on 'em. They were looking into putting underwater, submarine-detection stations in the ocean: like a little building, with guys in it, and listening devices to listen for Russian subs, at that time. They were testing people to determine under what conditions they would last in those stations. It didn't take long, for the guys in total darkness to get out. I don't know what the experiment was called. They didn't clue us in, in that regard. We were just there to make sure that nobody left their rooms, or came or went, without authorization. I was there for about a month and a half.

From there, I went to Naval Air Station, Oceana, at Virginia Beach, Virginia, where I was trained as an Aviation Firefighter. I spent maybe two months there, and, after I was trained, they sent me about 20 to 30 miles south to Naval Air Landing Field Fentress, Virginia. I was a firefighter there, where they would train pilots for landing on a carrier. They would talk to the pilots in the air and the pilots would come down, touch down on the runway, and take off again. We rolled out on a few house fires and a barn fire, in the area, and on a couple of crashes. I was there, until early 1967. While I was there, I earned my high school GED.

Then I got orders to go to the *USS Intrepid* CVS-11. It's the one that's now a museum, in New York. When I got my orders to the *Intrepid*, the chief that was with us at Fentress got his orders to go to the *Forestall*, and after he got there, there was an explosion on it, in July 1967, and he was killed.

Aboard the *Intrepid*, I worked in the engine room, as a machinist's mate. I was trained as a fire fighter, but they put me in the engine room. My rating, when I first joined, was fireman, which is in the engine room. I worked the throttle boards: they're like a gas pedal. Orders for different speeds came, on the engine order telegraph, and they'd ring a bell, and you'd put your ear to what was like a pipe, from the bridge all the way down to the engine room. And of course, they would joke sometimes and you'd put your ear to the pipe and someone, on the bridge, would pour water into it.

While I was on the *Intrepid*, I signed up for Navy Special Operations, and, when we were in port again, I got orders to go to PBR boats: you know, the plastic ones like in the movie Apocalypse Now. They were Patrol Boat River. They changed my orders, while I was on leave, and ordered me to report to Mare Island, in Vallejo, California. I looked at the orders and said, what the hell is Valley-Jo?

When I got out there, they were forming a new unit called the Mobile Riverine Force. It was gonna be probably the first time, since the Civil War, where the Navy and the Army worked together. My main training was at Mare Island, and then they sent us to San Clemente Island, for gunnery training, with big guns, like 105mm howitzers, 20mm, 50mms, 80mm mortars, and stuff like that.

Then I went to Whidby Island, in Washington, for my SERE training: that's Survival, Evasion, Resistance, Escape. That's where they play the enemy and put cha in prison, and beat the shit out of you. You went in, with a hood over your face, so you couldn't see where you were goin'. They put you into two types of boxes. One was a four feet by four, by four, and you were supposed to stand in it. If they caught you sittin' down, they'd pull you out and beat the crap out a ya. They had one box that was adjustable, from 3-1/2 to maybe four feet long to only two feet high and maybe two feet across. They had you cross your legs and kneel down and then they'd squeeze you into that box. They'd hold you under water, for a long time. They'd water-board you. They'd question you and try to speak and give more than your name, rank, and serial number. They'd punch you. They had different stances that were very painful. They'd hit you across the stomach and back with a broom handle: interesting to say the least. It was no fun.

Then I got shipped off to Vietnam. We flew into Dong Tam, in the Mekong River delta. It was the main base for the Riverine and the 9th Infantry Division. Then they flew us up to Vung Tau to pick up our boat. I was on a

Tango boat. It was T-131-8, and I was in charge of the engines and was the M19 gunner aboard it.

Tango boats were armored troop carriers. They were like the ones that troops landed from in Normandy. My boat was in River Squadron 13, River Division Alpha 131. We also had Alpha boats. We called them our little destroyers. We had Zippo boats. Those were the ones with flame throwers on 'em. And we had monitors with 105mm tank turrets on front. Then there was the command boat, which had a little building on it where the top officers would be.

We did joint operations with the 9th Infantry Division and ARVN units. My first combat was in May '68. We'd take the boats down canals. In the lead was always a sweep boat sweeping mines. There would be a monitor behind them. Then the Tangos. Alpha boats used to be mine sweepers, but the armor on them was real thin: only a quarter inch steel, and they were losing a lot of 'em they were armed with two 20mm machine guns and an M-60 on the stern, so they put them in the middle of the boat columns, for their firepower.

We started out carrying the 9th Infantry, but then they turned us into minesweepers. We usually led the pack, and we did get sunk: we hit a mine. So, did the other boat that pulled up alongside us.

We started out with a canvas top, over the well deck, where the Army would have been normally. The canvas top was to prevent rain from filling the well deck. The Navy eventually replaced all the canvas tops with flight decks, so they could land Bell UH-1 Hueys and OH-6 Cayuse or LOACH helicopters on them for whatever reasons they wanted to. The helicopter was bigger than the boat. The boats were only 13-ft across and 56-ft long.

The Huey's were usually the medivacs comin' in to pick up wounded and dead. In a LOACH, an officer would fly with a pilot, and then they'd direct troops that were on the ground.

On a lot of those canals you'd go down, our gun barrels would be in the trees beside the canal: the canals were that narrow. It was like goin' down a lane and a half in a road. So, when you got into a fire fight, you were definitely toast. They almost always shot the first shot. We lost a lot of guys. The Purple Heart rate was about 90% for the sailors of the Mobile Riverine Force.

We went out almost every day, on a joint Army-Navy operation or on a search-and-destroy mission, by ourselves. Every time we would go on search-and-destroy or on a joint Army, Navy operation we would get into a firefight. If you get into a fire fight every day, your boat's gonna get hit. The Viet Cong had RPG-7s, B40s, B50s, and recoilless rifles they would shoot at us from spider holes. A spider hole is like a tunnel dug into the canal bank, just above the water line. They'd shoot a rocket at cha from it. You could see the rocket coming out, so I'd give 'em one right back, with a LAW rocket. You'd see the rocket going in and a big explosion. The dirt would fly and water would go into there.

One time we carried a National Geographic photographer with us, and he took a lot of pictures that were in National Geographic.

On July 13, 1968, we were at the head of a column of assault boats heading up river to extract soldiers of the 4th Battalion, 39th Infantry and carry them to a landing zone to be helicoptered back to their base camp. We led the column up the Song Tien River and into the Song Ba Rai to a large bend where the river changes names and becomes the Dong Ba Rai. The wide river bend was nicknamed Snoopy's Nose, by the sailors, because, on a map, it looked like the nose of the Snoopy, the dog in the Peanut's cartoons.

Viet Cong used the land within the bend to ambush us. There were only about two acres there. Even when our engines were muffled, they could hear them as far away as a mile. We moved at about 6 knots an hour and they had a lot of time to get ready to attack us.

The first time we around Snoopy's Nose, we had 20 to 30 boats in our column: enough to surround the place. The VC waited until we surrounded it and then they fired on boats and hid. The jungle on Snoopy's Nose was dense, and our boats opened fire on the place. Because we were almost in a circle, some of our rounds went through the jungle and hit our own boats on the other side. We figured out quickly that the enemy didn't have 50-cal. guns there, and that we were firing on each other. After that experience, we had one boat move around the place and beach and fire into the jungle, while the other went around and fired only if fired upon.

The VC had figured out how we operated and counted us doing the same thing every time, and we did. It worked for them, and every time, we had to fight our way out. Even after a B52 air strike they ambushed us. They always ambushed us going in and coming out. Of all the places that we went, it was the worst.

We moved north of Snoopy's Nose and loaded the troops, with no opposition and headed back to move south around Snoopy's Nose. As we passed it, we received fire, from both river banks. Our crews' rapidly returned fire and suppressed enemy fire. The unit commander had the 4-39th landed on both sides of the Song Ba Rai, to find the Viet Cong. We coated the banks with fire and the infantry landed.

While my boat, T131-8, was beached, we adjusted her position and an underwater explosion blew a hole in the hull, under the starboard fuel tank, and the engine room flooded.

Viet Cong fire was heavy and when Tango boat 131-5 landed the men of Alpha Company, it received enemy automatic weapons fire and a HEAT round, a high explosive anti-tank round, hit the M 19, 40mm grenade launcher. It killed the gunner and made the gun inoperable. A second round hit the 131-5, on the starboard side, below the 20mm gun. It damaged and made a hole in the armor.

After Tango boat 131-13 landed it troops, it came alongside Tango 8 to help off load guns and equipment, and was sunk next to Tango 8. No one was hurt, but Tango 13 had an 18-inch wide hole in the port shaft area. Tango 131-8 and Tango 131-13 were unable to make way and remained beached while several other assault boats beached alongside them to set up a protective perimeter around the boats and crews.

Monitor 111-3, a Zippo monitor, sprayed the land near us with napalm-like material. Monitor 111-3 had an M10-8 flamethrower and could send napalm across any canal and some rivers. 111-3 emptied its flammable material and was relieved, by Monitor 91-2 and boat A-92-6, from the Riverine Unit Alpha.

Monitor 111-3 went back down river to our mother ship, escorted by Tango 111-1, which had an Army flame thrower unit aboard. This operation went on all day, and our mother ship, at that time, was the *USS Wyndham County,* LST-1170. She stood by, in a nearby river, to refuel boats, as they ran low on fuel.

Several boats remained beached all night, near 131-8 and 131-13, as salvage work went on. The work was done by men that arrived, from *Wyndham,* and the ship provided food and drinks to the boats' crews. *Wyndham* also moved its anchorage nearer to the beached boats and fired 40 rounds, from her 3-inch gun, to support the boats out that night.

During the night, two sailors were posted on watch, on each of the two sunken boats. Bobby Dean Dawson, a Gunners Mate 3, from a southern state, and I were on our boat, and on watch for the whole night. We had small arms and grenades and were there to prevent Viet Cong sappers from blowing up the boats. At about 1:30 or two in the morning, when it was real dark, we heard movement, in front of the boat's bow and challenged the sound. We received no answer and fired away. The enemy fired back. That went on for about an hour. When daylight broke, 9th Infantry soldiers swept the area in front of the boats. They didn't find any bodies, but did find a blood-soaked backpack and a lot of blood.

Enough repairs had been made to the two beached boats, and each was moved off the beach separately and secured to two other Tango boats, one on each side, and moved back to the base for more repairs. When the boats were raised out of the water, wire was found wrapped around the screw propellers and propeller shafts. The wire had connected to the propellers under water and, once that was done the propellers had wound the mines against the hull and the mines had exploded.

When the Navy said okay you guys, your replacements are here and you're going home, I only had three months to go. I wanted to stay in the Navy, and was going to re-up. I said I would, if I could stay with my unit, and they said, no, you've gotta go home. I said that's nuts. I want to re-up and I want to stay in Special Ops, but they said I had to go home. So, I did not re-up, and they sent me to Treasure Island, in California, right by Alcatraz.

When the U.S. was disbanding units, some of the river sailors became Army snipers.

When I arrived at Treasure Island, in May of '69, I didn't look like a sailor. I was dressed in green and was wearing a beret. They didn't know what to do with me for two and a half months, so they sent me to the brig, which was run by the Marines. I was a runner taking prisoners from the holding barracks, when they first got there, to the brig, and from the brig to court and back to jail. The Marines were as mean to me as they were to the prisoners. I was a Machinists Mate 3rd Class, when I was released from active duty, in July 1969, and when I was honorably discharged July 1972.

I had a great time in the service. I tried to go into the Army, when Desert Storm happened, in January 1991, but they said I'd have to join the reserves in Ohio. They said the next unit to go is supposed to come from Ohio, and I said, if it doesn't happen I'll be stuck goin' to the reserves in Ohio. So, I didn't join.

I have PTSD. We didn't know what it was, when we first got out. They had another name for it. I had the same re-occurring dream every night. We were the first troops to go into the U Minh Forest, in the Mekong River delta. As we were going in, it was Christmas, and there was supposed to be a cease fire, for a few days. We didn't have any soldiers with us. We were goin' in there, on a search-and-destroy mission, but, because of the cease fire, we were at the mouth of the canal going into the forest and were beached. That night the Viet Cong mortared us, so we went on in. So much for the truce!

As we were goin' into the canal, all we saw was young kids and old men and women comin' out in sampans, by the droves. There was no way between them. So, we knew we were goin' into a very strong VC held-area, and it wasn't going to be good.

We got in a fire fight, and got shot up pretty good. When we got to the end the canal it was like a narrow stream, and where it came out of the forest it was just wide enough for the boats. There was thick vegetation, at the end, like mangrove and stuff like that. We had wounded, and called for a medivac, and a Huey came in with a red cross on it. We were still taking small arms fire from the VC.

The Huey pilot was told to set down on the boat next to us. No one was shootin' at us, at that particular moment. The Huey came down and landed on the deck of a Tango boat, and the door guy got out, and a VC opened up with an AK-47. So, the Huey pilot took off. The door guy grabbed the skid, and he's hanging from the skid, as the Huey takes off, over land, like a bat out of hell. I got on the radio and was hollerin' your guys on the skid. About a quarter mile in and way up, the guy drops. I imagine he is unaccounted for: MIA.

On the way out of the forest it was ten times worse than goin' in, because they were really ready for us. Comin' out: this is the part that I dream about. I was just doin' my duty. The canal was so narrow, not more than four feet to the bank, and there was a sampan coming directly at us, with a woman in it that was holdin' a baby in one arm. When she got right in front of out boat, she reached down and grabbed a damn satchel. I knew what it was. She was goin' to throw that damn satchel bomb into the boat.

I was sittin' on my gun. I had an M-16 and a LAW rocket with me, like normal. So, I took the M-16, and I shot her. Unfortunately, she was holding that baby in her arms to cover her, as a shield, so I shot 'em both. The sampan floated on by my boat, and someone in the boat behind me threw a grenade in it to sink it and insure there was no one else that was going to attack us. To this day, I still see that, and nothing's gonna change that.

When we got home, at San Francisco airport, there were anti-war hippies there that called us baby killers. Technically, yeah, I did kill a baby. It hurts me to even talk about that shit. The VA gave me meds, but I tell them there's nothing you can do, nothing you can say to help. I know what I did. I had to do it. I'd do it again, for my crew. I wouldn't let her kill my guys. But the fact that the baby was killed bothers me: just bothers me. The PTSD disability rating the VA gave me is 70%.

During a fire fight, I got shrapnel, in the shoulder, and, because of the adrenalin in me, I didn't realize I was shot, until after the action. I looked at my shoulder and it was bleeding a little. It didn't bleed a lot, because the heat of the shrapnel cauterized part of it. When we got back to the mother ship, I went to the ship's sick bay, where a medic dug down, and he took two pieces out, and said there's another one in there, but I can't get it out. He said it'll fester up and come out. It never did. What had happened was an AK round came into the turret and went beside my head and hit the back of the turret. The gun turrets were 5/8-inch-thick armor-plated steel. Pieces of the round bounced back and went into me.

Another guy got shot, in that fire fight, and the medic gave us forms saying we were wounded in action.

We took the forms up to my officer, on the mother ship, and there were two Lieutenants there that day. My Lieutenant said, 'Oh, Christ! You want a Purple Heart for that? You guys can have Purple Hearts or what's in that can.' We looked at the big ol' can, and we said we'll take what's in that can. We thought he was joking. Turns out there were M&Ms in it. I guess he never turned the paper work in. I know I never received my Purple Heart.

About three or four years ago, a medical specialist diagnosed me with throat cancer caused by Agent Orange exposure, in Vietnam. I had chemo and I had radiation: very high doses of each. The doctor wanted to cut a hole in my throat and put a tube in me, but I said no. I'll go out, before I'll do that.

The medals and awards I got are a Combat Action Ribbon, a Vietnam Service medal with a silver battle star, a Navy Achievement Medal with a combat V for valor, a Navy Unit Commendation Ribbon with two bronze stars, a Republic of Vietnam Meritorious Unit Citation, which is a Gallantry Cross Medal of first class color with Palm, and a Republic of Vietnam Meritorious Unit Citation, which is a Civil Action Medal of first class color with Palm.

The Navy Achievement Medal was awarded for the successful combat missions that I was involved in that went deep into enemy territory daily.

When I got out of the Navy, I went home to my folks, in Michigan, and worked with my dad, for four months or so, installing gas units: liquid nitrogen and liquid oxygen, in hospitals and steel factories. In November of '69, I hired in with Detroit Edison and became a lineman, for 40 years. I retired in 2008, and live in Livonia, Michigan. Since then I've done some traveling.

I'm divorced. I've been married four times. The first marriage was in 1970 to a local girl. That lasted three years. A year later I got married again. She lived in Michigan, but was from Ohio. That lasted three years. Then a year off, and I got married again. The woman that was divorced and lived in Michigan. She was originally from

Germany. That lasted three years, and we got divorced. I was single for a year, and then I re-married to another Michigan girl. That lasted for 12 years. We were divorced a good 15-years ago.

With my first wife, I have a daughter. JoAnn Moulton is her married name. With my second wife, I have a son. His name is Ralph Albert Bigelow. He has two girls. They are Natalie and Whitney.

I'm on the board of directors of The Mobile Riverine Force Association. Adm. Elmo Zumwalt was a member of our association, and attended our re-unions every year, until his death, in 2000. He and his wife dined with us, and we had a few cocktails together many times. He is truly missed by all of us.

I'm a life member of the VFW, the American Legion, AMVETS, the Vietnam Veterans of America, and the DAV. I'm a member of the Moose; a member of the Fraternal Order of Eagles, and I'm a lifetime member of the Intrepid museum, in New York: the *USS Intrepid*, and a life member of the former crew members association. I'm also a mason. I'm a member of Wayne Lodge, No.112, Free and Accepted Masons of Michigan, and I'm a Shriner, and a member of Moslem Shrine Temple, Southfield, Michigan. I also donate every month to the Wounded Warriors Project.

Next month I'm goin' to New York, for a few days, to go the Intrepid. In June, it'll be 50 years since I was on it. So, I figured I'd better get down there and see it, if I'm going to do it.

This photo of Ralph Howard Bigelow was taken while he was in Vietnam on river duty.

A Zippo boat of the U.S. Navy's Mobile Riverine Force sends a stream of napalm on a suspected enemy position, in Vietnam.

This photo shows a Zippo boat, immediately after action, in about July 1968. The bodies of two U.S. sailors killed in action lie on the boat's fore-deck. In the background, a Vietnamese boy studies the situation.

'This photo was taken the first day that I had a new Mark 19, 40mm grenade launcher mounted in my gun turret to replace my 50-cal. machine gun.

When the Mark 19 was available, the Navy brought two over with the two guys that invented it. They took my 50-cal. and put the first one on my turret.

A 40mm grenade launcher has electric feed and shot a good 100-yards level. The round is a lot more powerful than the round fired by hand-held 40mm grenade launchers. When the guy that invented the gun went out with me to test it, he pointed out a Conex box 50- to 60-yards away and said to shoot at it. So, I raised the M19's barrel way up high, and the guy said not to; just aim at the box. I lowered the barrel and aimed at the box and blew the crap out of it.

The gun was fed by an electric feeder that supplied 600 rounds from a big canister linked to two 20mm ammo cans with M19 ammo in them, and I had another 100 rounds, on a belt connected to the 600. I also had a LAW rocket launcher, and an M-16, and could shoot those when needed.

I asked him what possessed him to invent this gun, and he said Korea. He said 10 well placed rounds can clear off everybody on a football field. He said, if they had had this gun in Korea, when the enemy was doin' their mass charges, they could have devastated them.'

'Here I am, with my new AK-47 rifle, the morning after I got it. How I got it involved two Tango boats.

One boat had two Army guys on it that operated a 4-ft searchlight that could use infrared or white light. My boat had one Army sniper and two other Army guys that operated a portable radar and listening device. With their listening device, they could hear a vehicle up to five miles away and voices half a mile away. We went out, at night, and beached our boats and waited to ambush VC. This proved effective, on the main river, when both boats went out together, but, in a narrow canal, we had to do ambushes by ourselves.

One night, in a canal, we beached our boat, on a bend in the canal. Our boat was alone, and we looked like part of the bend. One of the Army guys told me they heard a sampan coming toward us and said there were two people in it. He said he could tell that they had weapons, and told me to wake up the sniper. The canal was only 25-ft across, and I told him I could take care of the unwelcome visitors. I squatted down on the stern of our boat, with an Ithaca, 12-guage, pump-action shotgun, and as the sampan came around the bend they were about 20-ft away. I fired two shots and killed both VC. I retrieved their AK-47s and gave one to one of the Army guys.'

Ralph Bigelow searches a village, after his unit engaged in a fire fight with enemy personnel in it.

Sailors of the Navy's Mobile Riverine Force, Squadrons 9 and 11 are mustered, at their base, to receive Purple Hearts and some Silver Stars, in late 1967. About 90% of the men in the Navy's Mobile Riverine Force were awarded Purple Hearts. Many were awarded to men killed in action.

# Robert Clyde "Bob" Stephenson

interview of September 13, 2017

My name is Robert Clyde Stephenson. I was born October 23, 1947, in Appleton, Wisconsin.

My dad's name is Clyde Stephenson, He is alive and well at 97-years old. During World War II, he married my mother, and she moved from Appleton out to Seattle and worked as Rosie the Riveter on B-17 bombers. After World War II, he was an electrical contractor. They moved back to Appleton, after the war, and he had a little union company, with about 25 electricians.

My mother was Elayne Stephenson. Her maiden name was Storm. She passed away three years ago, at 94. They had been married 72 years.

I have two older brothers, we were two years apart. I went to a local high school when I graduated from high school in 1965, I was 17, and my parents wanted me to go to college. My two older brothers were going to Marquette University, in Milwaukee, my oldest brother, Larry, Lawrence, went onto medical school and became a doctor. Larry is now chief of cardio-thoracic surgery, at Detroit Medical Center. He's 74-years old and is chair of the department. He was in the Army Reserve and was in Desert Storm, and retired as a bird Colonel.

Larry wrote quite a few books, about heart surgery, with C. Everett Coop, the former U.S. surgeon general, from 1982 to 1989.

My other brother, Rollie Stephenson went into engineering. His full name is Roland Glenwood Stephenson. I went down to Marquette for a semester, and I really hated college, I was a pretty wild guy, so I decided since I'd get drafted, I'd join the military. Rollie was named after my dad's two brothers who were killed in World War II. The three of us get together quite a bit.

My dad was a Marine. I believe he enlisted early in 1940. He was at Pearl Harbor, when the Japanese attacked there. He and a small group of Marines were at a firing range, at that time, preparing to train Navy personnel in small arms. They were the first to return fire and did so within 10-minutes of when the Jap attack began and were credited with shooting down six of the 26 Jap planes that were shot down. By the time the war ended and he finished his Marine Corps service, he was a master sergeant. He is 97 now and one of the very few that was at Pearl, when it was bombed and also at Peleliu.

When I told him, I was going to enlist, he said to me, 'Son, if you're going to go in the military why don't you enlist for a school. And do me a favor and don't join the Marines.' So, much to his chagrin, I joined the Army for airborne infantry and Special Forces, in June of 1966. I thought it would be exciting, and it was.

I signed up with a friend of mine, in what the Army called the Buddy Program. Once we got to Basic Training, I never saw my buddy again in the Army. I went to Ft. Polk, Louisiana, for Basic Training. It was supposed to be for eight weeks, but I had appendicitis and my appendix was removed. After that they gave me a 10-day leave and I came home for a couple of days. When I went back, I started the training over, so I had about 12-weeks of basic.

They had a course there called Quick Kill, and we spent a week or two in the swamps there marching along. As we moved along targets would pop up and we shot at them with live ammo. It got to the point where we were pretty good at shooting from the hip. When I went home on leave, after that, the first pheasant I shot was with a hip shot.

After Ft. Polk, I was assigned to Ft. Ord, California, for my Advanced Individual Training. It was training in map reading, squad maneuvers, familiarization with mortars and 50-cal. machine guns and other matters related to the infantry.

Then I was signed up to go to Special Forces School, and there wasn't an opening, so they had me in a holding company for a couple of months. Then it came through that my background clearance didn't clear to go to Special Forces. The reason was that I had 13 speeding tickets when I was in high school. They said apparently, I couldn't listen to orders, but they did want me to go to OCS, Officer Candidate School.

Meanwhile, they sent me to Jump School, because I was signed up to be a paratrooper. I went to Ft. Benning, Georgia, to three weeks of jump school. When I finished jump school, I was supposed to go to OCS, but there wasn't an opening for me, at that time.

OCS was six-months long, and once you graduated, you had to sign a new, two-year commitment. I had enlisted for three years originally. If I went through officer's school, because of the delays, I would be in the Army more than three years, and I didn't want to be. So, I gave then a notice that I didn't want to go to officer's school; I just wanted to go to an infantry company. My military occupation specialty was 11B, which was light weapons infantry. Everybody with that MOS was getting sent to Vietnam.

Instead of sending me to Vietnam, they sent me to Ft. Bragg to the 82nd Airborne Division. When I got there, I was assigned to B Company, 1st Battalion, 505th Infantry. Most of the guys there were airborne guys coming back from Vietnam. I was one of the few that had not been to Vietnam.

While I was there, the only exciting thing that happened was that we were called into duty in Detroit when massive riots happened there, at the end of July in 1967. The city police couldn't control the rioters, so the governor sent in the state police and National Guard, and the National Guard couldn't control it.

The 82nd Airborne is always on ready alert for deployment to anywhere in the world. The division is divided into three phases, and I happened to be in the phase in which each man is packed and ready to move. At about midnight they told us we were going somewhere, but they wouldn't tell us where. They trucked us over to the Pope air base and put us on C-130s. We had our M-16s and, they loaded live ammo on the tailgate of the aircraft.

When they told us, we were going to Detroit, we were shocked, because there were rumors that we were going someplace overseas. We landed at Selfridge Air Force Base, just north of Detroit, and went by truck, in the middle of the night, and took over a school. They got us organized and took us out on the street and there were building everywhere that had been burned.

I was right next to a fire truck, a hook and ladder, guarding it, and one of the firemen was shot by a sniper and falls and lands about four feet from me. I turned and I saw where the guy shot from, but I was only a Pfc. and we weren't allowed to lock and load our weapons without an officer's order. I see this guy shooting out of a corner window on the third floor of this old apartment building, and I grabbed two other guys and told them there was a sniper over there and let's go get him. We ran up the back-fire escape, and by the time we got to that door, we were all locked and loaded and we kicked the door in and there were two black guys in there with rifles, and they were drunk and had wine bottles with them.

Detroit police were often with the Army guys, and worked with us when they could. We dragged the snipers down the stairs to the street, and as soon as we came out of the building, there was a Detroit cop. We turned them over to the police.

We were there for two weeks and out on the streets every day. Those riots went on for five days. The rioters were black, and the riots were among the most violent and destructive riots in U.S. history. When the bloodshed, burning, and looting ended 43 people were dead, 342 people had been injured, and about 1,400 buildings had been burned.

When it was over, we each got a commendation certificate, for our duty there, and I got five days off, so I went home to see some friends. Then I went back to Ft. Bragg. In about December of 1967, I got orders for Vietnam. I was in the 82nd Airborne Division, but I was assigned to the 173rd Airborne Division, which was supposed to leave out of Oakland on January 15th, after a 30-day leave. So, I went out to California with a friend for a couple of days, and then I went to Oakland and reported in.

We flew right away to Vietnam, on a Braniff 707 airplane, and landed at Bien Hoa in the middle of a clear day. I got off the airplane, and they had people there looking for the soldiers arriving for their units. I go to the 173rd guy, and he said all the 173rd guys are reporting to the 101st Airborne Division. I was assigned to Delta Company, 2nd Battalion, 506th Infantry.

When we got to Vietnam, we were in the 101st Airborne Division Replacement Center, and they sent us to Phan Rang, for a week of training on ambushes and other field activities. Phan Rang is right on the ocean and was protected by the Australian Army and South Korean troops. Then I got sent to my unit, at Phuoc Vihn. When I got to Phuoc Vihn there were only about two or three people in our company area, because the rest were down in Saigon, fighting at the embassy during the Tet Offensive.

A few days later, the rest of our unit came back to our base camp, at Phuoc Vihn, and I got tied in with the rest of the gang. I was asked what position I wanted. There are not that many different ones in an infantry platoon, and I said I wanted to be a rifleman, a grenadier, or a machine gunner. What about a radioman, I was asked, and I said no, I'd had no radio training in Advanced Infantry Training, because I was sick for a couple of days and missed it. They said the radioman was just shot, so you've got to be the radioman.

So, I became an RTO, a radio telephone operator and carried a PRC-25 radio telephone. It was sort of a boxy radio compared to what the Army uses nowadays. A radioman was pretty obvious at that time with it on his back and the antenna sticking up.

We ran a lot of operations, at that time, around Bien Hoa, in what was called the Rocket Belt, because a lot of South Vietnamese cities like Bien Hoa and Saigon were getting rocketed by the North Vietnamese Army, the NVA. That area is not real thick jungle like in the Central Highlands. It's lowland and a combination of rice paddies and hamlets. It's almost like northern Wisconsin woods: just a lot warmer.

On May 21, we were called in to rescue a Special Forces group of five guys that was surrounded by a battalion of NVA. We got choppered in real close to where they were.

We ended up moving into a major NVA base camp. There were a lot of fire fights and shooting going on. My platoon sergeant, at the time was Sgt. Belanger, and he got shot seriously in the shoulder. It was the same burst of fire, from an AK-47, that shot my antenna and shot the cord off my radio hand set. Sgt. Belanger got medivac out.

The guy that shot at us was a rear-guard guy trying to hold us back to give the NVA time to escape. He was sniping at us, so we wouldn't move forward. After our platoon sergeant was shot, I could see this guy pop up about every 30 seconds and he would shoot about 10 or 15 rounds and duck down again. He was hiding behind one of those giant termite hills that was about eight-feet high.

I was about 25 feet from this guy, and through the brush I could see when he popped up. The termite hill was so steep that I knew he would not see me, if I ran up behind it, on the other side of where he was. He had shot my platoon sergeant and shot my antenna and hand set cord, and I figured I had better get rid of this guy.

Right after the next time the sniper popped up, fired, and dropped down, I ran up on the other side of the termite hill. Then I took a grenade, pulled the pin and let the safety handle pop, counted two seconds, and threw it over the top. After I threw it and it went off, I ran around the hill, which was only about four steps and I saw the grenade had killed the sniper, but I put a magazine of M-16 ammo into the guy to make sure he was dead. I got a Bronze Star with a V for that. The Army called it for shooting a "machine gunner".

I got a total of three Bronze Stars. Two were with Vs and one was without. If you were in the infantry six months in a combat zone, you got a Bronze Star. You got one for if you were in a combat zone, just for showing up.

In that area, we ran into both NVA and VC, Viet Cong. The NVA were sort of the hard-core guys with the uniforms, and the VC were the pajama guys with the little pointed hats.

We were in a lot of little skirmishes; nothing major, and were in that area until about May 27, when we went to Dak To up in the Central Highlands and not too far from the Cambodian and Laotian borders. We stayed in bunkers, at Dak To, one night and we got on these real small airplanes called Caribous. The sides were just canvas. They could land on a real short runway. They flew us to a Montagnard village called Dak Pek.

If you look at an April 1968 issue of National Geographic, there is a long article about Dak Pek. Helicopters picked us up, at Dak Pek, and took us further up to a mountain top from where we could over-see the Ho Chi Mihn trail coming down from Laos and Cambodia. If you look at a map and find where those three countries meet, that's right where we were. We ran patrols out of there for a few weeks. We were really up high. That was the only place in South Viet Nam where we were above the clouds and it really got cold.

The hill we were on had trails going down each end, but the sides were really steep. If you tried to climb down the sides to go down in the valley, it would take you about three hours to get down and eight hours to get back up. Down in the valley, at night, you could see vehicles moving. We didn't have any artillery support where we were, but there was a unit on another hill, near Dak Pek, that had 4.2-inch mortars, and we could call in mortar support rounds on the trail.

We had a four-duce mortar support, which is a big mortar, with 4.2-inch mortar rounds.

There was solid traffic in the valley. It was like Highway 41 going up to the Packer game. When the mortar rounds began to fall all the vehicle lights would go out for an hour or two, and then they'd start coming back on. So, we would send patrols out during the day to see what we hit. One time we killed five or six elephants that had 122mm rockets strapped to their sides. About five or six got away.

Every night NVA would probe the ends of the hill top, where our listening posts were at. They were an early warning system. We were dug into the side of the hill and it was so steep they couldn't attack us from the sides.

Every hour each listening post would do a situation report. The RTO at the company command post would say sit rep, and if everything was okay, the radioman at each listening post would click his hand set once. If they think they heard something, they'd click it twice. If they know for sure they got some movement, they'd click it three times. Each outpost and company command post could hear that, and it put everyone on alert.

We typically had one or two ambush patrols out, and they were called Tiger-1 and Tiger-2, and we would do a sit rep with them too.

Every night the NVA would try to find our listening posts. In the morning the men in a listening post might go out and find the perimeter wire cut or the claymore mines turned around to face us, or a mine would be gone. It was pretty hard on your nerves, if you were in a listening post. Anyone that said he was not scared was a dam liar.

In the jungle, the NVA knew about where we were and they constantly tried to find our position. You could hear them talking, and if you were going through the jungle and getting close to a big group of NVA, you could smell 'em. They could smell us too.

During the couple of weeks, we were at Dak Pek, we had no real fire fights. It was all just probing, by the NVA. In June, we were sent back to Phuoc Vihn and ran more patrols in that area. We were in skirmishes and fire fights there, with some NVA, but mainly with small groups of VCs.

Around July, we left Phuoc Vihn, and we went to OPCOM, that is Operations Control, of the 25th Infantry Division. Even thought we were the 101st Airborne Division, we were now part of the 25th Infantry Division. This was in the area west of Saigon called either the Iron Triangle or Parrots Beak. The area had a lot of booby traps and tunnels and they were in a lot of daily contacts and fire fights with NVA troops.

One day, I stepped into a punji pit. Fortunately, it was filled with water, and the bamboo was somewhat flexible. It cut my pants leg, but never cut the skin of my leg. It was so bad that we lost a point man almost every day, for a month, just from booby traps. A lot of the booby traps were made with our own bombs and ammunition that the VC or NVA would find up in the vines or trees, in the jungle. It was ordnance that had never hit the ground. I've seen bombs dropped by airplanes that never made it through and was hanging up in the trees.

There's two radio operators in a platoon, and, on September 15th, the Captain, the company commander, moved me from the platoon to be his radio operator.
My assistant radio operator was Randy Thompson, took my position and a new guy took his.

On September 16, 1968, my platoon walked into a daytime ambush, in the Cu Chi area. I missed it, because I was with the Captain, but as soon as we heard all hell break loose, about 100 meters away, we went to help them. The patrol was walking from jungle to then cross a rice paddy that was bordered by bushes. The NVA opened up with machine guns on the guys crossing the rice paddies. The surviving patrol members jumped over a berm behind the bushes and onto an ox trail for protection. The NVA had two machine guns set up on that sides of the trail and they opened up with crisscrossing fire and killed or wounded everyone in the platoon.

We lost six or eight guys dead. My best buddy Randy Thompson was killed. He was from Columbus, Ohio. Sgt. Douglas Gaines, a black E-7, which had been my platoon sergeant, was fatally wounded, and he died in my arms. He was from G     Gainesville, Florida.

Another man killed, in that ambush, was Lt. Marshall Traylor. I was his radio operator, for a few months, before this ambush.

One day, we were walking down a trail, in the Central Highlands, and about two feet off the trail a North Vietnamese pops up in a spider hole, like a jack-in-the-box, and he pointed a rifle at the back of my Lieutenant. I was like five feet away from this guy and had my thumb on my M-16's selector switch. I put it on full automatic, in a split second: we called that on rock and roll, and pulled the trigger and dumped a magazine in him.

It took us about 10-minutes to get to the ambush site, and by the time we got there, the ambush was over and the NVA were gone. Most of us stayed with the bodies, while some of the men went after the NVA. That was unusual, because whenever there was a fire fight, you were told not to chase the enemy. But everyone was so pissed off about what happened that some of the guys went after the enemy.

It turned out that most of the enemy were NVA and VC. They went about a half mile away. Everything over there is in meters, so they went maybe a click away, which is 1000 meters and then disappeared into tunnels. One of the helicopter guys spotted where they all disappeared into a small entrance.

We went over to see what we could do about getting them out of the tunnels. The little village near it was called Trang Bang. We put some CS gas, a very strong tear gas, down and that didn't work. We must have dropped about

50 frag grenades down the hole and we could still crawl up to the entrance of the tunnel and hear people talking.

We were doing this for a couple of hours and trying to figure how we were going to get them out. The battalion commander called for my Captain, and my Captain was busy, so I'm on the phone with the battalion commander. He says, 'What the hell are you guys doing?'

And I said, 'We're trying to get VC out of tunnels. Quite a few went in there.' I said, 'Why don't you send us about 300-lbs of C-4 explosive or else a flame thrower?'

About 15-minutes to a half-hour later, a helicopter comes and give us 50-lb boxes of C-4. We took two 50-lb boxes of C-4 and put them in sandbags. We crawled into the hole and shoved in the first C-4 bag with no detonator. We put another C-4 bag with a detonator right behind it. One man had a 50-ft cord, from a Claymore, and as soon as our men got out of the tunnel, he blew up the C-4. The explosion blew a piece of earth about the size of a house straight up in the air, in what looked like slow motion. It turned over and came back down. There were bodies and trees, and AK-47s, and all kinds of shit layin' all over.

From September 14 to September 19, we got 32 replacements in our company. That was about a third to a fourth of our company, because so many men get wounded or killed.

We spent a month or so in and around Cu Chi on patrols. Then, on August 30th we began a big battle in that area, after we surrounded a battalion of 300 to 500 North Vietnamese. The battle went on for four days. We had all the companies in our battalion engaged: A Company, B Company, C Company and D Company. We formed what they called the cordon to enclose the enemy, and the North Vietnamese were trying to get out of there. Each night the fighting was worse than the night before. RPGs would fly over your head and hit a tree. We did not open up at night with our weapons, because the muzzle flash would disclose our positions.

At night, our artillery fired flares and a C-47s circled the area and kicked parachute flares out. Every once in a while, the timing would be wrong, and it would be completely black. Otherwise we had light all night long.

I had a radio and was on a battalion net, so I could hear all the other companies' conversations. I remember one time when it was completely dark for about five minutes, and the Captain of Charlie Company got on the battalion net to the airplane and said, 'God damn it, I don't care if you have to jump out of the plane with a flashlight. I want some light out here.'

Our artillery pounded the area, and our different companies kept moving in. Finally, after about the fourth day we made it in to the middle. We didn't have any prisoners. Every one of the enemy was dead, and most of them blown apart. I'm going to guess the battalion lost 10 to 15 guys dead on that operation and another 40 to 50 guys wounded. I never heard a name mentioned for that battle.

From September 20 to the 29th, we were back at our base camp, at Phuoc Vinh. In early October, they moved us to Camp Evans and Camp Eagle, which were very close to each other, in I Corps. There we finally tied in with the rest of the division. On October 13th, we were sent up to Fire Support Base Birmingham, and on October 21st, we were moved to Fire Support Base Bastogne. On November 3rd, we were at Panzer II, on November 6th, we were at Camp Eagle, and on November 7th we were at Camp Evans. We made each move by helicopter in daylight. All those bases were in or near the Ah Shau Valley: a bad area. I'm not sure why we went from one to the other, other than to run patrols looking for the NVA

All that time, in the Central Highlands, we had a lot of small fire fights and NVA sniping at us. The fire fights were short. If one lasted over 15 minutes, it was a big deal. They would ambush us, in the jungle, and in a few minutes, they'd be gone.

In November, I was promoted to sergeant, and on December 2nd, I went to Hawaii, on R & R.I came back on

December 10th. At Christmas, I was at Camp Evans, and the Captain said I had been in the field longer than anyone else, and he made me supply sergeant. The job was in the rear, and I had to send supplies to the company by helicopter. Every second or third night, the supply sergeant, at a pre-determined time, after the platoons were settled in, would call each platoon, on the radio, for supply requests. The only things you were allowed to request were ammunition, parts for a weapon, water, or a replacement for a ripped boot or some clothing article.

When you're the supply sergeant, you are usually in the rear with only the XO, the executive officer. I stayed in a little supply hut that was about the size of a two-car garage, and once I got the re-supply order, I'd get it ready for the next day's helicopter, and send it out on the helicopter. One day, I was sitting in the supply shack with some of the supplies and reading this magazine, and I hear the screen door close. I look up, and all I can see is a helmet. I stand up and it's a new Lieutenant, and he chews me out. He says, don't you know how to salute a Lieutenant? And he went on and on. So, I saluted him and apologized.

He said he was being assigned to my company as one of the platoon leaders. I need you to tell me what I should take with me on the next re-supply helicopter. I only had about a week left in country, before I was leaving, and this guy pissed me off the way he chewed me out. So, I told him what he had to carry, and when he left, he looked like a loaded pack mule. He had more crap on him, including old, broken M-72 LAWs, flashlights that didn't work, and all kinds of useless crap.

The next night, when I did the re-supply order, I got to this new guy, on the radio, and he says to me, '4XRay,' that was my code name for radio use, 'tomorrow's my birthday. Is there any way I can get a birthday cake out here?'

I said, 'You're in luck. I'm baking tonight, over at the mess hall. Yeah! I'll whip one up for you.'

Then he said, 'There's a little PX over there. Can you go over and get me some Tiparillos?'

I said, 'Oh, you betcha'.' I said, 'I'll get you a couple of packs of 'em.' All of a sudden, the Captain cuts in, on the radio, and says, 'God damn it, Stephenson. Quit fucking around with the new Lieutenant.' I had so little time left, that I was sure I would never see the guy again.

About a week or two after Christmas, I went to the 101st Replacement Camp in Saigon, and then flew back to Travis Air Force Base in Oakland, California. I had a 30-day leave and then reported back to the 82nd Airborne Division, at Ft. Bragg. I ran into a bunch of guys I had been over in Vietnam with, so we all rented a five-bedroom mobile home together. We were all sergeants, and we each had only a few months left. We were on jump status, so we were able to get a few more parachute jumps in.

My estimate is that my company, D Company, 2nd Battalion, 506th Airborne Infantry, 101st Airborne Division, was in violent contacts or firefights between 30 and 45 time, while I was with them in Vietnam.

While I was in the Army, I received the Combat Infantryman Badge, the Bronze Star with V device and first Oak Leaf Cluster, the Air Medal, the Parachute Badge, the Vietnam Service Medal, the Vietnam Campaign Medal, the Army Commendation Medal, a Bronze Star with no V device, and the Expert Badge with rifle and machine gun bars.

On September 26, 1971, I married a local girl named Martha Vanderhyden. I didn't know her, before I went in the Army. We've been married 46 years. We have three children, two boys and one girl. The oldest is Robert Clyde Stephenson, Jr. The second one is Timothy Phillip Stephenson, and my daughter is Sara Jane Lornson. Each of them have three kids, so we have nine grandchildren. We have four granddaughters and five grandsons.

I had done a lot of electrical work, for my dad's company, before I went into the Army, and they finally read my statement of pre-military experiences and assigned me as the maintenance guy for the 82nd division. I was the only electrician on the base. Every day I'd get a bunch of work orders to fix lights or other electrical matters. Anything that was more than I could do, I left for the post engineers to do.

When I got out of the Army, on June 14, 1969, I went to summer school, at the University of Wisconsin, in Oshkosh. Then I came back to Appleton and went into a four-year electrician apprenticeship, at the technical college. I ended up becoming an electrician.

In 1972, my brother Rollie myself and two investors started an electrical construction company. I owned 20% of his company, Rollie had 60% and the other men owned the rest. At that time, I went to work for my dad's company.

The company Rollie headed and I owned 20% of was a non-union electrical company, and after 13 years with my dad's company, I went to work with my brother. I spent about 30 years there. When I joined that company, it had 10 guys and my specialty was the industrial end, and my brother took the commercial end. It worked out quite well, with all the paper mills up there. When I left the company in 2006, we had 1500 electricians. Now the company has over 2500 electricians.

After I retired from my brother's company, I had a small company for about six years. We did mainly government work: VA hospitals throughout the country. When I turned 65, I had a couple of law suits going against the government, and I retired. About 2-1/2-years later I had to do something, and right now I work over at Lowe's, where I'm the electrical pro.

I belong to the VFW; American Legion; Vietnam Veterans of America, Chapter 351; the Fox Valley Vietnam Vets, which is in the Fox River Valley, here in Wisconsin; the 101st Airborne Division Association; the 506th Infantry Association, the Disabled American Veterans. I'm pretty active with all these organizations.

I've was in Rotary Club for a number of years, but I had to quit it, because I didn't have enough time. When I was in business, I belonged to a group called Associated Builders and Contractors for about 25 years. I was the state president of that, and the national president, for the Electrical Contractors, for about five years.

I was not physically wounded, but I do have a 60% VA disability rating, by the VA, and go to the VA for psycho-therapy. Part of the rating is PTSD, part of it is Agent Orange, and part of it is for tremors in my right and left hands. I get lot of comments about how much my hands shake.

We have a Veterans Court, in Outagamie County, for veterans that come back from Iraq and Afghanistan and get in trouble with the law. The court is not for serious crimes like murder and rape. The court has about 30 mentors they can assign a veteran to for a two-year program, instead of prison. I've been dealing with a couple of guys, as a mentor, on a volunteer basis. This is my brief story as best that I can recall.

Robert Clyde "Bob" Stephenson, in South Viet Nam

Robert Clyde "Bob" Stephenson, on right, with an unidentified comrade, in South Viet Nam

# James Lee Patin
interview of September 4, 2016

My name is James Lee Patin. I was born February 20, 1949, in Port Arthur, Texas.

My dad was a senior and I'm a junior. He ran the machine shop, at an oil refinery, for what is now Unocal. It was Union 76, when he worked for it. My mother's maiden name was Florence Aline Hackney. She was a homemaker. Both my dad and her were from Port Arthur.

I've got one sister. Her name is Judy Ann. She lives in Jackson, Mississippi, and she is over all the nuclear power plants that Entergy owns. She is four years younger than I am.

I went to William B. Travis Elementary School, Thomas A. Edison Junior High School, and graduated from Thomas Jefferson High School, in 1967. All were in Port Arthur. I went one semester to Lamar College and did welding locally.

My daddy was a Navy vet. He was at Normandy, and in 1967, the year in which I turned 18 and was going to graduate from high school, Vietnam was heatin' up hot and heavy. He talked me into joining the Navy Reserve, so I would not have to go to Vietnam. In the Navy Reserve, you did a two-year active duty tour and four years of reserve.

I was called to go to active duty in 1968. They sent me to San Diego, California, for my two-year active duty, and I'm walkin' around looking at all this big-ass ships and this that and the other. And if it didn't move, some poor son of a bitch was paintin' it, and, if it moved it was bein' saluted. I said, 'This ain't for me!'

The Navy interviews everybody in it to try to put them in a spot they will like and where they won't cause any problem. When they interviewed me, I asked, if they had anything smaller that the big ships there. The classifier said, 'Oh, yeah! Ya like t' hunt?'

I said, 'Yeah.'

He said, 'All I can tell you right now is this will entail a tour of 12 months in country, in Vietnam, and it's nearly ninety-somethin' percent volunteer. I've got to run a security clearance on you. Go do whatever you want to do, and I'll see you at 8 o'clock in the morning.'

I went back at 8 o'clock in the morning and he gave me my orders, which were for 12 months or the duration. He also gave me 30-days leave, so I went back home. Then I reported to Naval Inshore Operations Center, at Mare Island Naval Reservation, near Vallejo, California. That was 1968. They sent us to Camp Roberts, an Army base in the middle of the California desert, to blow stuff up. They brought us back to Mare Island and we did some more trainin'. Then they sent us to Whidbey Island, in Puget Sound, for a week of SERE, which stands for survival, evasion, resistance, escape. It was about the closest thing I can think to Hell Week. It was no fun.

Then they sent us to Vietnam. We arrived there first part of August 1968. Our boats came over on merchant Marine ships. My boat cost the government half a million dollars. All these boats, with the exception of one, were converted LCM6s. They was designed and built during World War II to carry Sherman tanks or troops from ships off shore to the beachhead.

Some of them were armored and had a ramp that could be lowered and they carried troops. Others they cut the ramp off and put bows on 'em. We even had one called a Monitor that had a 105mm howitzer on it and one called a Zippo that had two flame throwers mounted on the bow. It looked like every time they built one they put a bigger gun on it.

We got the boats and, being as they were brand new, we outfitted them. We was what the Navy calls "plank owners", which means members of the first crew. We were part of the 'Brown-water Navy' assault units that operated from January 1967, until we turned the boats over to the South Vietnamese, in 1970. January 1967 was when our assault units became official. That was when the 2nd

Brigade of the 9th Infantry Division arrived and joined with the Navy's Task Force 117 to form the Mobile Riverine Force. I was in River Assault Squadron 15, one of two squadrons in River Assault Division 152.

The powers that be decided that they would take the war to the Viet Cong, because we wasn't killin' enough of 'em. So, at that time, they took the 2nd Brigade of the Army's 9th Infantry Division and they shipped them to Dong Tam, and they operated primarily out of there. With the soldiers, there were 5,000 of us based at Dong Tam.

Dong Tam was a shore base on the north bank of the Mekong River, near My Tho. It was made by dredging river mud and sand and pouring it on to a rice paddy. In 1966 and 1967, Army engineers built up an area there more than a square mile in size and five to 10 feet above the river.

We carried men of the 9th Infantry Division's 2nd Brigade up rivers, inserted them somewhere, let them make a sweep, and then picked them up and took them someplace else. We moved them around the Mekong Delta. We had to fight through ambushes to get to where we had to insert them and then fight our way back. We worked III and IV Corps: mostly IV Corps.

The Ho Chi Mihn trail came down through Laos and Cambodia and had several offshoots that went into South Viet Nam. The last one, as far south as the trails went, was into the U Minh Forest. There had not been a white man in that area, since the French left. The Viet Cong had all kinds of weapons, ammunition, support facilities, and supplies there, and we took it back from 'em. Best I can remember, it took us two, roughly week-long operations to get them out.

We didn't worry too much when we was in a big, wide, *wide* river. All the VC could do was set up a mortar unit, at night to try to hit us, or float a bomb down and stick it on the hull. They sunk a couple of our boats that way. But when we entered the smaller, narrower streams, flak jackets went on and so did the steel helmets. Our boats were 18-foot wide and 50-somethin' foot long. We lived on 'em. We went up rivers where the trees and vegetation on the banks hit both sides of the boat. Our top speed was 6 knots, and we were kind of like ducks in a shootin' gallery.

On March the 30th, 1969, I was wounded, by an RPG explosion, while we were on a narrow river. There're different type of rounds they can put in RPGs. They shoot them out of what kinda looks like a bazooka. They accounted for more U.S. casualties, on the river, than any other thing the Viet Cong or NVA had. One went off, about 6, 8 ft. from me, on my right-hand side and it got shrapnel in my arm and hand. We got out of that firefight and pulled the stuff out with a pair of needle-nose pliers, put band aides all over it, and never left the place. Finished the operation and made it on back, and then I went up to sick bay and let 'em make sure my tetanus shot was current. I didn't leave my boat and take no R & R. I was afraid, if I did, I wouldn't want to come back.

My boat was a Command Communication Boat. It was scheduled to have a crew of 11, but we operated with nine. We was cross-trained on everything in the boat. Each man could do everybody else's job. We always left two back, at Dong Tam, in the attrition pool. On the bow, it had a 20mm on the left side and a 20mm on the right and a little higher, in the center, it had a grenade launcher. When we were aboard those boats, we were lucky if we had a pair of pants that had legs in 'em.

Our top speed was six knots. You can't outrun nothin' at six-knots an hour. That slow speed is why they built the river boats as heavy as they did. The boats did a pretty good job of what they were supposed to do, as long as they didn't get mined or a rocket hit 'em in a soft spot.

When we started goin' further and deeper into the delta than that, we started workin' with the ARVN, which is Army of Vietnam, and the Vietnamese Marines.

At the end of December 1970, we turned all of our boats over to the South Vietnamese. While these Vietnamese were runnin' these boats, we had American advisors who would ride with 'em. They was former boat people themselves, so they knew what the hell they were doin' and what to expect.

After we turned our boats over to the South Vietnamese, I was appointed to staff and given a little Boston Whaler with a 40 hp Evinrude motor on it. We had one particular weapon, a Mark 19 grenade launcher, which fires 350 rounds a minute. In one-minute's time, you can empty the drum magazine. The reason why I was assigned to staff was because there was two of us at that time that knew that particular weapon inside out and could fix it in our sleep. The other guy decided he'd extend for six months, so he was home on 30-days leave, so they kept my ass longer.

After the North overran the South, all the boats that we give 'em were captured by the North Vietnam Army.

During those war years the Navy lost 2,558 men killed in action and the Coast Guard lost seven. Of those Navy men killed in action 106 or 108 were in the brown-water Navy. In 1968 or '69, Time magazine said the casualty rate on them boats was over 70%. Eight of our sailors won Navy Crosses and one sailor won the Medal of Honor. During that time, the 2nd Brigade of the Army's 9th Infantry Division lost 2,624 men killed in action.

Then they shipped me home. I didn't let anybody know I was home, and I spent the night at the airport, in Dallas, because I wanted to get the hell out of California. We weren't greeted very well. When we got off the plane, here come all the people spittin' at us and yellin' baby killer and a lot of other crap. I had on a new set of jungle greens, and new boots, and a camouflaged beret. I got out of there, before I really got in trouble.

I stayed home for 30-days leave, and reported to a destroyer out of Long Beach, California. When I reported to it, I was one-day over the hill, and so drunk they had to carry me up the gang plank. They told me, 'Gunner you got it made. They dun unloaded all the ammunition. They gonna take this thing to San Diego and sink it.'

I said, 'Well, I don't need to be on it then.' Then they found me a rack; throw'd my old drunken ass in it. The bugle went off in the morning to wake everybody up. I just rolled over and went back to sleep.

The next thing I know, the chief petty officer that I was gonna work under was kickin' me in the ass and sayin','Cowboy, get your ass out of that rack.'

I looked at him and said, 'What in the hell are you doin' here?' He said he was fixin' to ask me the same thing. Both he and I served together, in Vietnam.

If you was from Texas, you was either "Tex" or "Cowboy". They called me "Cowboy". All the Nam people know me as "Cowboy", and everybody else knows me as "Lightnin'". A welder boss tagged that on me on a pipeline, one day, because he said, 'I ain't never seen anybody weld that fast. I gonna call you "Lightnin'", and the name stuck.

The chief petty officer took me to the air-conditioned personnel office and said, 'You work for the personnel man now. If anybody gives you any shit, you tell them come find me. Ain't nobody that's gone through what we went through's gonna to clean bilges and all that crap, so they can sink this piece of shit.'

The Navy made a big mistake when they disbanded our teams and sent anybody that had a lengthy enlistment left t' the fleet. We were not fleet sailors. We stayed in trouble. We saluted nobody, we did what we wanted t' do, and didn't listen to nobody.

I had maybe a hundred and some days left on my two-year active duty requirement. They told me, 'If you want t' leave early, go ahead and leave.' The first thing I typed was my early discharge. When I went into the Navy, I was an E-1, seaman recruit. When I got out, I was a gunner's mate third class, E-4. When my separation papers were approved, I caught an airplane and come home.

In the Navy, I earned a Purple Heart, Navy Achievement Medal with Combat V. I don't know how many naval unit citations and presidential unit citations I've got. I just don't remember.

When I got out, that's when I got married to my first wife. I was 21, when I married her. Her and I went to high school together. We grew up together. I went back to Lamar College, for a semester and then figured I could make more money weldin' and workin' construction. I sold industrial supplies fur Drago Supply, the largest metal supply company in that part of the country.

My wife and I had two children, and I knew somethin' was wrong, and I didn't want t' be around an' hurt any of them, so I divorced her and left. We were married for 12 years. She got a bachelor's degree and a master's degree and was a school teacher. She's retired now. I quit my job and went to pipe lining.

My son's name is Jeremy an' my daughter's name is Jennifer, an' she has a daughter by the name of Kaleigh that just turned 13. My daughter got married and stayed in Port Arthur, until she and her husband bought a place just about due east of me, about 100 miles. My son and I do not talk. The last time I saw my son was when my mother passed away. He's married and has an adopted son.

I married an idiot the second time. She was from Buna, Texas. She worked, at the time I met her, for a major oil company. She'd piss off a stop sign. I'd work all year long and make a little over a hundred thousand dollars, and she'd spend a hundred and fifty. I finally had enough of it. First thing I could get my hands on was my 30-cal. M1 carbine. I did a John Wayne through a set of French Doors that I'd just finished installin', tryin' to get a shot at her, and she made it out the back door before I could kill her. I packed my shit and left. We were living in Vidor, Texas then and had been married for about 10 years. We had no children.

I have only one photo left of when I was in Vietnam. My second wife destroyed every other one.

During these years, I was a welding advisor for Eutectic Castelin, an outfit out of Lucerne, Switzerland, that had an office on Long Island, New York. They laid a bunch of us off, so I put a welding truck together, and I went back to work. I was a pipe fabricator and a pipeline welder, in oil fields. I hated them places. They dangerous.

I married my third wife, and was married for a couple of years. We split in December of '96. I have no comment on her.

I came to Waco, in '97. I was called to work on a pipeline, in a little town not too far from where I live right now. I met my current wife. I was single—livin out of a travel trailer. It'd take me 30 minutes to put everything I owned in the thing and go down the road. We get along real good. We've been married almost 16 years. She's retired. She was a housewife and worked in convenience stores and took care of elderly people. She was divorced and has three children: two girls and a boy.

Her youngest daughter is an RN. I don't know what her oldest daughter does. Her son is her youngest child. He is a law enforcement official in Kerrville, Texas.

About 11 or 12 years ago, the VA told me I had worked all I can work, mentally and physically. I'm 100% total and permanent disabled, due to PTSD, hearin' loss, and Type 2 Diabetes, thanks to Agent Orange. There's somethin' else, but I forgot what it is. I got a list of ailments a mile long. I stay home most of the time.

After I came home, I self-medicated, just like a whole bunch of us that came back did. There were drugs and the alcohol. I had PTSD, but the VA didn't discover my PTSD; another Vietnam vet did. He said I had PTSD, an' I said, 'What the hell is that?'

He said, 'You're f___ed up in the head, you dumb ass!' He says, 'Any of the young kids that went over there came back screwed up. Some terrible things happened.

'No! I don't want to talk about it. What part of "no' don't you understand?'

I was tryin' to quit self-medicatin' when I went to the VA. I had about a year and a half of therapy with the VA, about 14, 15 years ago. They didn't know how to treat it. They'd give yuh a hand full of drugs and say, 'Eat these an' let me how yuh feel.' We were Guinea pigs. My life was a true roller coaster. The VA helped me, and I've been clean ever since. I don't do anything now but drink a beer every now and then.

I'm a member of the Mobile Riverine Force Association, and a lifetime member of the Vietnam Veterans of America and the Military Order of the Purple Heart. I'm very active in the American Legion in Waco, and that's about all that I'v'e time to do.

Members of the Mobile Riverine Force Association are pretty close. The members are from different boats, different times, different tours, and we've got members scattered pretty well throughout the United States. We've got some 9th Infantry guys in there. We talk every morning, on the computer. An' if any of us don't show up for a few days, phones go t' ringin'. We're still close.

James Lee Patin, is in the crews' quarters, aboard a 60-ft long Command Communication Boat of the U.S. Navy's "brown-water Navy", in South Viet Nam. His left-hand rests on a Navy-issue, Smith and Wesson, 38-cal., six-shot revolver.

The same compartment holds 11 or 12 bunks at one end and radio and navigation equipment at the other.

Patin's job was weapons repair and weapons maintenance, but the crew were cross-trained, so that each could perform the work of other crew members.

Patin said, 'January 1967 was when our assault units became official. That was when the 2nd Brigade of the 9th Infantry Division arrived and joined with the Navy's Task Force 117 to form the Mobile Riverine Force. I was in River Assault Squadron 15, one of two squadrons in River Assault Division 152.'

# Thomas Lee Reilly, II
interview of August 18, 2013

My name is Tom Reilly, actually Thomas Lee Reilly II. I was born on February 27, 1945, in Kalamazoo, Michigan.

My mother's maiden name was Naomi Audrey Perreault. She was from Brooklyn, New York. Her father was a credit manager for Graybar Electric, and he transferred to Atlanta, with his family. That's where my mother met and married my dad. She went to live in Kalamazoo, when my dad was stationed there, in the army, and I was the end result. I was about a year old, when Japan surrendered, in 1945. Dad was preparing for the invasion of Japan. After the army, dad came back and picked up his job with Sears, and my mother kept on being a housewife.

Before she married, my mother worked for Metro-Goldwyn-Mayer as a secretary. In fact, they did her wedding for her.

My family originated, on my father's side, in Chicago, Illinois. We were with Sears Roebuck and Company, and, of course, their headquarters is still in Chicago. In 1941, my father's father and his family came down from, Chicago to Atlanta, to help found Sears, Roebuck and Company in Atlanta. It was the store in Ponce de Leon Avenue, and the building still stands today. From there, some of my uncles went to places like Greensboro North Carolina. But by and large, we stayed with Sears till my father's untimely death in 1951: I was six-years old.

I went to Lady of Assumption grammar school, Cross Keys High School, graduated from Oglethorpe University with a Bachelor of Business Administration degree, in 1967. By 1968, I was in an infantry unit. I volunteered for the draft. Oglethorpe University offered me a draft-exempt job recruiting, as I recall. And I thought about recruiting for the college, but I wanted to serve my country, just like my father had done; just like my uncles had done. So, I declined the job offer. Graduated in June of '67 and waited. And by October of '67, I was drafted into the United States Army.

After I was drafted, I went to Basic Training, at Ft. Benning, Georgia, and went to Advanced Infantry Training, at Ft. Dix, New Jersey. I attended Officer Candidate School, at Ft. Benning, in the spring of 1968. It was a disgrace. It was the sorriest experience that I had in the service.

They had had to lower the standards for the soldiers, because people just weren't showing up to serve in the army. Nobody wanted to play soldier any more. So, we wound up with a bunch of bums, sociopaths, bullies, thieves, and crooks in the Officer Candidate School. And most Vietnam veterans and college graduates took one look and said they wanted no part of this. The course was six months long, and I had been in OCS for about two months, when I refused to stay in it.

At that time, there were very few college graduates, in the enlisted ranks. There were very few college graduates in the OCS program that I could see. People weren't going.

Years later, I would learn that the lack of volunteers had led to a lowering of standards for the officer corps, resulting in widespread, thievery, blackmail, incompetence, and abuse. It was the only school that I ever experienced designed to kill its graduates. Punks were replacing soldiers as officers to the detriment of all concerned. No one can survive with both sides gunning for you.

The end result of that was that I ended up, at Ft. Benning, Georgia, trained only in the infantry, as far as the army was concerned, and at the height of the Vietnam War. It did not take long before I got orders to go to Vietnam.

I went on leave, I think, for two months and then came back and took an airplane flight to Anchorage, Alaska; to Tokyo, Japan; then down to either Tan Son Nhut or Bien Hoa airfield near Saigon. At that point, they put us through a processing center to get us out there. And I'd seen enough of the army, by then, to know that you had to be your own advocate. So, I started asking around about units and such and was told about the 199th Light Infantry Brigade, which was right there in Long Binh Post, in IV Corps. And some guy was kind enough to mark me down for the 199th Light Infantry Brigade.

We had about a week's orientation, at brigade headquarters, in about August 1968, and, during that time, they showed us something about guard dogs, for example, and they told us something about the kind of lives we'd be leading out there in the infantry. Two of us went in: John Boring of Maryland and myself. We had both been at Officer Candidate School and wanted no part of it. Both of us wound up sent to the infantry at the same time, as a result. At the last minute, John was snaked off to the Finance Corps. He had a business background too, and I went on into the infantry.

The monsoon takes place, in Vietnam, from roughly June to December. I got in there in July 1968. The rest of the time, from January into June, it is just as dry as dry can be. It turns into a regular dust bowl, especially in the paddy country. But in the paddy country, during the wet season, all the paddy fields become completely filled with mud. And you're talking mud that is anything from knee to waist deep, and it can go for miles. It smelled as if there had been a lot of water buffalo there for a very long time. And we had to go through it.

If you were the first one through the mud, it wasn't too bad. But this was the kind of mud, where the more you churned it, the stickier it got. The last guy in line had a real problem. It could take your boot off with the laces still laced. I was bigger than most, but quite frankly, it was hard. But I stayed with it and kept on going through it, and eventually the mud dried up: but it took six months.

In the daytime, we might go out on a patrol: just the platoon. A platoon had four squads and a total of about 25 men. A company, of course, is something like a hundred men. Of course, troop strength would vary. There would normally be four companies out there, with some men on base guarding it. There was an Alpha, Bravo, Charlie, Delta, which were infantry, and Echo Company, which was the mortars. The mortars tended to stay behind.

We set up ambushes at night. Usually it was a squad-sized ambush, but sometimes platoon-sized too. When a platoon went out they would set up at least two ambushes.

We went out and found a designated site to set up for any Viet Cong we might be able to kill. We would bring a radio with us. We would have one guard, and every hour we would change guards. So, we were in the underbrush, waiting for some Viet Cong to come along the road or something. If we were squad size, there would be a radio and about 10, 15 guys. There would be a squad leader, riflemen, ammo bearers, and a radio-telephone operator.

And we would wait out there all night, and there would be someone awake all night. He would wake up the others, if the Viet Cong came along. But night after night, day after day nothing happened at all. We didn't take one casualty; we didn't have any trouble at all. The one exception to that was a fire fight on September 7, 1968.

We had encountered a squad of Viet Cong the day before, on September 6th. It was the first time I was under fire, and I was not in a position to use my grenade launcher due to the tree line, so I sought cover behind a dirt pile, until the small arms fire was over. The very next day we were again on RAG boats, returning from an operation or sweep where I had been walking as point man.

A RAG boat was a Higgins boat with a metal roof over its open sides, and I was taking my customary pre-weekend sun bath on the roof of one of these converted amphibious landing craft. The whining sound of bullets: a sound I never liked, and a rocket propelled grenade swishing over my head killed the sun bathe in a hurry: no pun intended. I grabbed a rifle, several bandoleers of ammunition, and an officer's helmet and started laying fire on the VC position while the RAG boats maneuvered in a figure-eight evasive tactic. That was the first time I thought I had a close call.

Eventually a helicopter gunship circled overhead, cheered on by us all. One of our soldiers stood up right in front of me, just as I was getting ready to empty another magazine at the enemy. I froze in position, still sighting along his spine, until he got back down. I remember saying to myself, I'm actually shooting at people, before switching back to semi-automatic, from automatic fire, to get more control. We searched both banks of the river, the Saigon or Mekong, without finding any sign of our opponents.

After that, there was total silence, and then, after that, they declared a halt to bombing North Viet Nam. I remember writing my family very tongue in cheek saying, it looks like trick or treat. October 31st, Halloween, is going to take on a whole new venue this year, because we knew, as soon as they stopped bombing that would let the flood gates open up. From July through October, we didn't take one casualty. Bombing North Vietnam stopped on November 1st, and in November and December, we lost approximately a third of the whole company killed or wounded, just like that. Like they couldn't see it coming! And that was the time we had it worst.

We lost a couple of people when our unit was ambushed. Viet Cong were digging in, in full sight of our soldiers; set up and opened fire, and our soldiers didn't do a thing. I don't believe we even got a shot off. Bob Needham was telling the sergeant, that the Vietnamese setting up over there don't look right, and the sergeant said to ignore them. A moment later the VC opened up on us.

A man named Larry Wycroft, from Oklahoma, was shot, but not fatally wounded. But he was so convinced, in the hospital, that he was going to die that he did some days later. He was our first death. Several others got wounded, and none of them came back to the unit.

And the pace of casualties just picked up after that. Not long after that, my squad leader Dennis Haynes had taken the place of a sick soldier, at the last minute, at what was called an LP or listening post. He and John Miller were out there. Dennis is from Palmyra, Pennsylvania, and John Miller is from Detroit, Michigan. We didn't have the complete story, until a few years ago, but the Viet Cong had three snipers that fired 90 rounds all of a sudden, out of the darkness, at Dennis and at John, who were half in water, by a rice paddy dike.

The Viet Cong emptied each of their AK-47 magazines at them. Of their 90 rounds, only two found their mark, and they found it in Dennis Haynes' head. He was shot twice, and John Miller thought he was dead and was getting ready to leave. Then Dennis moved, so John knew he had to get him back. He kept Dennis' head out of the water, and Johnny Fielding, a man from a small town, in Alabama, came up, and he and John Miller put Dennis on a poncho and slid him over the mud out of harm's way and kept his head out of that paddy water. If paddy water had gotten into that wound, as filthy as that stuff was, who knows what would have happened.

Dennis was taken out, and he was medevaced, by helicopter. At first, when he was taken to the hospital, they put him behind a curtain. That means they were leaving him there to die. They would come in and talk to the people that were going to die and help them any way they could. At the last minute, a man named John Baldwin was asked to go in there and work on Dennis, as best he might. He was a chest surgeon; this was a head wound. He patched up Dennis, as best he could, and Dennis survived.

He is partially paralyzed, on one side; he has lost some of his peripheral vision, but he went on to have a successful career, at the University of Pennsylvania Medical Center, as a draftsman. He went on to have his family. He went on to inspire thousands of people that saw an award-winning documentary on him done by CBS 21 out of Harrisburg, Pennsylvania. And he and I have never lost touch with each other.

We had first been told that Dennis was wounded, but he was recovering nicely. We were all very relieved, at that. We didn't know his real condition. I sent him a letter, and that's how come we stayed in touch.

There were six other times when I feel I had close calls. One was in November 1968, at a fire base, near the Cambodian border. Bob Needham and I had to run around an incoming cluster of mortar rounds to get to our gear in case of a ground attack.

Another close call happened to me some time from December 7th to 13th, 1968. We were in on stand down, for a rest at our Long Binh headquarters and watching a USO show complete with a very thin Vietnamese go-go dancer. The Viet Cong hit our base with a rocket attack, beginning with our ammo dump. The explosion looked like a major fireworks display back home. One of the rockets shredded the roof and an upper room in our two-story barracks, where normally several soldiers would have been watching TV. As it was, they were a distance away watching the USO show instead. The rocket missed where I was by about fifty feet. After the attack, I started to drink a can of soda and found it only half full, and shrapnel, from the exploding rocket was in the bottom. I had to drink it very carefully to avoid drinking the shrapnel along with the liquid.

On about December 12th, 1968, we had come across indications of a squad of Viet Cong, near the Cambodian border, and were chasing. December 13th found me staring at a set of barefoot VC footprints, one of which still had some water running into it from a nearby puddle. On December 14th we exchanged small arms fire with VC. We were lying flat on the ground while a VC bunker was being blown up, and a rocket propelled grenade was launched at us, by VC. The RPG splashed into a pond right next to me and just lay there under water, fizzing like a giant Alka-Seltzer tablet. That was a close call, because, if that RPG had landed near me on dry earth, it would have shredded me.

Then we started to chase those VC, and I remember, we were crossing a river, and I heard small arms fire again as we encountered them off in the distance. On that particular day, I was the very last man to cross that river. I got across the river; I got up in position, and we waited, and then we moved out in pursuit of this squad of Viet Cong. All of the military manuals tell you never to pursue your enemy in a straight line, because that sets up a pattern and the enemy can anticipate your moves.

We pursued them for three days, in a straight line. And we might as well have had neon signs and dancing girls out there telling them where we were. What the VC did, we found out soon enough, was pretty clever, I think. On December 14th, I was sent an extra radio, since I was a radio-telephone operator. And I remember, with my radio being strapped to my back, and looking over to one side, and there's a whole lot of tiny, barefoot footprints. One of the barefoot footprints was next to a puddle left over from the monsoon rains, and the water was still leaking into the footprint. That's how recent that was. I thought, this can't be good, and we went off and pursued them some more.

The Viet Cong were amazing outdoorsmen, and I think those footprints were left there deliberately, in a haphazard pattern to make us stop, look, and bunch up. The reason I say this is because of what happened the next day, December 15th. On that day, we were coming to a creek, and this creek had a single-log bridge, maybe a foot around, that you could walk on over the creek. I wasn't too sure of my balance with my radio on my back, so I went into the creek and held on to the bridge and got across hand over hand. The water was up to my waist, but the radio was dry. Got kidded a little bit, but the radio was dry.

I got up to the top of the other side of the creek and the men were bunching up. John Miller was the point man, and what he told me, many years later, was that he found more of those footprints all over the place, and he stopped and sent back word not to bunch up on the creek. The message never got to us.

The VC had rigged a Bouncing Betty land mine to be set off when a trip wire hidden in some tree branches over the log bridge was disturbed. The Bouncing Betty is a mine that springs up and blows up.

When it went off, I had just had turned around to say something to the platoon sergeant, and the mine bounced up right behind Jesse Miles who was between the mine and me. It exploded, shredding Jesse. He caught the full blast. My radio caught every bit of the rest of it, but one piece that I could feel in my lower left back, next to my spine. I went down, and as I went down, I saw this tree, in front of me, turn into this little green cloud, because there was so much shrapnel racing through it. That was when I got my first Purple Heart.

John Miller got the radio off my back. I was sarcastically wishing people a 'Merry Christmas', as they stepped over me, dripping with water, to help ward off any ground attack from our front. Then I smelled smoke and heard the crackle of flames. One of our smoke grenades had set off a brush fire which was moving towards some other wounded men. I got my feet under me, found out that I wasn't paralyzed, and went over with Captain Wiggins to scoop water into our helmets, from some leftover monsoon puddles, and put out the fire, saving the wounded men.

I was in the hospital, in Cam Rahn Bay, for a month, and became the librarian at the hospital, and stayed there, until it was time to come back. I came back in January 1969, and got into the field. By now the monsoon was gone. It was as dry as dry could be. The dust was everywhere—tons of dust.

We now had a confirmed coward as a squad leader. He had replaced Dennis Haynes. He was nowhere near as good as Dennis. Bum, bully, coward, you name it. He was ordering us around, getting nasty, and losing his temper all the time. And I remember him telling me to hand him his helmet. It was about 10 feet from him. I'd had it. I picked up his helmet, and I handed it to him, by throwing it at his head, sort of like a discus. It was a steel pot with a liner in it going at high speed. I would have got him, and of course it would have been an accident, but he saw it coming and turned back and grabbed that helmet just before it got to his head. He was standing, and the helmet's momentum was enough to spin him around and put him on the ground. He threatened me with a work detail and walked off. Nobody went for any details. And that was the last time, I think, we had any trouble with him.

Capt. Wiggins came up to me, and we were having a chat, just the two of us. And he had found out about an opening for a war correspondent for the battalion and asked me if I'd be interested in the job. I'd done book reviews, in college, which of course eminently qualified me for that work. I said yes. I became a war correspondent in February, 1969.

It turned out that the head of the outfit that I was going to be attached to, at brigade headquarters, was a complete idiot. I heard bad things about him, and I just didn't show up for the assignment. I started being a war correspondent, but on my own, in the field. I would take a camera with me, as well as my rifle, when I went out with infantry troops. I'd look for pictures, look for stories, process everything and send it in, and then get roaring drunk with some of my infantry buddies, and go out and do the whole thing over again.

And all the while, this complete idiot who was supposed to be my boss, was looking for me. I finally got snaked into his office and found out that his version of a war correspondent job was some kind of a third-string typist that did the left-over typing from the other guys. I knew a Major, by then, in the public information office. The Major and I did a little dog-and-pony show we rehearsed, for the Captain. I had been in the Captain's office for less than a day, but I overheard the Major say to the Captain, 'What is he doing sitting here doing typing?' The Major gives me a broad wink, on his way out the door, and the Captain calls me into his office and tries to justify all the things he's doing.

And I say, 'No sir, that's not the way it's done.'

Finally, his words to me were, 'You pack your bag, and you don't come back here—ever.'

The next day, I went back out into the field. I found half a hut, at battalion, to live in. That was at Fire Support Base Stephanie, and the routine was the same. I'd go out looking for stories and pictures all week. Come in to brigade headquarters, at Long Binh, once a week: type the stories, on a typewriter, and process the pictures; find my infantry buddies; get drunk, real drunk; sleep it off, and go out and do the same thing. I did that for six months.

In March--April, 1968, when I had become the war correspondent for our battalion, I was on an operation with my Alpha Company, Third Battalion, 7th Infantry. Our Kit Carson Scout, Dinh, had just removed and disabled a booby trap. A Kit Carson Scout was a Viet Cong that had come over to our side and worked for us as a scout. Dinh was good. Unfortunately, when the U.S. left Vietnam, we left in a great rush, and he was left there. As we started to walk past the site, a loud whining noise started coming from the nearby underbrush. With no thought, no hesitation beyond a quick head shake, I dropped to the ground, just as the explosion sent shrapnel ripping into every man in front of me.

The seventh close call I had happened early in April, 1969, when a hand grenade booby trap blew up over an overgrown ridge line. A piece of shrapnel flew over the ridge straight for my chest. I threw my right arm up over my chest, at the sound of the explosion. The shrapnel hit my arm, cut across it, and bounced harmlessly off my shirt. Shrapnel was flying everywhere, but the only other man hit like me didn't throw his arm up. Shrapnel penetrated his chest, nicked his vena cava, and killed him on his feet. Usually these booby traps took out 10 to 15 people at a time. Thirteen to 15 men were killed or wounded that time. I was the only casualty to walk away.

The way in which I was first given the Bronze Star will give you an idea of the quality of soldier in the army. I got it from a guy that was despised, and I found out why. I was looking for the Bronze Star they were supposed to get me, and an officer called this sergeant to find out if he had it, and the sergeant's words to the officer were, 'Send the young punk over here.' He didn't even know me. I went over to him and he took the Bronze Star, which he had, in a case, and threw it at me across the desk and said, 'Here. From now on, check with us the first time.' I looked at him and said thanks and walked out.

I mentioned that in a letter home. My dad died when I was six, and my mother could be very conscientious. She wrote the XO, the executive officer of the brigade about that. She quoted my letter, because I told her what happened. The XO calls me into his office; says 'Tell me what happened.' So, I told him. That was in July of 1969. He gets the whole story from me, and he says, 'Send in the sergeant,' who was seated outside, 'for disciplinary action.'

So, I go outside and say, 'Sarge, the XO wants to see you', and went right on out the door. Not long after that, we had the formal ceremony with all due military honors for me and several other people getting our Bronze Stars.

I kept on being a war correspondent, and finally the Colonel said, 'You're one of four people in the whole battalion that has been wounded twice.' I think I had only a few weeks to go in-country. I trained my successor, whose name was John Smith, and went on R and R, in Thailand, and came back and had about a week left. I got my Bronze Star, in a ceremony and had a week's Rest and Recreation, R and R, in Japan, just before I went back to the United States.

After that, it was pretty much time to go home. But I'd seen enough of what power does to the right people, and the wrong people. It was an Army policy in Vietnam that no one could be promoted from Captain to Major without serving as an infantry company commander. Many such men sent to command companies had held only desk jobs, and it was hard to see how they had even held the desk job, they were so incompetent in the field. We repeatedly saw how power could bring out the best in a good person and the worst in a bad person.

Soldiers don't have a lot of good things to anticipate. Some of the good things were mail from home; USO shows; sleep; dryness; camaraderie; R and R; leave; going beyond the call of duty; recognition; honorable discharge; and stories to tell.

From July 1968 to July 1969, I had served with an infantry unit, in the Vietnam War. 1st Squad, 1st Platoon, Charlie Company, 3rd Battalion, 7th Infantry of the 199th Light Infantry Brigade. I served first as a regular infantry soldier, for six months; then as a war correspondent for the United States Army, for six months. During that time, I received the Bronze Star Medal, two Purple Hearts, and the Combat Infantryman's Badge. I also earned the Vietnamese Cross for Gallantry, the Good Conduct Medal, the Vietnam tour and the Vietnam campaign medals.

I got home, and walked into my family's home, which is in Atlanta, about three miles from here, and on the TV in the den, I saw men walking on the moon. It was July 20th, 1969.

I met Margie when I was working for an insurance company. I knew, by the second date, I wanted to marry her. She was Marjorie Lucille Eager then. Didn't want to rush, so I waited for six weeks, before I proposed. I called her Margaret, by mistake, until after I proposed. Even so, she said yes, and we've been married for 43 years as of last June.

In 1973, we had a son, Mark, who is going to be forty October 15th. And then Melissa, our daughter, was born on March 25th, 1977. They both have successful careers. They both married in haste; divorced in haste; and married real winners the second time. They have three children, two boys and one girl, and three step children, so we have six grandchildren: five boys and one girl, and they all live nearby.

I wound up being a business analyst for Dunn & Bradstreet Corporation. Stayed there till I peaked out, salary-wise, and then launched a career as a credit manager which I stayed at for the next 16 years. But I was caught in a downsizing in 1990, the peak of my career. For the next seven years after that I found out, if you really want to work, there's work. I would have a full-time job in the daytime and a part-time job nights and weekends. And Margie kept her job throughout all this. For seven years, that's how we did it. If the full-time job got phased out, I would take the part-time job and activate that to full-time and go find another part-time job. Then I got in with the phone company: Bell South Mobility, which was bought by Cingular Wireless, in about 2001. Cingular Wireless lasted about five years, before it became AT&T.

By that time, I was old enough and rich enough to retire. I liked investing. So, I did. I was 58-years-old. I tried conventional retirement for two months, and about went crazy, so I went ahead and started working at Barnes & Noble, in the warehouse, hauling books out of the trucks and processing them into the store. I loved it. I did that for six years, until they started having electronic books. I wasn't even laid off: my hours just went away. We're still on great terms.

Then I started serving on three different boards of directors. I'm the habitat coordinator for the National Wildlife Federation, in this area. And church work, thrift shop, the gym, and family and friends. I play my dulcimer during a Wednesday church service at the Ashton Woods Convalescent Center. Even in a wheelchair and with their eyes closed, some of the patients can still sing 'Amazing Grace' with me during the Communion service-- a rare, wonderful moment, every time.

I have also been involved with the City of Brookhaven, which was created on about July 29th of 2012. Before that time, I went out to get voters out. I attended a lot of zoning meetings and did a lot of letter writing and communication. And I also agreed to co-chair the 'Brookhaven Yes' Task Force, a temporary committee formed to inventory all parks in the future City of Brookhaven area. We did a photographic survey first; then a written survey evaluating the parks. We noted what was needed, and submitted all that to the new Brookhaven City Council. Now, on September 3rd, they're going to hire a parks and recreation director who hopefully will pick up where all of this left off.

I've been active in zoning for 35 years in DeKalb County, and plan to continue that with the City of Brookhaven. I am the secretary of a group called The Ashford Alliance, which is a zoning advocacy group. That's one of the three board of directorships that I have. Before that I was involved in zoning as a private citizen to the head of an activist group, which saved the Fisher Mansion, on Chamblee-Dunwoody Road. It was the ancestral home of Dr. Luther Fisher, who founded Crawford Long Hospital. My church was getting ready to destroy the mansion, claiming it was no longer fit for human habitation. We had several experts and knew better. We were able to go to the newspapers and the congregation and to TV and finally get legislation passed so, instead of destroying the historic Fisher Mansion, it is now on the National Register of Historic Places.

Margie and I have also traveled a lot. We go to a capital and sightsee there, and then visit the countryside. That's the way we like to visit different countries.

I never applied for compensation for Post-Traumatic Stress Disorder, but it has been a disorder among troops ever since there's been war and conflict. It goes by different names. It was soldier's heart, during Lincolns War; shell shock, in World War I; combat fatigue, during World War II; and in Vietnam it went by several names. It started out as delayed stress reaction. Post-traumatic stress disorder is the most common term now. Delayed stress reaction is the most accurate term for it, in my opinion. It's not uncommon to have soldiers suffer from this, just because of their experience in war.

It consists of recurring flashbacks of what's happened; sudden attacks of tension and anxiety; and instability vocational and emotional. And what tends to happen, in a normal pattern for this, is that you have some of this initially, for a year, after you get back from active duty. Then for 10 years it will go fairly dormant, and then, 10 years later, for some reason, it will start again. Then, after that 11th-year anniversary, it tends to go ahead and level off and pretty much recede. Now, the memories never entirely go away. You'd be less than human, if they did.

The most painful one I can remember happened in July of 1969. I was a war correspondent on the last month of my tour, and at night, outside of our battalion headquarters, near Can Giuoc, southwest of Saigon, American soldiers ran into a squad of six Viet Cong outside our battalion headquarters, and they opened up on each other. We heard the firing, and they got to the point where they called in helicopter gunships. What we did not know at the time was that our battalion executive officer had not correctly identified his target.

The six Viet Cong escaped from the area in something called a Lambretta, which is a three-wheeled, French-made vehicle. What was left behind, where they had been, were 21 Vietnamese children: the oldest a girl of 14. Our Cobra helicopter gunships went in a circle firing as they went. We were told they were firing at the Viet Cong who had just engaged our unit. I watched the whole thing, from the side of the road, near our Battalion Headquarters. I could even hear them, over a radio, in a jeep nearby, joking with each other as they fired, not knowing that they were killing children.

I had taken up residence with the medics temporarily, between field assignments. Later that night, all of a sudden, all the medics were called out in a hurry to respond to an emergency. I knew not to go with them. I knew it couldn't be good. And that's when we found out about the massacre. Twenty-one village children were killed, by mistake. The girl of 14's leg had been blown off, by one of our machine gun bullets, and she had bled out though the stump.

The whole story finally came out. I went and visited Can Guioc the next day. Of course, everything had been cleaned up. But for 35 years, after that, I could not tell you what I've just told you now, without just choking off, in mid-sentence, even in front of an audience. Ten years later, in about 1979, I started having dreams where I could see my own children being killed in the place of those Vietnamese children. And that really scared the stuffing out of me. It was a nightmare that haunted me for a year before it disappeared.

The fact that I can talk about it now indicates that, over time, these things do get better. But you'd be less than human, I think, to ever completely get over something like that. I had to become a father myself to realize how their parents must have felt. It's hard. It never quite goes away.

When I think about the Vietnam War, I think it could not have been won the way it was fought. And I think about that, when I think about the wars in Iraq and Afghanistan. I'm very conscious, looking at the historical record, that whenever a conventional force is deployed against an unconventional or guerrilla force, the deciding factor isn't tactics or strategy: it's time. In these wars, whoever lasts longer wins. And about 85% of the time the guerrillas win, because they're the ones that have been there for hundreds or thousands of years, when the opposition shows up, and they're the ones that'll be there hundreds or thousands of years after the opposition leaves.

The only times I know of when military incursions turned out successfully, was when the invading force never left, such as the Spanish Conquistadores and the Korean War. I honestly think what happened to us was inevitable. It wasn't so much a matter of what would happen, but when it would happen. We did the best we could getting out when we did, and I think how that war ended is always going to be part of our collective memory, as Vietnam veterans.

If the wars in Iraq and Afghanistan end the same way, I think it will be a horrible, devastating blow, not only for the veterans of those wars, but especially for us, because we'll have seen three guerrilla wars end the same way in our lifetimes.

The best approach I know of for fighting a guerrilla war comes not from the 1960s and the United States, but from a man named Sun Tzu, in China, in around 600 BC. He was a Chinese warlord who wrote a book called *The Art of War*. He says when you're in a war like that, you get in, you win, and then you leave. We could have won it, by going directly to the source of the problem: not South Viet Nam, but North Viet Nam. You cut off the snake's head; the rest of the snake dies. We didn't do that. It was misplaced priorities over and over again.

The four Reilly brothers pose outside their home in Atlanta, Georgia, in 1942, while on leave. Left to right are Ray Reilly, Jack Reilly, Thomas Lee Reilly (the father of Thomas L. Reilly II), and Enos Reilly.

Ray served with infantry, in Germany; Jack was a truck driver, in North Africa, and received the Soldier's Medal, for putting out a fire in a truck laden with explosives; Thomas was a supervisor of a Military Police training unit, which was preparing for the invasion of Japan, when the war ended; and Enos was a medic, in Europe.

The second assault wave of 3rd Battalion, 7th Infantry Regiment, fly through smoke-grenade haze, as an Army medic watches. This US Army photo, by Thomas L. Reilly appeared in *Pacific Stars and Stripes*.

Spec. 4 Thomas L. Reilly II (right) salutes, after receiving a Bronze Star Medal, in Vietnam, in July 1969.

An element of Charlie Company, 3rd Battalion, 7th Infantry Regiment, cross a water body, in the Mekong Delta, during spring 1969. The officer in charge is standing. On the rear right side of the boat is a Kit Carson Scout.

*U.S. Army Photo by Thomas L. Reilly*

An ammo bearer of Alpha Company, 3rd Battalion, 7th Infantry Regiment is stuck in waist-deep Mekong Delta mud and is ready to hand a can of M-60 ammo to another soldier to lighten his weight. Once he handed off the ammo, he also handed off his M-16 assault rifle and other easily removable gear to other soldiers who helped him out of the mud. In addition to M-60 ammo, this soldier carries the normal issue of 100 rounds for his rifle and four grenades. He also has Rosary beads around his helmet, which are visible just above the brim. Thomas L. Reilly said, 'Sometimes, the mud was so thick we had to tie a rope around a man to get him out.'

*U.S. Army Photo by Thomas L. Reilly*

In a rice-paddy area, in the Mekong Delta, men of Alpha Company, 3rd Battalion, 7th Infantry, wade into waist-deep water. What appears to be dry land is bog.

*U.S. Army Photo by Thomas L. Reilly*

Men of Alpha Company, 3rd Battalion, 7th Infantry Regiment, wade across a muddy Mekong Delta creek. Note the PRICK-25 radio on the back of the nearest man and the mosquito-repellant container on the left side of his helmet. The man behind him is carrying anM-79 grenade launcher.

*Photo by Thomas L. Reilly*

In dry season, during May or June 1969, men of Alpha Company, 3rd Battalion, 7th Regiment, search for Viet Cong, amongst nipa palms, in the Mekong Delta. Note the self-made flack apron worn by the man on the right.

*U.S. Army Photo by Thomas L. Reilly*

Spec. 4 Thomas L. Reilly, back home in Georgia, on July 20, 1969, after a year in Vietnam, 'I got home, and walked into my family's home, which is in Atlanta, about three miles from here, and on the TV in the den, I saw men walking on the moon. It was July 20th, 1969.'

# Michael Albert Harris
## Interview of September 16, 2016

My name s Michael Albert Harris. I was born in Seattle, Washington, in August 1948.

My father's name was Albert Thomas Harris. He was from the Coos Bay, Oregon, area. He had miscellaneous jobs and then ended up being a milk man. My mother's name was Glyness Edna Harris. Her maiden name was Butts. She was from International Falls, Minnesota. After they were married, she worked at Safeway as a clerk, for many years and then was a housewife.

I have one brother. His name is Jan Arthur Harris. He is two years older then.

My dad got a job, on the dams, on the Columbia River for a season. Then our family moved to North Bend, Oregon, around 1951. Dad worked in some lumber mills, before he got a permanent job delivering milk house to house, in North Bend, Coos Bay, and the surrounding communities. My brother and I went to Coos River Grade School, Marshfield Junior High School and Marshfield High School. I finished high school, in June, 1966.

Then I worked in the hay fields and earned enough money to pay for a couple of semesters at Oregon State University. I wanted to be a physical education teacher and coach. My grades got lower than I expected, and I got my draft notice. My brother had decided to go into the Navy ahead of me, so I decided to join the Navy. I enlisted for four years. My primary purpose was to say out of Vietnam.

I went into the Navy, in June of '67, and went to boot camp, in San Diego. I qualified as a radioman, and they sent me to Basic Electricity and Electronics School and then on to Radioman 'A' School, and then, after that, International Speed Morse Code School. All of that was in San Diego.

While I was in Radioman School, it came time to fill out a dream sheet for where we wanted our next duty station to be, and everybody put exotic places and never got 'em. Our instructor was a very good man, and he was a radioman chief, and he appealed to our class for radiomen, in Vietnam, because the attrition rate was bad and they needed help. That was about in November of '67, and I just wrote down Vietnam river boats and ended up getting those orders.

I finished up the schooling there and then had a 30-day leave, and then reported to the Naval Inshore Operations Training Center, at Mare Island Naval Shipyard, in Vallejo, California. We had small craft training, gunnery training, survival school: all that stuff. It was intensive and about three months. We were sent to Camp Roberts, California, for gunnery training, and then we were sent to Whidbey Island, Washington, for survival, evasion, resistance, and escape training.

We finished all the training, and I shipped out for Vietnam, on July 20 1968. It was a long flight over. A lot of anticipation of what was gonna happen. We were well trained, but not trained enough for combat itself. We landed in Hawaii and then the Philippines, and arrived in Saigon. Our new, riverine boats weren't fully built yet, so they put us on an attack transport, the *USS Bexar* APA 237, to billet until our boats arrived from the U.S. The Bexar was a mile or two off the coast of Vung Tau. My boat was one of the first four that arrived, so I only stayed on that ship for about two weeks.

My boat was an armored troop carrier. Our top speed was six knots an hour. They called them Tango boats, and they were one, two three, and five. I don't know why four wasn't in there. Anyway, a merchant ship showed up, and we were put aboard it, and we sailed up to Saigon. They tied up there and lifted our boats off and into the water. We were moved from there to a little place called Nha Be.

I'm not sure, if we were towed there or went under our own power. When we got them, the boats had no oil or fuel. We had boxes and boxes of stuff to open and use to fit the boat for combat. We also did some outfitting, at a place called Cat Lo.

Once we got the boats operational, we were able to go out Rung Sat Special Zone. It was an area that was very heavily defoliated with Agent Orange. It was kind of a mangrove marsh, and there was a lot of Viet Cong in there, and we went in and we just went in there and fired our weapons at will.

My Squadron was River Assault Squadron 15, and my division was River Assault Division 152. There were two divisions in a squadron. In my squadron, there were divisions 151 and 152. One-five-one boats were already operational, and we were forming up. When we were outfitted they said we were chopped: like chopped chicken, to River Assault Squadron 13 to do combat operations, while the rest of our division boats were arriving and getting outfitted. We transited down to Dong Tam. That was a major staging area for the Navy's Mobile Riverine Force and the Army's 9th Infantry.

So, in the first operation we were in, during the first week of September 1968, we were baptized by fire. Several were wounded. We were carrying troops and inserting them to look for Viet Cong. That was about three or three and one-half weeks after I arrived in Vietnam.

Once we were outfitted and went out and experienced our first firefight, it was rather sobering, because we had wounded. They told us, in training, that some guys would be wounded and some killed. The reality began to set in.

Once our division got all filled up with boats and ready for action, we went out on several very large operations with a large amount of boats. Sometimes 30, 35 boats. They sent us down to the U Mihn Forest. Not many American military had been there ever, and it was a very hostile area. It was a staging area for the Viet Cong and

North Vietnamese, because they had had such a free use of it. Nobody bothered them there, and all of a sudden, we come in and all hell breaks loose. We were ambushed every day: sometimes two three times a day. We took a lot of casualties down there. The Viet Cong used water mines and were able to sink some of the boats.

One very vivid memory is we got in a very serious ambush, and we pulled back out to re-supply, and re-fuel, and everything. Then we were sent back down the same river, which was maybe 40- to 50-ft wide. The Viet Cong or North Vietnamese or both had taken palm trees maybe eight- to 12-in. wide and stuck them in the bottom of the river, in an X pattern, so our boats couldn't pass 'em. It was an engineering feat, done overnight. I don't know how they did it, and I marvel that they did it.

They called up my boat to push against them, to see if we could push 'em out. This was a 60-ton boat, and we couldn't push 'em out. The tree trunks would just bend over and come back. So, they had to bring in an EOD team, and Explosive Ordnance Division team, to blow them out of there, so we could go down that river, and, of course, we got in more ambushes.

We operated quite a while, in the U Minh Forest and then, on the way out, the officers decided to drop my boat, Tango 1 and Tango 10, at a little Vietnamese naval base, at Rach Soi. In retrospect, I figured out, it was the beginning of a very massive operation called Operation Sealords, which began on October 8, 1968. The purpose of this was to stop enemy interdiction, and weaponry, and supplies coming from Cambodia into South Viet Nam.

That was at about the end of the time that we really did large boat operations. In late November 1968, they broke us up into small units, and we spread out all along the Cambodian border, and did our best to stop the infiltration. My boat was at Rach Soi for eight to ten weeks.

We were chopped to river patrol force, Task Force 116, and we operated there, until the first week of January 1969. Their boats were PBRs, Patrol Boats River. They were 31-ft fiberglass craft with twin Jacuzzi engines, so their boats were very fast and our boats were very slow. The purpose of our time there was to alternate night operations. Tango 1 would go out one night and Tango 10 the next night. We'd hook up with the PBRs and go on night patrols. It was pretty suicidal. It was a bad operation, because we were so slow and only had one boat. The rivers were about 75-yards wide, and the PBRs were very fast.

We operated a lot on narrower waterways. A river 75-yards wide is not very wide when the enemy has rockets. We transited a lot from rivers to canals and operated on canals that had been hand dug, in the 15th century. When you were on a canal, you went in a straight line. You couldn't maneuver the way you could in a river. Canals were bad, because they knew you were comin', and they'd set up for you. My boat was in an ambush where one of the PBRs got hit and was on fire, and we were able to help put it out, but out boat was never hit.

Luckily, we didn't have any major ambushes, until December 27th 1968. Tango 10 was out for the night operating an' the enemy ambushed, and they took four rocket-propelled grenades. They killed a seaman named Barry Barber. He was hit in the chest with an RPG, a rocket propelled grenade, and it unfortunately blew his body all over the boat. Several other sailors were wounded on the boat, and they lost an engine. We heard on the radio that they had one killed and several wounded. It was just awful. They were screaming for help and trying to get out of the ambush. They took me off of a PBR to get on Tango 10 to help them to get back to the little base at Rach Soi.

Anyway, they made it back to the base, and they tied up next to our boat, and I'll never forget it. I could smell all the blood and cordite. The next day, my crew had to go in and clean up Tango 10. We were the only ones available to clean it up. It was just an awful mess. I mean, parts of Barry's body and shell casings were all over the boat. It was just a bloody mess. It was just awful.

The medevac chopper had come in the night before, after the ambush, and had taken the large pieces of his body, but there were still pieces all over the boat. We put the parts in a 20mm ammunition can and then we had a small kind of a service lowered them into the water and sunk it. That was all we could do. That was a horrible situation.

The afternoon before the night on which Tango 10 was hit, they asked us to go out, but we had backed into a river bank and bent one of our shafts and screws and we couldn't go out, so Tango 10 went out in our place. The guy that got killed was in the same gun position that I was on, in my boat.

After that, the officers decided that they better move us back to the main group, at the Mobile Riverine Base, where the main ships that we tied up to were in the river. It was probably the Mekong, in the vicinity of Dong Tam. We got a little down time there, and then we continued on various operations month after month.

We were called out on different operations. We went down to the U Minh another time and they sunk two of our boats with water-borne mines that would come in and were detonated from the river bank. They would just wait, until a boat got over the mine and then set it off. They sunk Tango 151-5. We lost two sailors, on that one. And then they sunk ASPB133-2, an assault support patrol boat, and we lost two or three there.

Obviously, the enemy had a good water mine team down there, because they were getting to us with the sinking. They would try to damage a boat badly enough that the other boats would have to stay in the ambush area, and we'd just fight it out with them, while we tried to rescue our wounded and the boat.

I think it was sometime later, we went out to the Twin Sisters or Three Sisters area, and it was really different. It was really flat, and we got into a few ambushes. I remember one time there was enemy spotted fleeing from us. One of our boats was called a monitor, and it had a 105mm howitzer on the bow. They actually used the howitzer to fire at the enemy, at two miles. I'm not sure of the success, but it was the first time that indirect fire was used from one of our boats. Usually the monitors fired directly into the river banks and bunkers.

The enemy built some pretty sophisticated bunkers, even some concrete bunkers. They would just wait for us to come by and shoot us. They had RPGs and recoilless rifles. Some of the recoilless rifles were 106mm. They were pretty big weapons. They were a crew-served weapon, and they could be shot at quite a distance and hit one of our boats. The weapon's crew could be far from us and not risk getting killed by our weaponry.

Operations like that just went on month after month.

To be promoted from E-3 to E-4, you had to have a year in rank. I remember, around February 1969, the Navy cut time in rank to six months, for men in combat. So, I made E-4, in six months, and I made E-5, in six months. So, I was an E-5, a radioman second class or RM2, in one year and nine months, which was pretty unheard of, other than in combat. At that point, they asked me to become a volunteer naval advisor on Vietnamese naval boats to help them, and I just told 'em no way. I'd had enough combat, in eight months that I didn't feel like I wanted to be on a boat with Vietnamese only.

At that point, at Dong Tam, we had about 400 men, in our division or maybe it was our squadron. Anyway, we had 222 Purple Hearts, in my division, in eight months. I think we ended up with 385 Purple Hearts. Of course, several guys were wounded twice or three times, and we even had one guy wounded four times. In addition to the wounded, in our River Assault Squadron 15, we had a dozen or more men killed.

It was either late '68 or early to mid '69 *Newsweek* ran an article on our river boats, and said the casualty rate was at about 70%, including killed and wounded. The casualty rate was very high, because our boats were kinda like tanks, you know. They'd take an incoming round, and just about everybody in the vicinity was wounded. The RPG and recoilless rifle rounds would burn right through everything and blow up inside the boats.

Speakin' of the man that was wounded a fourth time, his last name was O'Briant. He was also a radioman, and he received his third wound out in a remote area, during an ambush. I remember watchin' a helicopter come in, and it was a unique helicopter. We'd never had an Air Force Husky helicopter, for medivac, and this was kind of a boxy helicopter with two rotors. We had waited for maybe over an hour for them to come, and they came in and they picked up the wounded, including O'Briant. When they were flying away from the deck of the Tango boat, the enemy hit the helicopter and wounded O'Briant a fourth time, so he had four Purple Hearts.

After I turned down the offer to volunteer to be on a Vietnamese boat, we carried on with the operations. There were so many of them. When we worked down south, we moved U.S. 9th Infantry troops, Vietnamese Marines, and Vietnamese regional forces. During my tour, we probably moved U.S. troops only about eight times, because the other squadrons had the 9th Infantry taken care of.

I went on R & R to Australia, and late May of '69, for about a 10-day period. When I got back, my boat, Tango 152-1, was out on an operation, so they put me on Tango 152-2. Well, that was kind of a fateful thing, because I went out and we got ambushed two times, and it wasn't even my boat. I had close calls both times.

One happened when we had been put back at the Mobile Riverine base, and, on June 13th of 1969, they just grabbed a bunch of boats suddenly and said we're goin' on an operation to pick up 9th Infantry troops. We transit for maybe five, six miles, along the Ong Muong Canal, in Kien Hoa province. We're nearing the place where we're going to pick them up, and we got ambushed heavily. Tango 152-4 took two RPGs, and they were loaded with Army troops. The two rockets killed four Army, on board, and wounded 30 some, including U.S. Navy personnel that were wounded too. That was pretty rough, with only a month to go.

Two days later, June 15th, 1969, we're in the same area, and we got ambushed again. We're eight boats there to pick up a company of 9th Infantry troops, on the east bank, and, as the ramp on my boat was going down, the ramp cable snapped, and the ramp just dropped on the river bank. We were, in essence, dead in the water, and we couldn't go anywhere. The enemy ambushed us, at the very same time.

Our division's commanding officer, Lt. Thomas Gunning Kelley, pulled his monitor in about 30 yards from my boat and fired three howitzer rounds in front of our boat to deter any enemy coming toward us. When the howitzer fired, I was out with a chain hoist, hooking up the ramp to hoist it up manually. I was out in front of those muzzle blasts, and they darned near knocked me over. They deafened my left ear. I couldn't hear anything with it for two or three days.

I rigged up the chain hoist, and in the interim the monitor boat that Lt. Kelley was on turned to the east bank of the river and moved over. When they got in an exposed position, the enemy was down the river quite a ways with a recoilless rifle, and they hit the monitor right in the coxswain's flat and knocked the Lieutenant and the boat Captain down severely wounded. And they shot a second round, and hit 'em. The boat was so disabled that it drifted into the river bank, with nobody at the helm. One of the gunners saw what was happening and was able to back the boat off the bank, where the enemy was right in front of them. He backed the boat away.

I was told that Lt. Kelley had taken shrapnel in the left side of his head that took a huge chunk of his skull off, and his right eye was actually hanging down on his cheek. He continued to insist on guiding the troops, in this fire fight. Later he received the Medal of Honor, for his actions that day. I was decorated, for that day, with the Bronze Star with V for valor, for exposing myself by getting out and cranking this half-ton ramp up, so we could get off the river bank.

I went back to Vietnam six times, from 1990 to 2010, and I actually got the co-ordinates for that ambush site and went down there, and where there was two rivers that divided, at a peninsula, the Viet Cong had built a memorial to the Viet Cong on that peninsula, the memorial was about 12-ft high and on it there were bronze figures of three soldiers—one with a recoilless rifle, one with an RPG, and one with an AK-47. It was really surprising, because it was exactly where we got ambushed.

Another time, we were out on an operation, and my boat loaded troops and backed off into the middle of this small river, and I'm up on top of the boat, and I just happened to look to my left, and there a Viet Cong soldier stood up and fired an RPG at my boat. And there's just nothing you can do. It starts in slow motion. I watched him. He took his time. He aimed, I saw the smoke come off the back of the tube and the rocket comin' at us. We had a miniature flight deck where a helicopter could land, and it missed our flight deck by about six inches. It hit a palm tree, on the other side of the river and knocked it down.

I called in to the boat's officer, and he said, 'Where'd it come from? Where'd it come from?' And I told him right where this guy was. We had a boat called a "Zippo" boat that had napalm, and it nosed over there and shot napalm in there. They went in after and checked, and there was two dead Viet Cong in the hole. The VC learned that they could shoot, at 75 yards, up through our flight deck and hit everybody in the boat at one shot. He was off just a bit, but it cost him his life.

I recall quite a bit, about my tour, but for some reason, when the American crew came to replace us on our boat, I can't remember them or what transpired at all. We turned the boat over to them, and we were put at Dong Tam. I'm sitting there drinking a beer on a screened-in of the enlisted men's club, on I think July 10th of '69, and I hear a 107mm rocket, and I turned around and looked, and it was coming cross the horizon in my direction. It landed in the middle of a group of 9th Infantry troops that were being moved back to the U.S., due to the Vietnamization program. It killed three of them and shrapnel just come all over beside me, but I didn't get hit. It was just miraculous.

It was the day before I left to go to Saigon. We got to Saigon, and the billet that we were supposed to stay in, the Annapolis Hotel, was hit, by Viet Cong sappers, the day before, and blew the whole front of it off, so we couldn't stay there. I was just so frightened, by the time I got on the airplane to leave that I thought I'd never get out of that place. I left, on July 15th, 1969, so I was actually there in country for one week short of a year.

I was 19-years old, when I arrived in Vietnam and 20-years old most of the time I was there. I left Vietnam July 15th, in '69, and went home on leave. Then the Navy sent me to 35mm motion picture operator school, in San Diego. I never used any of it. After I got out of the service, I could watch a movie and tell when the next reel was gonna be starting.

My next duty station was the Naval Communications Station, on Guam. And when I got to Guam, the Captain of the base I was on and the personnel people made me prove that I was in combat, even though I had received a medal for valor. While I was there, I wrote a couple of letters to the commander, and I estimated that I was in somethin' like 25 ambushes, in Vietnam, and in several rocket and mortar attacks. I wrote the letter, because a new ribbon came out, in February of '69, right in the middle of our tour. It was the Combat Action Ribbon. When I was discharged, I got my records, and saw the Combat Action Ribbon was there the whole time, but they didn't see it.

I was a Radioman 2nd Class, which at Guam, would qualify me to be a watch supervisor, for maybe five or six guys. I had gone from Radioman School to combat, on river boats, using voice circuits and machine guns. In our well deck, we had two 50-cal. and four 30-cal. machine guns, and, depending on where the ambush was, I could go to port or starboard and fire those weapons. I got to Guam and I didn't know anything about ship to shore and shore to shore communications. So, they had to start re-training me, and it was pretty miserable, because I didn't know what post-traumatic stress was, but I had it raw, and I'm trying to learn all this stuff. It was very difficult. I wanted actually to be back in Vietnam, where I didn't have to deal with the spit shine and all that regulation that they had.

In Vietnam, we got away with quite a bit. Adm. Elmo Zumwalt allowed us to grow beards. If we were to go on one of the Navy barracks ships there in the river, which were a Mobile Riverine base, we had to have the uniform of the day on, and none of us wanted to do that. We just had cut offs, and boots and stuff, so we just mainly stayed on our river boats the entire year. We went aboard, on occasion, but it was a pain to get all dressed up according to the rules. Thompson, our boat Captain, would go aboard the ship and be able to stay in nice accommodations. We figured once the boat Captain was off the boat, we could do anything we wanted, so we stayed on the boats when he was aboard the ship.

The barracks ships were in the main rivers, but they had to move around to avoid attacks and water mines. The 9th Infantry Division troops would stay on the ships, so we had, I think, two brigades of 9th Infantry troops that operated as Riverine Force infantry. They would stay in the ships, and when we got ready to go on an operation, we'd pull up to the pontoon, by the ship, and load the troops, and off we'd go.

My tour, on Guam, was 18 months, and it was a long, long time, on a beautiful island, for a 21-, 22-year old man with PTSD. The Guamanian people didn't like the military, because we were kind of infringing on their island. It always happens that way, and I don't blame them. Early on, I bought a brand-new Honda 350 motorcycle, so I could just ride around the island, for somethin' t' do. Guam is like 33 miles from north to south and maybe four or five miles wide. It's a big island, but it's little when you're stationed on it. We called it the rock.

When I got there, they were short-handed, in my division, so we had to do port and starboard duty for a long time. That meant 12 hours on duty and 12 hours off. Then we started getting' more personnel in, so they cut down to a 1, 1, 1, 32. We'd have a day watch, a mid watch, and an eve watch, and then we'd have 32 hours off. Then that advanced up to 1, 1, 1, 56. And then the real icing on the cake was when it came up to 1, 1, 1, 80, so we would do a day, and a mid, and an eve, and have 80 hours off, which was quite nice.

We operated ship to shore communication mainly. A lot of message traffic, from Vietnam, so I was keeping an eye on the river boats and what was happening there. It was pretty hard being away from the boats and having them still in action, and guys gettin' killed and wounded, and readin' it on a teletype-writer machine. But I got in a group of friends there, and we did what we could. I did a lot of golfing, on Guam, and hiking, and riding my motorcycle.

Being that I was an E-5, I could live off the base, so about three of us would rent a house off base. I was pretty much a hard-core alcoholic, by then. I didn't drink, until I was 19-years of age, and after that I really tore into it. Thankfully, I quit in 1976, so it's been 40 years, since I had alcohol now.

I decided to go out for intra-service football, because I was gaining some weight and didn't like it. The football team was equivalent to NAIA competition, I would think. It was very high caliber football. I just wanted to make the team, and I ended up being first string, as a cornerback, on the defense. It was quite interesting, because we started our first three games with one win, one loss, and one tie. And then we ended up the year with six wins, one loss, one tie, and won the island championship, which allowed our whole team to travel to Japan and play the intra-service champion of Japan. Unfortunately, we lost the game, in Japan, but we had a heck of a time on liberty.

There were men on the team that had tried out for the NFL. I remember this Anderson Air Force Base team had this running back that was 234 lbs. Just a monster guy, and I met him in a hole and the hole opened up, and hit him head on, and received a concussion out of it. Then I had a second concussion. It was in a fight. My brother was still in the Navy, and he was on Okinawa with a naval patrol air squadron. He was actually a yeoman, which is a paperwork guy, but he talked his Lieutenant into letting him fly over to Guam with the squadron. I think we hadn't seen each other for two years. We went to a club and a fight started, and one of the guys that my brother was with tried to pull me off of this guy, and the guy kicked me in the forehead. But we had a good time.

I got into some trouble, on Guam, because I was so rebellious. I just wanted the lack of discipline that we had on the river boats. The first day that I arrived at my watch section, there was a seaman draggin' a table – this is just an example – and so I kind of hustled over there and picked up the other end of it and helped him move it where he was movin' it. And I walked back, and the 1st Class Petty Officer that was showin' me around, just told me outright, 'You don't do that around here. You're an E-5 now.'

I just told him, 'Go to hell. If a guy's in need, I'll help him.'

I got into some trouble, just being rebellious, and it came down to where I had about 12 days to go, before I was shipped to the United States for discharge. I'm not real proud of this. We were out drinking, and in this little car, and I was in the back seat, and we passed an Air Force staff car. And it happened to be the commanding officer of Anderson Air Force Base, and being stupid, I stuck half of my torso out the window and gave him the finger.

The next day, I get this call to come in for a Captain's mast right away. I had to dress up in my whites, and I went in there. The Navy Captain is there that presented me with a medal for valor. A Colonel, from the Air Force base was sittin' behind me, with his aide. The

Captain asked me what I did, and I said, 'I don't know, Sir. I was drunk.' And he basically let me off. He told me he could keep me there, and that was terrible, because I wanted out of the Navy so bad. But he didn't take a stripe, and he let me go home for discharge. Stuff like that happened because I just hated the Navy, after a while.

I was discharged, on March 10th, 1971. I was at Treasure Island Naval Base, there at San Francisco, and my brother had been discharged from the Navy and he was living very close to there, in Sunnyvale, California. He would come up and get me, while I was on base waiting for discharge, and somehow my name didn't get on the roster for duty. So, he would just get me and we'd go out drinkin' and he'd drop me back off. I think I was there for about a week. Then I was discharged. It was one of the happiest days of my life. Of course, I was an alcoholic, and I couldn't control much. I'd saved a whole lot of money, and just blew it on booze and everything.

The awards I won, in the Navy are a Bronze Star with a V device; a Navy Achievement Medal with V device; Combat Action Ribbon; Presidential Unit Citation Ribbon; Navy Unit Commendation Ribbon with a star, for a second award; a Meritorious Unit Commendation, while at the Naval Communications Station, on Guam; National Defense Service Medal; Vietnam Service Medal , with four stars, for four campaigns; Republic of Vietnam Meritorious Unit Citation: a Gallantry Cross with Palm; Republic of Vietnam Meritorious Unit Citation, for Civil Actions, First Class Color, with Palm; and a Republic of Vietnam Campaign Medal with 1960s device.

The diagnosis for Post-Traumatic Stress Disorder wasn't really official until 1981. So, I had 10 years of just goin' around suffering. I couldn't maintain relationships. I didn't care. I fought against the police. I finally quit drinking alcohol, in 1976. But I was still so lonely. I was sick. You know, the Vietnam vets, we just kind of stayed in the shadow.

I quit drinking, because I was fearful I was going to kill somebody through vehicular homicide or in a fight or somethin' like that and be caged up for the rest of my life. I just committed myself to quit, and the way that I did it was I went around to all my drinking buddies, and I told them outright that I'm quitting. That just gave my pride the strength to work through it. It was a tough thing to do, but I was able to finally get away from it.

I worked at odds and ends. I worked for my cousin for two or three years, up in Washington and got some building experience. I only lasted for three or four months, in California, and I had to get out of there. It was too confining for me. Being from Oregon, you've got all the streams, and rivers, and mountains. Down there it was just nothin' but walls of people.

Then an opening came, in 1974, which was two years before I quit drinking, to go through the Carpenters Apprentice School with the Veterans Administration. While I did that, I had to be in the local carpenters' union, and be sent out of there on jobs. The VA upgraded my pay to a journeyman wage throughout the process, so it was a pretty good deal, but I was still drinking and struggling with the studies. We studied all aspects of building. But I made it through, and my whole intention was to learn enough to start a business on my own, so, if I wanted to go fishing, I'd just have to ask myself.

I was rebellious enough that I thought the instructor was teaching way over the level that he should be for apprentice carpenters. So, I went before the board, with him present, and told them what I felt about his instruction. He was a great instructor, but he was like a Picasso instead of a regular painter. They decided not to give me my journeyman card, because I was going to go out and start my own business anyway, and I did.

I had my construction business, from 1977 to 1990, and pretty much did re-model work and pretty much treaded water and maintained my post-traumatic stress disorder: not making a lot of money. Just making enough to get by, and maintain my stress level.

In 1985, I found Freddy Breeland, a good buddy I had in Vietnam, on the river boats. He was also a radioman. I had tried to find him for years, and, as it turned out, he also was trying to find me. I finally made the right phone call, and I found him in Canonsburg, Mississippi. I will never forget, we're talkin' to each other and he was weeping. I could tell he was weeping, because he had been tryin' t' find me for so long, and he knew that he had reached my father, but my father was too drunk to help him.

I took time, between jobs, and I drove down to Mississippi to be with him, for a couple of weeks and reminisce. His wife and son were scheduled to go on vacation with neighbors. He was much like me: just kind of an isolate, home-body: just keep the stress down. His wife and son went with neighbors up to Nashville, Tennessee, and left us there by ourselves. We had a good time. I can never forget, when I was getting' ready t' leave, I could just see the tears in his eyes, because we had such a comradery with the battles and rivers and everything.

I went back home and we'd have like three-way conversations. He and his wife would get on different phones, at their house, and I'd be on my phone, for an hour or two and just have a good time. And then, January 30, 1986, his wife called me about 5:30 in the morning. I kind of ribbed her, at first about calling so early. I thought she just forgot the time zone, but she had bad information. Freddy had been in a car accident the day before and he wasn't expected to live. The car had rolled and had damaged him bad. He died the next day. That was in 1986.

It was just a terrible time for her and the son, and everybody, and so I tried to help as much as I could spiritually and financially, for the next following months. Several months later, I ended up asking her to marry me, and ended up raising his son Jason Breeland, from 13-years old on up to graduation from Marshfield High School, in

1990, and Eastern Oregon University 1994. And now Connie and I have been married for 30 years.

She was from Winnsboro, Louisiana. She and Freddy were married for 14 years, until the tragic accident. The boy is 33 or 34 now.

I didn't marry until I was 38. I had many years of struggling alone and trying to maintain myself. I was actually resistant to God, because I felt that he'd dealt me a bad card. I had quit alcohol, but then I kind of replaced it with a recreational drug. I had used the drug for four or five years, and then I had quit. I had gone 40 days without using any drugs, and I slipped up and indulged again. And I was just in a very bad place, because I was so sick of myself for givin' in again. About that time, one weekend, my buddy came with his wife. This was in 1981.

He grew up in the Catholic Church: a very strong Catholic family, but he and a brother and a sister had stepped out of the Catholic Church and had gone evangelical Christian. Their family really ostracized them, for doin' it, but it turned out well. He shows up, and he's telling me over and over that weekend that he knows that Jesus is God, and I just got so sick of him, because I didn't want anything to do with God. I didn't have any upbringing with God. After he left, about two or three days later, I was so angry, I just put my fist in the air, and I said, 'God, if you are real, make yourself real to me.' And nothing happened. And so, I just figured I'm gonna die and then rot in a grave, and worms are gonna eat me. I didn't have any hope at all. It was just a real dismal situation.

About two days later, I'm sitting at my kitchen table, and God spoke to me. He said, 'Flush your drugs down the toilet.' I objected.

I said, 'What about Randy, my friend? He uses them too.'

And He said, 'Flush them down the toilet. He doesn't need them either.' It took me probably about an hour to flush all the stuff I had down the toilet, because it wouldn't sink very well.

That was the beginning of my Christian walk. I was 33, single, and a carpenter, when I accepted Jesus into my life. After that radical salvation experience, I began studying the Bible, and this friend of mine that was sayin' that Jesus is God, hooked me up with his younger brother, who was 10-years younger than him, and we studied the Bible for years on end. I couldn't explain it. We just ate the word of God for years.

Finally, in 1985, it happened with Freddy and Connie, and then Connie and I married, in 1986. When I felt like I was healed enough myself, I started a Point Man Ministries outpost, in Coos Bay, Oregon. It was an offshoot of Point Man International Ministries. The outposts were for military veterans. All you had to do to be in it was to have a heart, and a phone, and a desire to help your brother veterans. I started that late in 1988, and it's still active 26 years later.

I was very active in it, until three years ago, when we moved from Coos Bay up to Monroe, Oregon. I'm not in touch with them as much now. Others have taken it on. When I started it up, in '88, Hank, a Christian man came, and his pastor had sent him to check if I was valid or not. Hank found out right away that I was authentic and stayed with me. Others came and we had a very successful outpost.

I had planned a trip back to Vietnam, and had it all set up, and then the president of Point Man Ministries, asked me, in '89, if I would form teams from Point Man to take over to southeast Asia to work, as a mission. I really felt bad about it, at first, because I had already had a trip back set up, and I would have to cancel it. I decided God wanted me to do that, so I started formulating teams. I took two or three teams over to work in Thailand, and in Burma.

Most of the team members were Vietnam veterans, and, after the teams were finished with their short-term missionary work, I'd take some of the members into Vietnam to areas where they had been during the Vietnam War.

While I was there, I felt a calling for long-term mission work. I mentioned it to my wife and she just said, 'Well, you could go and do whatever you want, but just build me a house, and I'll stay here. I just couldn't do it on my own.'

I never talked to her about it. I just prayed about it. One day I came down from the bedroom, and she was at the kitchen table with a big grin on her face. I asked, 'What's up?'

And she said, 'I heard from God.'

We moved to Bangkok, Thailand, in January of 1990 to go long-term mission work. Our target was southeast Asia. We worked there, but just a few short months, and my wife was diagnosed with cancer. I was far from her, at the time, and I had a long bus ride back to Bangkok to be with her. The enemy, Satan, the devil, tried to lie to me the whole way that she was gonna die. I fought against him, and I got to Bangkok, and she just collapsed in my arms. All we could do was pray and believe.

I was so sweaty from the trip that I took a shower. While I'm in the shower, I asked God outright, 'Give me a scripture. Give me some support of some kind.'

A voice said, 'Romans, chapter eight.'

I said, 'No. I want a scripture.'

And he gave me Romans, chapter eight, verse 32, just bam! Like that! I read it, and it was so comforting. Basically, it says nothing can come against us, with God. Connie had surgery a couple of weeks later, and she's been cancer free now for 26 years. So, God took care of it.

We worked over there till August of 1997, when we came back to the U.S. to live full time. She's an X-ray, MRI technician, so she could find work, and I did odd jobs, and finally became an accredited Veterans Service Representative to represent veterans before the VA. I've been doing that for probably 16 years now. It's a volunteer position, and I don't receive any pay for it. In 2009, I really had to start cuttin' back, because I was puttin' in 12-, 14-

hour days, and burning myself out. I do mostly advising and counseling now, instead of the actual paper work.

It's interesting, as a side note, that Lt. Kelley that received the Medal of Honor, he was able to convince the Navy to let him stay on active duty. He was the only officer to command a war vessel, at sea, with one eye. He eventually became a Captain and retired. He ended up in the Massachusetts Veterans Administration and worked his way up to be the commissioner, the top man, there. The point is that we were decorated in the same ambush, and we've worked very hard to help our fellow veterans.

I was diagnosed with PTSD. I first went in for an evaluation, in 1983, and I was rated disabled. Then, through the years, and all the claims that I filed for my concussions in service, I ended up being rated 100% disabled, in 1998. That has given us some monetary support. My wife worked, until about 2010, so we're fine.

I belong to very few organizations. The Point Man International Ministries is one. Vietnam Veterans of America, and I'm the webmaster for the Mobile Riverine Force Association. I'm was not wounded, so I don't belong to the Purple Heart Association, which is fine with me. I did get hit, one time, with shrapnel in the helmet just above my forehead, and it put a dent in my helmet.

I hunt and fish yearly. I hunt mule deer and Rocky Mountain elk, in eastern Oregon. When I do not draw a tag over there, I hunt black tail deer and Roosevelt elk, in western Oregon. I primarily fish rivers for steelhead and rivers and lakes for rainbow and brown trout.

Michael Albert Harris, at Rach Soi, South Viet Nam, in December 1968

Connie and Michael Harris, in Bangkok, in December 1992

# Kirk Steaven Baldwin Leavesley
interview of January 6, 2017

My name is Kirk Steaven Baldwin Leavesley. I was born July 23, 1950, in Winnipeg, Manitoba.

When I was born, my mother was in the hospital, and she told her mother that she wanted to name me Kurt. My granny was from Glasgow and had worked in one of the factories, in Scotland, in World War I. My nana went and registered my birth and decided no kid of hers was going to be named a German name, so she registered me as Kirk. Baldwin was my grandmother's maiden name.

My dad's name was Leonard Ernest Leavesley. He was a radiator mechanic. His mother was from Ireland, and he came from a family of about 12 kids. Eleven kids were born to his mother's first husband, which was named McSweeney. He died. My dad was the only child of her second husband, which was Leavesley, which is an English name. My dad's mother was in Canada, when she married him. That side of the family is an interesting mix of people.

My mother's maiden name was Una Angela Baldwin. She was a housewife. My father's family was riddled with addiction of all sorts. My mother came from a pretty staid Scottish family, so my background was quite dysfunctional. My father was an alcoholic.

I have one sister. Her name is Kelly. She's five years younger.

I went to public schools in Winnipeg. I achieved the level of grade 10. I had skipped two years. At the age of 14, I hit the road, and didn't come back until 1963. I traveled all over the U.S. and Canada. In Vancouver, I lived on the streets.

When I was working, as a bus boy, in Niagara Falls, New York, I met these people from Cuyahoga Falls, Ohio. He was an osteopathic physician and surgeon. Their last name was Zalen. They took me in, and, of course, I lied to them and told them I was 18, when I was like 14, and I looked like I was 10. I think I told them my father was insane and my mother was dead. I stayed with them for about six months. The Zalen family vouched for me and helped me with a lot, including getting a job at a Howard Johnson restaurant, as a cook. They insisted that I register. That's how I ended up getting registered for the draft, when I was only 17-years old.

I was back in Canada, when I was 17, and I decided that I had no idea who I was, what I was, where I was going, what life was all about. I figured that I needed a little discipline, so maybe I'd join the Marines. I enlisted in Minneapolis, in October of 1967, and they flew us down to boot camp, in San Diego, California.

I remember getting off the plane and then they mustered us up on the field. The bus drove up and the drill instructor marched us on to the bus. Once we were on the bus, life as I knew it was over. I had no idea how my life would change, and, of course, it did. Boot camp was brutal, because we had some vicious drill instructors, but, as vicious as it was, it was a defiant streak in me that just said you're never going to beat me.

We went through boot camp, for 12 or 13 weeks. Towards the end, when we were standing in line to have a photo of our boot platoon taken: Third Battalion, Platoon 3096, and the real mean drill instructor come up to me, and he gets his face right in my face, and he's screamin' at me and the spittle's flyin' in my face, and he says, 'Leavesley, if I ever catch you smilin' again, I 'm gonna jam your pearly teeth down your throat. Of course, everybody in the line is ramrod straight; starin' straight ahead. Then he leaves, and I try not to laugh, 'cause I think the guy's like an idiot.

I had no idea what he was talkin' about, till we went in and we got the photo. Well, there's our drill instructor in front and 80 guys from the platoon in back, and there's one guy in the photo smilin'. Everybody's lookin' mean and grim, and there I was smiling.

Infantry Training Regiment, ITR, was in San Onofre, California. That's where they trained us in all the weapons. They get you up at three or four in the morning and march you up into the hills, in your full gear and the M16, and you hike around all the hills. It's like you're out in a war zone. They put you in a Quonset hut and you go in with your gas mask and take it off, and you get to play with flame throwers and all those fun toys. I really liked ITR. During ITR, I was assigned artillery, as a military occupation specialty.

In 1968, they sent me to Camp Lejeune. A lot of my memories of Lejeune are getting up at 6 o'clock, putting the utilities on, going out by 6:30 AM, for a work crew, and half an hour later we'd be soaking with sweat, because the humidity would be so high.

They had tested me, and found I had an aptitude for mathematics, so I got sent from there to Ft. Sill, Oklahoma, to study ballistic meteorology, which is the effect weather has on the missiles and artillery. There was a Marine Colonel that was in charge of all the Marines that went to school there, and the school was from 2 April to 10 June 1968.

That's when I got into some mischief, for sure. Ft. Sill is north of Dallas, Texas, and there were many nights when three of us drove all the way to Dallas, party all night; drive back in the morning, and then go to school all day. And then repeat and repeat that routine. Man, I can't believe how many times we did that. I don't know how we managed to do it.

One guy I did this with was a sergeant. He had been to Vietnam already. He didn't talk about it much.

Then I went back to Camp Lejeune, and I was sent to Camp Pendleton, and then I got deployed to Vietnam, in September '68. We flew over, and I was friends with this kid from Minnesota. He was a big farm kid. He'd never experienced the world, and was kind of naive about life.

We landed, in Saigon, and, from Saigon, they flew us up to Da Nang, which was kind of like the big staging area. Eventually, we were deployed to Dong Ha, which was just south of the DMZ. All the time I was in Vietnam, I was in that area of I Corps. I was with Headquarters Battery, 12th Marine Regiment, 3rd Marine Division.

When we first got there, they sent us to work, in the mess, for the first month. The kid from Minnesota was workin' in the main mess, and I was workin' in the officers' mess. Sirens sounded, because we were being attacked by artillery. Previous to this, it was like it was a big joke, but this is where it all came together for me. We went out into the trenches, which were maybe four feet deep, and this guy from Minnesota and I were sitting in this trench talking. Beside us are an E-9 and another high ranking enlisted non-com. There was this tremendous boom, when a mortar round landed right on the edge of the trench and blew their brains and guts all over us, and left us with our ears ringing.

The Marines were used a lot as a recon work. They'd send in maybe in four-man teams, with limited fire power, which is why a lot of them got killed. If the enemy discovered them, they didn't have much fire power with them to defend themselves. Their purpose was strictly to go in and to observe: to recon. That's why, if they did encounter the enemy, it usually didn't end up well for the Americans. I mainly caught night patrol, night ambush, day patrol, and night listening post duty.

From there, I ended up working about three or four months in FSCC, fire support co-ordination control, in a bunker, in Dong Ha. It looked almost like a briefing room. It had a map of the whole region, and we would be advised of the location of any friendly troops that were in the area. There were many tactics to clear areas, and they included artillery fire, B-52 bombing runs, and air-strafing runs with multiple 50-cal. machine guns that blanketed a grid area. Our purpose was to ensure there were no friendly troops in targeted areas. The missions could not begin, until they were cleared by us.

They had incredible fire power, and they'd just literally shred areas. We had to keep track of where all friendly troops were and insure there were none in the areas being attacked with air or artillery. I had to co-ordinate with squads that were out and maintain the big map. Everything was bunkered there, because we were always under fire. You were five clicks, less than five miles, from the DMZ, so the NVA could just fire right into your area.

Just because you had a job, like the FSCC, that didn't stop them from sending me out on another job in the daytime. During the daytime, they'd send me out on mine sweeps. We didn't just have one job. On those mine sweeps is where I really got to know the Vietnamese people. Maybe 12 guys would go out, in a couple of trucks. Our job was to clear areas of suspected mines. That's where we would see a lot of Vietnamese people in the villages. You got to know the people, and they had such a tough life. You'd meet the children who'd been maimed by illness, and mines, and through the war. It was kind of heartbreaking. It was shitty!

When I was a kid, I used to watch movies with Stewart Grainger and other stars in the jungle, and I used to think it was so exciting, so romantic. Well, when you get into the middle of a jungle with hundreds of leaches and bugs, and you've got to literally cut your way through the jungle, it's got to be the most horrid place ever. There is nothing romantic about it.

Then, for the next two to three months, I was out, in the jungle, as a forward observer. I was deployed to one of the little posts with maybe 100 sq. meters enclosed. There you would go out with squads to locate enemy troops and to call in artillery on them.

We did not use proximity fuses in mortar rounds that I know of. We had cluster bombs that were timed so that they would explode at a certain level above the ground.

They would explode and you would get this whole bee-cluster effect on the ground below.

The Army had a main base called Camp Carroll, right in the jungle. The base was taking artillery fire, and nobody knew where it was comin' from, until they discovered it was coming from a mountain called Dong Ha south of the DMZ. The mountain was the largest land mass, in the area. The NVA was entrenched in that mountain and had set up artillery and were just havin' their way with us. They were firing at will. Because of how they had cycled their attacks, it was very difficult to determine where their fire was coming from.

When we finally found them, they sent in troops to capture the mountain, which they did. They sent in the air force and they bombed and strafed. Then the troops came up the mountain, and there were a fair number of people killed going up the mountain to take it.

I was in the second wave that went in. I got flown in to the top of the mountain, after they dislodged the enemy, and we set up our artillery. The guns were either 105mm or 155mm howitzers. I was actually using the stuff I'd been trained for: doing the mathematics for firing the guns accurately.

There were also 8-inch guns, but those were mainly used by the Navy. We used them. The Navy would fire from off shore, from the South China Sea, and they were accurate and effective.

I was up there for probably a month, and that was one of the scariest times, because we got cut off, surrounded by the enemy. They couldn't fly in water, so we were short of water. Any time they tried to send in water, on helicopters, we'd get mortar fire. The enemy were entrenched throughout the mountain and moved their mortar emplacements. As a result, it was very difficult to determine where mortar fire was coming from. We were short of water, and the jungle was dry, and up on the mountain you were exposed.

During that period, everybody had to go out on patrols right around the mountain. We also had night listening posts, where four guys go out to a designated area. There's no verbal communication. You key a code in your radio and check in via your radio every so often. You sit there all night and your purpose is to observe any enemy activity. You're not to engage. If you see anything noteworthy, you radio it through codes. Listening posts were the absolute worst, because you couldn't do nothing: just sit, listen, and look.

After I got off the mountain I was working out of one of the small posts, and was sent out on night ambushes, which are quite different, ey? They would send us out, and tell us our location and the grid point where we had to go, maybe three to five kilometers, to where there was known enemy infiltration or enemy activity. We would set up, and our purpose was to engage the enemy. We killed people. There wasn't a lot of captures. That's the reality. We didn't try to capture anybody for information. I saw a lot of pretty terrible stuff go down.

Later in '69, I worked for artillery, in another bunker in Dong Ha, and my boss was a Major. He was absolutely this fanatical security freak. The assignment was called intelligence, and there were two of us working for him in the bunker. He was a tyrant. There were two parts to the job.

One was electronic listening posts that allowed us to monitor enemy movement throughout the DMZ. The listening posts were sensors planted in the ground. We monitored enemy infiltration routes and known enemy activity, and provided information to other units. That was a big part of the job.

The second part of the job was the most interesting and the one that I really liked. I had to acquaint myself with all the enemy artillery, because when we took artillery fire, we had to run out to the crater, collect fragments of the shell and set up a reverse azimuth reading to determine the angle of penetration. The shell fragments help you to identify the type of shell, which in turn helps you to identify the type of gun was used to fire it. Now you know the range of that gun. That allows you to take the return azimuth reading and return fire, by estimating the position of the enemy gun that fired it. I became really good at identifying all that enemy artillery and weapons that were used.

On October 3, 1969, I made Lance corporal, E-3.

In probably November, December '69, I contracted malaria, and ended up on the *USS Repose* for a month. You had to take this pill every day, and you had to take this big one once a week to prevent malaria. I was religious about taking them, because I didn't want to get sick, and I came down with malaria.

When I was on the *USS Repose*, I got a medical book from a doctor, and I read up on malaria, and I discovered that none of that shit really protected the men properly. As a matter of fact, at the time that I was in Vietnam, probably while I was sittin' on the boat, the university in my home town, called the University of Manitoba, was contracted, by the U.S., to provide research on malaria vaccination. They didn't have adequate malaria prevention. The government had really lied to us. If you got bit by a malaria-infected mosquito, you were going to get malaria. The pills were a placebo.

There are three different kinds of malaria. I had falci malaria, which is the worst kind. It's the hardest to cure, but once cured, it's very unlikely to return. There's a malaria type called vivax, which is rather easy to cure, but it constantly recurs. People can die from the recurring type, because, with each recurring round of fever and chills, you get weaker and weaker.

An interesting note is that, even though they put you in the hospital, and everybody knew that you had malaria, they couldn't treat you, until they identified exactly what type of malaria you had. So, you were classified as FUO, for a fever of unknown origin.

You would feel okay, until the parasite split. When it split, is when you would have the fever and chills. That would happen every 24 hours, and your temperature would go up to 105 degrees Fahrenheit, and you would shake uncontrollably. This period would last three to four hours. Your fever would get so high it would be dangerous. What they would do, when you were sick, you're shakin', you're burnin' up, was take you and put you in a shower and rain cold water on you. I can laugh about it now, but I wasn't laughin' when they were doin' it to you.

Before I was treated, I'd go through the four-hour period of chills and fever, and I'd spend the next eight hours recovering, and I'd be walkin' along the deck, just tryin' to pull myself together, and I'd just start to feel good, but I'd know that within a couple of more hours, it's gonna happen all over again.

They had to take blood, at a specific time, to identify the virus, and it took them almost two weeks to identify which virus I had. Once it was identified, I was treated.

After that, I went back to the base and I was given a job that brought me in contact with the Vietnamese people, and I really liked it. I would fly out to a village with a medivac team, and the medics would provide medical treatment for all the people in the village. When we'd get to the village, we'd set up a little station, and the whole village would line up. I was one of several Marines there to provide protection for the medical team. That was a really interesting job. I liked that.

In the summer of 1969, I went to Thailand on a seven-day R & R, and I also signed up, for another six months, in Vietnam. The only reason I did that, was because I had time left to serve, and I couldn't stand the discipline in the States; I couldn't stand the spit and polish bull shit. If you signed up for another six months, you got 30 days free anywhere you wanted to go in the world, and I wanted to go to Australia.

We were doin' a perimeter patrol, at the bigger base camp five klicks from the DMZ, and we came upon an old shell casing. Unfortunately, because I had experience, I was lookin' at it, but it was a booby trap, and it went off in my face. It had gun powder in it, and the gun powder fizzed up and burned my hands, my face, and the hair off my head. The other guy beside me just had his hands burned a bit.

There I was with my hands all bandaged, three or four weeks before I was to go on the 30-day leave to Australia. It was pretty painful, and the only way to kill the pain was to get drunk. They gave you Darvon and stuff like that: didn't even work. So, you just got falling down drunk, and then you couldn't feel anything. I remember a buddy of mine from Texas and I were drinkin' and we got into a fight, and he lets me have one in the face, and he peeled a couple of inches off my cheek. Then he kind of looks at me, and we kind of had this moment of clarity.

I was quite the sight, I can tell you, because there were newbies that came to Vietnam and got off the plane, while I was waiting for a flight out. They took one look at me, and it was like holy shit.

Everything healed okay, but for the longest time, I use to have a problem in winter. My face would get all mottled, but for whatever reason, it's never bothered me since.

After I was wounded and recovered enough, I returned to duty and for the six months I'd extended. And then I was flown to Japan to Hawaii to Alaska to Philadelphia Naval Hospital. I arrived there, in December 1969 and was there for about two months. While I was there, I completed my high school education. I was released, by the hospital, and discharged by the Marines, on February 17, 1970, and I came back to Winnipeg. I was still healing, ey, even while I was home, at my parents' house.

I had been in touch with my parents. My mom knew I had joined the Marines and was very supportive of me when I was in the Marines. She sent me like little Care packages. When you're in the jungle, you get stuff like jungle rot. It's really hard to keep your feet in good shape. Fungus was a big problem, and my mom would send me this stuff that I put on my feet. It really protected my feet from getting any kind of disease.

While I was in the Marines, I earned the Combat Action Ribbon and the basic campaign medals.

When I came home, I had PTSD, but back then we didn't know what it was. I had a hyper-sensitivity to sound, which is one of the trademarks of PTSD. My reflexes were razor sharp, and were attuned to the slightest sound, probably for the first year. It really wasn't until two years that I kind of settled back down. I really considered myself fortunate, in some ways, even though I was an alcoholic and a drug addict, because, in many ways I was able to get through a lot of that on my own and deal with it.

I became a drug addict and used a lot of drugs, in Vietnam. They were issuing amphetamines, but there was heroin and all kinds of drugs available. I can blame my addiction on Vietnam, but as I look back, with my understanding of addiction, I was set up for that before I went to Vietnam. I got the drugs in Vietnam: the heroin, the opium, and all the pot, but the seeds had already been set, before I went.

It was really the way I grew up. I grew up in an alcoholic environment. I grew up with complex drama, and never feeling safe. My father was a pretty violent guy, and I was drinkin' before I went over there. In Vietnam drugs were everywhere, and a large percentage of service personnel there were usin' 'em. Most people were doin' drugs or drinkin' alcohol. As I like to say, when reality is such as it is, who wouldn't drink.

Eventually, I was able to understand what kind of happened to me over there, and I went on to become an addiction counselor, and I also specialized in PTSD.

After I was home, I got into the hotel business, as a night auditor, 'cause I was good with math, ey. In 1971, I met a woman that I liked, and I married her. In that five years what happened was I did all kinds of work. I worked as a musician. I'm a singer-guitar player. I took my new wife and packed everything into a baggage trailer I made, and I moved to British Columbia, because I wanted to be a professional musician. Didn't know a soul there.

We lived in a place called Crescent Beach, which is south of Vancouver and close to the U.S. border. I got connected, in Vancouver, and did a lot of different kinds of work, and worked with a lot of bands and did a lot of touring. While I was there, I also really got into the drugs and alcohol, and my marriage fell apart after about five years.

I had done a lot of drugs, when I was in B.C., including heroin again. I also had periods of sobriety, but I was definitely an alcoholic, but didn't think of myself as one. I definitely had a problem, but didn't think of myself as having a problem.

I came back to Winnipeg and got into the hotel business again and met Val who was an alcoholic. During that time, I stopped using drugs, and actually stayed drug free. I worked in the hotel business for a year or two, and then I went to work for Xerox and worked for Xerox for three years. I became very successful, at Xerox, and married Val in the beginning of the '80s, because I had won a trip to Italy and I could take her, if she was my wife. We'd been living together, but the marriage was a disaster. I never should have done it, but she got pregnant, and I have a son named Dirk Logan James Leavesley, who is now 37. I also have a daughter named De'ja, from the first marriage. De'ja is 43.

Then my sales manager's father started a company, so I went with them selling printing. I worked with them for 20 years. I had started to use drugs again, while also using alcohol. The job included taking customers to lunch, and my addition just got worse and worse, and I crashed and burned. It was a pretty bleak period. I finally came to an end, in December of 1995. That's when everything changed. I woke up, and I saw where my life was going. I saw I was probably going to rob and steal, and cheat, and lie from every friend I had, and from every family member I had. Those thoughts made me want to kill myself. God came into my head: I call it the God thought, and says call the hospital.

I called up a buddy of mine, and he took me to the detox unit of the provincial hospital, on January 2, 1996. That was the beginning of my journey back to recovery, and I've been sober ever since. I'd been sober not quite a year, when I declared bankruptcy. In the fall of '96, I lost my house. Life hasn't been perfect, but it's been a good journey since.

Drugs aren't that great. Initially, they're the solution. But the solution then becomes the problem. Drugs help the user to cope initially, but they then become his problem.

When I came out of the hospital, I did not go back to the printing company. What I hate about business is the bull shit. You know, I sold a hundred grand this year; I gotta do a hundred and twenty next year. I gotta do this. I gotta do that. What about the reality of what you're doing? There is a sense of grow, grow, grow, but to what purpose? Our society is a consumer society, and people tell us that we have to consume and the economy has to grow. We don't really need to, but we're being pressured to do it. People are caught up in a vicious cycle and take on debt.

About two or three years after I was in recovery, I began to start playing music again, and I started singing, because I was mainly a singer. I got together playing with people I got connected with. I made my living off and on, the past 20 years, as a musician. But the difference was this time I wasn't drinkin' and I wasn't using drugs. I found going to the job not so great.

For the next five years, I worked as a contractor, for a security company, and I sold security systems. It was great, because I would take three to five leads a day that had been generated and go out and meet with those contacts. I did that from '96 to 2000.

In 2000, I went to work, as a general sales manager, for a printing company. I worked for a guy I had hired, when he was young, who became a partner in his own printing company, which was bought out by a bigger concern. He was the V.P. of the bigger concern, and he knew I could do a good job. He wanted me to come in and take five companies that they had bought and manage the combined sales team. I did that, and worked for them for two years, until about 2001, when I became really sick with hepatitis C. I was only at stage 3, so it wasn't that bad: my liver wasn't compromised, but I really suffered from the symptoms of the disease. I was fatigued, my immune system was lowered, I got sick easily, and I had brain fog. I could walk into a room and not remember why I went there.

I applied for disability and they turned me down. It took me five years and five appeals to get it. I did the appeals myself. They finally gave me Canada Pension Plan Disability, and I was on Canada disability for five years. In the meantime, I was in good condition, because the company that I was with had an insurance plan that paid me disability. In 2002 or three I took a clinical trial that was a year-long treatment regime of weekly injections of PEGylated Interferon and 12 mg of Ribavirin each morning and the same each afternoon. For that whole year, I was so sick, that I did not feel like getting out of bed to go to the bathroom.

But I forced myself to move, get out of bed, and get involved. The year is a bit of a blur. I actually met Brenda, my future wife, while I was on treatment. She is from Winnipeg. During that time, I was involved in recovery. I was involved in CA, Cocaine Anonymous; I ran two-12-step meetings, while I was that sick. And I also went to church and was involved in their Alpha Program, which was discovering Jesus. It was an introduction into Christianity. I met her at the Alpha Program.

When I finished treatment, I was kind of wacked out, from the treatments. It really affected me kind of mentally. It took me about four to five months to kind of level off. I had been on disability a year prior to going on treatment, and I was on disability while I was on treatment, and then for probably another three years after. Just as I was starting to feel better, I ran into an old friend who I'd met while doing AA or CA meetings out in jails. He was a member of one of the groups I was a member of, and he ran programs in the provincial jail. His name is Brian Patterson. He is now the executive director of a recovery center called Tamarack Recovery Centre Inc., in Winnipeg. He asked me to come on the board. I went on the board, and I was at one meeting, and he called me and offered me a job.

I was making a couple of grand a month tax free in disability. I didn't have to go back to work. They weren't telling me I had to go back to work, like they did early on, when I was really sick. I had an opportunity to get back into the work force, but it was a big leap, because I was going to give up the disability payments. I took that leap and gave up the disability payments. I had a lot of the skills they needed, and I worked there for a little over four years, as a counselor. I decided it was time to move on, and I left Tamarack.

My wife and I moved to Sandy Hook to a place that we used as a summer place. It was winterized, so we moved there year-round, for two years. The first seven months or so, I had some contract work, with a vocational re-hab company. I was helping people get back to work, but specializing in addictions.

A friend of mine, in the city, worked at a nice, high-end retirement home. She said, 'Kirk, why don't you come here and play music? We get lots of musicians here that are terrible. You could do a good job.' So, while I was living at Sandy Hook, I put together an hour-long set and practiced it. Then I went there and did it, and I've been doin' it ever since. Retirement homes, independent living homes, whatever they're called, pay about a hundred bucks an hour.

After the first year, I got so busy, that we decided to move into the city. We moved back into the city two years ago June. I average about 20 gigs a month. We live in a house in St. Boniface, a section of Winnipeg. I'm still involved with CA, sponsoring people, in service work and recovery. I know a lot of people all across Canada and the U.S. through CA.

I make my living full time now, as a musician. I've written a little over 20 songs, and I've got songs I've recorded, and I'm putting a band together to do them live and to record them. I've prepped about half of them and am ready to go. So, I'm actually in the process now, at 66, of recording this stuff and playing it live with a group. I'm looking for specific musicians, and I haven't found all of them yet.

I probably had about 300 color slides that I took in Vietnam. My grandfather was in World War I, and I had his little rattan foot locker, and I kept the slides in there. A few years ago, I gave the foot locker and all the photos I took in Vietnam to my son. Now he can't find the photos, but they'll turn up, probably before I'm dead.

I never ever did get connected with the Canadian Vietnam Veterans Association. I kind of thought about it, but it was kind of like I want to put all of this behind me.

Kirk Steaven Baldwin Leavesley, in San Diego, in 1967 or 1968

Kirk Leavesley, at Dong Ha, in 1969

Kirk Leavesley, in Winnipeg, in 1971

Kirk Leavesley, at home, in 2017

# Philip Leslie Spackman
### interview of March 9, 2017

Philip Leslie Spackman is my name. I was born at Emory Hospital, Atlanta, Georgia, 31 March 1948.

My dad was Arthur Houghton Spackman. He was from Buffalo, New York. He moved to Cleveland, Ohio, as a teenager, and finished high school there. He was a salesman for the 3M Company. I was born here, spent two years in Pittsburgh, two in Cleveland, Ohio, and then back here to stay, in 1953.

My mother was Elsie Jane Cottier. She was from Cleveland, Ohio. She attended Miami University, in Ohio, and studied journalism, but she ended up being a bride during the Second World War. My parents married, while my dad was in the Navy, training at Great Lakes Naval Station. He served in the Pacific, and my mother was a housewife, after they married, and eventually the mother of five.

My sister Hallie Kay was six years older than I, my brother Michael Geoffrey Spackman is 18 months younger, my sister Nancy Jane was six years younger, and my brother Terry Francis is 11-years younger.

I went to Avondale High School, in the City of Avondale Estates, in DeKalb County, Georgia. I finished there in June 1966. Then I attended college, at DeKalb College, in DeKalb County, Georgia. In February of 1967, I enlisted in the Army.

After basic training, at Ft. Benning, Georgia, and advanced training, reconnaissance training, and armored cavalry training, at Ft. Knox, Kentucky, I was selected to attend the Officer Candidate School, at Ft. Knox.

At Ft. Knox, there was a facility known as the Patton Museum. It was a mile and a tenth from the Officer Candidate School, and I would run it both ways. I spent 23 weeks in that school; 21 of those weeks, I was restricted to my home area, but I was allowed to go to the Patton

Museum on Saturdays and Sundays. I was restricted probably for being a smart-aleck southern boy. They were trying to rein me in a little, and eventually did.

This museum was very low key, but it was stocked with a lot of German hardware: Panthers, King Panther, all the Panzer equipment, field artillery pieces, and all the American equipment as well. It had a walk-around loft: a big loop around the building inside, where you could get above the display floor and look down on these displays.

It also had Patton's field trailer: about a 30-, 32-ft long, single axel trailer that they pulled with a road tractor, or some other device. Inside it were all of his maps of Europe. On one end of the little thing were his maps of Sicily and the boot of Italy, and there were notations and marks on them, and I took them to be original, and have no reason to doubt that they were. This was not like a professionally run museum. It was just a big warehouse with all his stuff and a bunch of equipment from World War II in it.

Very few people came to the museum and they were visitors and not soldiers there to read Patton's field reports and other documents. I was alone there most of the time.

In that trailer there were file cabinets; desk drawers. You could look at anything you pleased. Some documents were typed; some were hand-written. There were all manner of documents of a military commander. One action that I read about was the move that he had the 3td Army make to disengage six divisions from front line combat during the middle of winter, then wheel north to relieve the 101st Airborne, at Bastogne, all in an unexpectedly short time. All he asked of his men was don't bother to eat or sleep, just get there and save the Americans. His men responded, because they'd been trained for that kind of all-out assault action, and that's what they were good at. In the assault they were marvelous.

If I took one thing away from reading much of the material in that trailer, it was the thought that an aggressive force suffers less than a force on the defense. It stuck in my mind that you were less likely to be harmed attacking, than you would be defending. That applied to cavalry particularly. Cavalry is mobile, it is quicker than the big armor. You can change directions on a dime. You can flank and do all kinds of things with quick cavalry.

The difference between cavalry and armor is pure weight. Armor would be fighting vehicles 65-tons and heavier. Their weight restricts where they can and cannot go, and the modified M113 armored personnel carriers were a lot more capable in a variety of terrain than a tank. That was true, even in the highlands, where I was, which had a totally dry season and an incredibly wet monsoon season that made mechanized travel incredibly difficult.

I was commissioned, on December 15, 1967, and assigned to Ft. Rucker, Alabama, as a permanent party awaiting my deployment to Vietnam. On October 3, 1968, I completed jump school, at Ft. Benning, Georgia, and was presented my airborne wings. I took airborne training, because I thought I had a chance to be assigned to an airborne unit. Being a 20-year old, that intrigued me, but it didn't turn out that way. After that, I had leave, and then left on the way to Vietnam.

They flew us to Hawaii and on to Tan Son Nhut Air Base, and I was in Vietnam on November 1, 1968. I was assigned to the Americal Division, the 23rd U.S. Infantry Division, 11th Light Infantry Brigade. My command was 3rd Platoon, E Troop, 1st U.S. Cavalry.

At full strength, my platoon had eight modified M113 armored personnel carriers modified to be armored personnel assault vehicles and one mortar track with a 4.2-in mortar. Each vehicle was armed with two M-60 7.62mm machine guns and one modified Browning 50 cal. machine gun. The crew of each was four to five men. The mortar track had a five-man crew and often was assigned to base security. It didn't travel with us.

I was in combat, with my platoon right after I arrived.

I was 20 years of age, a Second Lieutenant, in command of a cavalry platoon that operated both independently doing reconnaissance in force and similar missions, and was also often assigned to various infantry units, in the brigade. The machines were modified so there was very little room in them, and we added sandbags and ammo cans in the interior, so there was even less room. We never hauled troops, except, once in a while, guys hopped on top.

I was the oldest man in my unit most of the time. My NCOs, God bless 'em all, came out of the NCO academies. Most of them drafted, but they had great aptitude, either mechanical or mental, and the NCO academies tuned them up, and they were excellent NCO, because they had the very best training on the machinery, the very best training on the weapon, and they were 20years old and thought they were bullet proof, which makes for a fine NCO.

My initial combat experience happened right after I arrived and was versus local Viet Cong. Combat against that particular opponent was always late in the day and of limited duration. That was determined by the nature of how he fought: what he had to fight with.

I was promoted to first Lieutenant 15 Dec 1968. By the spring of 1969, North Vietnamese regular army units, in battalion size were operating where I was, and they became my opponent. Combat against them was a very different concept, because they were well equipped, well trained, well-armed, and fought like an army, whereas the Viet Cong fought more like a street gang.

I don't have a list of operations in which I participated. The award citations I received each denote a village or hamlet where the action took place, but my cavalry unit was used a great deal like a fire department. If an adjacent infantry unit made contact with the enemy and I was within 10 km, they would call us. We'd rush to their aid with our fire power, so I often entered fights that were under way. The men we rushed to help may well have been on some big mission, but, for us, it was simply respond and participate.

Many soldiers that I know have said to me, 'How did you get in so many fights, in so short a time?' It was because I was mobile and had great communication and was very familiar with my area. I operated in it alone, as a unit, often. I was very familiar with where those machines would go and how to git 'em from one place to the next without comin' up on a creek that I couldn't ford or a railroad berm that was too steep to go over. That familiarity helped me, and I was part of an infantry brigade that had four battalions in the field; two or three of 'em around me most all the time. Once the North Vietnamese got involved, our battalions got involved pretty frequently, and they would call us, if we were close enough to help.

On March 9, 1969, my unit encountered a well-entrenched North Vietnamese force, which was unusual. We normally saw local, Viet Cong resistance, but this was a regular North Vietnamese army force that had chosen to engage an American rifle company head on. They set up a defilade, in a ditch that had a lot of vegetation around it and directly in the path of this infantry unit. They let the American unit get incredibly close, before they engaged them. That caused the infantry unit to be deployed less well than they would have liked to have been, and they were kind of in a knot. The company commander and his crew were pinned down in the center and some of the trailing elements worked their way on line and were putting effective fire on the North Vietnamese.

We were close by, and they called for help, and I was able to come the same path as the infantry had come. Upon arrival, they explained to me where the enemy was and how they couldn't do their fire and maneuver. They were in a pen. I was able to run my unit parallel to the ditch and apply all kinds of fire power to the insurgents and get 'em moving. I managed to silence one position and continued along the ditch engaging them with grenades. At that time, a North Vietnamese soldier stood up to fire an

RPG at us, but I threw a grenade at him and eliminated that threat. Once they got up and started moving, the American infantry was pretty effective against 'em, but when they were in that depression, it was hard to being fire on 'em. The Army awarded me a Bronze Star with V, for that action.

On March 15th, we went to help an infantry unit that had taken many casualties and was pinned down by a North Vietnamese force south of a place called Van Truong. But, with so many Americans being right in the front of this mess, we had to press the enemy and try to move him off his spot, so he wouldn't be a threat to the wounded. We were able to do that with some degree of success.

As we moved towards them, we came to an impenetrable dry stream bed that was heavily covered by vegetation, and the enemy was in it. The banks of that dry stream bed were so steep that our machines would have fallen in on their noses and flipped over on their tops, if we had tried to ride into them. It was not traversable.

The enemy chose that place, because they knew there was only one place to cross, and that was 15-km on down the stream bed.

We chose to modify our procedure a little bit, and had pretty good effect with it. We decided that we would ride along parallel to the stream bed, using hand grenades and the left-flank, 7.62mm machine gun. We quickly realized that the way our machine guns were mounted in their swivels and how close we were to the enemy prevented us from shooting straight down, which is where the enemy was.

In some places, along the banks, the vegetation was so dense that we could not be sure where the bank was. That caused us to weave away from the ditch, until we decided we could run that vegetation over. That allowed us to stay close enough to effectively engage with automatic rifles and hand grenades, which is what we did. The hand grenade is an incredibly effective weapon, in an enclosed area.

*Author's note: On 25 April 1969, a Silver Star Medal was awarded to 1st Lt. Philip Leslie Spackman. The citation reads:*

*'For gallantry in action against an armed hostile force in the Republic of Vietnam. First Lieutenant Spackman distinguished himself by intrepid actions on 15 March 1969 while serving as a vehicle commander with E Troop, 1st Cavalry. On that date, a friendly element was pinned down by an enemy force south of Van Truong. While moving toward the location to provide support, Lieutenant Spackman's platoon encountered a well-entrenched North Vietnamese Army force. The platoon was unable to move forward because of dense vegetation and could not maneuver its 50 caliber machine guns on the enemy positions. With complete disregard for his personal safety, Lieutenant Spackman raised himself high in his cupola and engaged the enemy with hand grenades and rifle fire. From his exposed position, he directed his men through the hostile trenches and detected enemy soldiers as they attempted to close in on his vehicle. He personally killed six insurgents at close range, despite hostile fire coming from every direction. Through his gallant actions, the unit was able to break through the enemy lines and provide assistance to the pinned down element. First Lieutenant Spackman's personal heroism, professional competence, and devotion to duty are in keeping with the highest traditions of the military service, and reflect great credit upon himself, the Americal Division, and the United States Army.'*

On March 24, 1969, an infantry unit, near Thuan Hoa, was pinned down by intense Viet Cong fire, and called to us for help. We provided the fire power necessary to take the pressure off of them and to do some real damage to the enemy. We overran the enemy's forward position and forced them to retreat. We stayed with the infantry, until they set up a secure night position.

My first Purple Heart was, ironically, the last shot fired, as darkness fell after that day. I literally saw the shooter, in the twilight, come out of the wood line and fire a single shot with a rifle, and I totally ignored him, in that he was 1000-yards away. And it hit me! What's the chance of that happening? He was aiming at my head, but he was so far away that he hit me in the lower leg. It startled me, but the bullet was not traveling at a high rate of speed when it struck me. The medic thought more nerve damage would occur, if they tried to take it out, so I do have it in my leg, as we speak. I was awarded an Oak Leaf Cluster to put on to my Bronze Star with V, for this action.

My platoon was on a convoy security mission, for fuel tankers, on May 12, 1969, on a dirt and paved road known as Highway 1 that ran north and south through our area. The tankers were carrying JP4 jet fuel, which is very flammable. My platoon had been ordered to place our vehicles scattered throughout their convoy, which was the worst-case scenario for me, with my people scattered apart. We could communicate with each other, but, if something happened in another part of the convoy, we could not get there. I didn't like it. I thought that was a misuse of my force.

I felt we would have been more effective deployed up and down the road, on higher ground, where we could see each other and communicate. I had learned many ways to travel and get on little promontories, where I thought I could have been effective. I thought we would have thwarted ambushes better with that tactic than driving along amongst a bunch of flammable material.

The truckers were trained to continue through an ambush, if possible. Once they reached the paved part, the fuel tankers were able to motor much more rapidly and did so, but they were prime ambush targets.

The enemy's tactic was to cause the lead tanker to catch fire and spill fuel, and then the roadway behind it would be in flames, because of spilled fuel. They did this with an RPG that punched a hole in the first tanker and caused jet fuel from that tanker to pour onto the paved road. The first RPG went into the fuel and was extinguished by the liquid fuel and lack of oxygen. When the second RPG hit 1000-yards further down the road, it hit above the first hole, with oxygen in the tank, it immediately ignited the tanker and all the road behind it.

This day, near Dien Troung, we were ambushed. An RPG hit the lead tanker and a little further down the road another hit it, and it lit up like a candle. At almost the same time, two or three drivers had been shot; the road was on fire; and other tankers caught fire, 'cause they had to drive through the flame to get past the point of the ambush. The convoy was in great disarray. It was an effective ambush, by a very small force. The paved roadway became so hot it melted.

In addition to hitting the fuel trucks, one of my machines took a direct hit right into the driver's compartment killing the driver. His machine went every which way: eventually in a ditch and up a slope, and almost tipped over. Every other crew member in it was wounded.

I managed to move my vehicle near them and fired my 50-cal. machine gun at the enemy. That enabled the wounded crew members to load in my vehicle. As you know, a 50-cal. machine gun is a reach-out-and-touch-you weapon accurate to a mile. If you can see it, you can hit it. That persuaded the enemy to leave quickly. While this was happening, I radioed for medevac helicopters to meet us at a secure landing zone, and when we arrived there, the wounded were carried to a field hospital for treatment. I was awarded a second Oak Leaf Cluster for the Bronze Star with V, for that action.

On May 17, an American infantry unit that I was close to, but not assigned to, engaged a North Vietnamese rifle company or better. This was west of Duc Pho. I think it was a weapons company, because they were loaded up with RPGs. The American's took a bunch of casualties immediately: had 15, 18 men on the ground, when they called me. They were having a hard time securin' the wounded: getting them out of harm's way.

When I arrived, they directed my attention to natural, earthen structures on a high creek bank that had at least two machine guns in it and RPGs. The bank enabled the enemy to move up and down the creek without being seen by our infantry. In order to fire on us, they had to work their way up the bank. When I arrived, the enemy were engaging the infantry unit, and didn't see us, until we attacked 'em. We caught 'em off guard.

I was able to run parallel to the creek and look down into it, and with the M60 machine guns on the flank of our machines, we placed very effective fire on them. There was no place for them to run. That day, I may have bagged more of them than I did on any other day. We made north of a dozen confirmed kills that day. This probably didn't take half an hour, but when I think back on it, it seemed like a lot longer, at that time. I was awarded an Oak Leaf Cluster on the Silver Star, for that action

*Author's Note: On 27 July 1969, a second Silver Star Medal, an Oak Leaf Cluster to put onto the medal, was awarded to 1st Lt. Philip Leslie Spackman. The citation reads:*

*'For gallantry in action against an armed hostile force in the Republic of Vietnam. First Lieutenant Spackman distinguished himself by intrepid actions on 17 May 1969 while serving as a platoon leader with E Troop, 1st Cavalry. On that date, the troop was working in conjunction with a friendly infantry unit on a search and clear mission west of Duc Pho when they encountered a well-entrenched enemy force. The insurgents inflicted heavy casualties on the friendly units in the initial contact. Realizing the urgency of the situation, Lieutenant*

*Spackman immediately regrouped his men and led an assault on an enemy fortification. Due to the fact that the maneuver was initiated without delay, the cavalry element was able to easily overrun the bunker position and eliminate the insurgents within. After this objective had been silenced, Lieutenant Spackman ordered his men to withdraw and secure a landing zone so that casualties could be extracted from the site. With complete disregard for his personal safety, Lieutenant Spackman remained in a forward position and provided continuous covering fire for the medevac aircraft. During this time, he came under intense rocket propelled grenade fire from two North Vietnamese Army soldiers located in a nearby grove of trees. Lieutenant Spackman quickly engaged them with his turret mounted machinegun and routed them from the area. His courageous actions were instrumental in minimizing casualties among his comrades and in the overall success of the mission. First Lieutenant Spackman's personal heroism, professional competence, and devotion to duty are in keeping with the highest traditions of the military service, and reflect great credit upon himself, the Americal Division, and the United States Army.'*

The Army Commendation Medal I received was a cumulative award. What it had to do with was Special Forces bases that were in the far western frontier of South Viet Nam. They were as close to the Laotian border as they could get 'em, and some of them might have been over. They had large, self-propelled howitzers, at these outposts. And, when the outposts became untenable, they had to save those guns or destroy them. This nice award had to do with us escorting a couple of bulldozers and a couple of other machines, and a bunch of Seabees, and going to this base getting the self-propelled part of those guns runnin' again, because they hadn't been run in a long time, and then escorting them back to our base. Fortunately, I didn't run into my opponent, while I was in that disarray. We came out with a lot of stuff. It looked like a circus. I think this is like a participation trophy.

*Author's note: On 1 July 1969 1st Lt. Spackman was awarded the Army Commendation Medal, for actions from 1 May 1969 to 26 May 1969. The award citation states that the award is 'For meritorious achievement in connection with military operations against a hostile force, in the Republic of Vietnam...By displaying a great desire to complete his mission, he set an example that inspired his comrades to strive for maximum efficiency.'*

On May 31, an American infantry unit operating in my area became engaged with a North Vietnamese rifle company or better and suffered a lot of casualties in its initial contact. In this case, the infantry commander and I had worked together numerous times. The American unit was face to face with the enemy and the enemy had concentrated its men in the middle of its line. The American commander was able to move his squads right and left of his center and leave me an opening in the middle of his line that allowed me to put together the classic armor wedge and run my machines right through into the middle of the enemy line. With that angle, we were able to get more machine guns on the enemy while moving. That worked out very effectively that day. For that action, I was awarded a second Oak Leaf Cluster to put on my Silver Star.

*Author's Note: On 24 August 1969, Silver Star Medal, second Oak Leaf Cluster, was awarded to 1st Lt. Philip Leslie Spackman. The citation reads:*

'For gallantry in action against an armed hostile force in the Republic of Vietnam. First Lieutenant Spackman distinguished himself by intrepid actions on 31 May 1969 while serving as a Platoon Leader with E Troop, 1st Cavalry. On that date, an element of the troop was *dispatched to assist a friendly infantry unit that was pinned down by a North Vietnamese Army heavy weapons company near Tap An Bac. Upon arrival at the point of contact, Lieutenant Spackman learned that the well-entrenched insurgents had inflicted numerous casualties on the infantry company. Quickly assessing the tactical situation, Lieutenant Spackman organized his platoon into a wedge formation and led an assault against the enemy positions. Several times during the advance, he dismounted his Armored Personnel Carrier to guide his men to the friendly soldiers. Once inside the enemy perimeter, Lieutenant Spackman ordered his platoon in a circular formation and directed their fire against the hostile fortifications. Under this covering fire, all casualties were quickly loaded aboard the vehicles. Lieutenant Spackman then led the platoon out of the area and to a secure rear location where the wounded could be safely evacuated. His courageous actions were instrumental in the swift extraction of his wounded comrades and in thwarting the enemy attack. First Lieutenant Spackman's personal heroism, professional competence, and devotion to duty are in keeping with the highest traditions of the military service, and reflect great credit upon himself, the Americal Division, and the United States Army.'*

Sometime in June, we were in an operation, in which one of my APCs was damaged by RPG fire. One of my men was wounded, in that operation, and taken to be treated. After the fighting ended, I learned that wounded Americans were being taken to a graveyard. It was a graveyard, in very low-lying country, and people were buried there in mounds. I went there to find out why there was not a medivac copter in there hauling these guys off.

We were laying the wounded out waitin' for an evac, and a fight was going on about 150-yards from there. I found my guy, and he told me he heard shots nearby and men crying out in that graveyard.

While I was on one knee talking to my man, I felt a powerful pinch in the flesh outside the right hipbone, without striking the bone. I heard the bullet hit the ground in front of me. Because of that, I knew the direction the shot came from and looked up at trees not half a football fields' length away, and there was this NVA guy sitting on a limb, like a deer hunter, not too high up in a tree, and without camouflage. He saw me, but I ended his term of service in that second. I kept his belt, for the longest time, because he had truly angered me. I was lucky. The bullet had gone through my flesh and not hit bone.

No one had seen the sniper, because of the battle noise and the fact that few people look up too far from the ground, when fighting is going on. The NVA was shootin' the wounded one after the other. Nobody was there to shield them or to do security there, other than the guy that was tryin' to call in helicopters.

In the Americal Division and in the 11th Light Infantry Brigade, they had a policy that, if you were in a combat line unit, and you received a third Purple Heart, they would do everything they could do to rotate you to the rear, for the remainder of your tour. They would find you another job, in Vietnam, out of harm's way, as best they could.

They did the paper work on my wound, and the company's first sergeant and I talked about it, and he said that, if I got a third Purple Heart, then they're gonna want you to come in here and help the XO, or maybe be the executive officer, till your tour ends. That would mean I would have to fool around with the mess hall and how many blankets we have, and whatever, and I said I don't want to do that. He said he would handle it. He took care of it from there. What he did, was he kept sendin' the orders for that medal, to various units in Korea and elsewhere. I never saw more of it, and that was the end of that.

July 2, 1969, was a day when my unit was doing a reconnaissance by force, without infantry, through an area that we did the same operation in too often and too consistently. I feel like we gave our enemy an advantage, by doing things habitually, which helps the ambush planner.

The enemy chose to set up an ambush, on this particular day, in a place where we often suspected there would be one. The machines had to traverse a dry stream bed, and when they did that they would be almost nose down initially, as they went down the stream's bank towards the stream bed, then in the stream bed, and then almost straight up, as they went up the opposite bank. They were very vulnerable when they did that, and that was part of the ambush.

Initially they fired RPGs and machine guns on the lead vehicle. My vehicle was the lead vehicle every day I was there, except that one. The track commander was shot dead, off the top and fell off. The crew were all wounded, by two RPGs that struck the thing. It was smoking, and fire danger was imminent to me.

I had my unit strung out behind the lead vehicle, and was able to reposition them and have them start putting effective fire on a large ditch that these gentlemen were using. Contrary to my training, I decided that I should dismount, with a rifle or machine gun and get, as fast as I could, to that vehicle to see if I could get people out of it before burned.

There was plenty of supporting fire, and I was able to run to the vehicle. I heard bullets goin' by, but I wasn't struck by one, and I was able to get the wounded out of the vehicle and around the side to where the vehicle would shield them from the gunfire. Upon returning to my vehicle, I repositioned it to where my 50-cal. would be more effective and left a NCO on that gun, while myself and two other crew members went and retrieved the wounded from that vehicle and brought 'em back behind our vehicle.

I became aware that the enemy was in the classic L-shaped ambush and behind me as well. They never fired a shot, until we brought the wounded behind me, where I thought they were secure. Then bullets started hittin' the APC, and we realized that there was a bunker of 'em 100-yards behind us. I decided to crank up and go get 'em. I had good luck with that, and the remaining enemy broke off contact.

It was a sad day, because good young men died. Many units tried to come and help. An infantry unit, from across the road, heard the fighting and could see it from the hillside they were on. They got organized and were trucked down to the road, put 'em on the ground, and then they came to try to assist. By that time, the situation had changed, but I never forgot that they came to help. I was awarded a Distinguished Service Cross for that action.

*Author's note: On 25 September 1969, a Distinguished Service Cross Medal was awarded to 1st Lt. Philip Leslie Spackman. The citation reads:*

'For extraordinary heroism in connection with military operations involving conflict with an armed hostile force in the Republic of Vietnam: First Lieutenant Spackman distinguished himself by exceptionally valorous actions on 2 July 1969 while serving as platoon leader during a unit patrol operation in the Rice Bowl district near An Lao. As the lead armored personnel carrier crossed a stream and penetrated a hedgerow, it was struck simultaneously by several hostile rocket grenades, wounding all the occupants. A hostile force of North Vietnamese began moving down the stream bed to cut off the damaged vehicle from the rest of the troop. Lieutenant Spackman immediately killed the nearest enemy soldier and repelled the rest of the assailants. While reinforcements secured the river crossing, he dashed to the vehicle through strafing automatic weapons fire and removed the casualties from exposure to direct fire. Then he and the less severely wounded carried the injured across the stream. Deploying the other vehicles along the river bank to engage the hostile positions beyond the hedgerow, he directed their firing as *well as that of the gunships which had arrived. He also established communications with and assisted the commander of an infantry element that had been airlifted near the enemy force. When the infantrymen began advancing on the communists' flank, Lieutenant Spackman maneuvered his armored personnel carriers on line and rolled toward the enemy positions. Encountering stiff resistance from one bunker, he directed his driver to rush the position. Firing from atop his tracked vehicle, Lieutenant Spackman pinned the enemy down until his vehicle passed by the position into which he threw several grenades, which destroyed the structure and killed the enemy. With the bunker eliminated, the enemy were routed from the area. First Lieutenant Spackman's extraordinary heroism and devotion to duty were in keeping with the highest traditions of the military service and reflect great credit upon himself, his unit, and the United States Army.'*

On August 11, 1969, I was wounded again. That was an action where a couple of my platoon's personnel carriers were disabled from rocket propelled grenades. My vehicle received an RPG through the hull, in the rear. It penetrated the battery box and went through both batteries and shot a lot of lead and sulfuric acid into the cab, and I suffered, as did my other two team mates, a hundred wounds in each leg, from lead from the batteries and aluminum from the hull, hot plastic, and sulfuric acid. That was a painful thing, although not fatal, and when the medics got to it, it was more painful: tryin' to pick all that stuff out of your flesh with tweezers. One of my team members took more of the stuff than we did: he was closer to where the RPG penetrated the hull, and he suffered a more grievous injury. We received Purple Hearts for those wounds.

This same action, on 11 August, also resulted in me being awarded the third Oak Leaf Cluster of the Bronze Star with V. We were working with an infantry unit that had engaged the enemy. This particular unit was small: a platoon size. It engaged a company plus of North Vietnamese, and was immediately at a disadvantage. When we arrived, the North Vietnamese were advancing. Generally, they would fight from a fixed position, but in this case, they thought they could over run this little outfit.

The North Vietnamese didn't know I was close, and infantry in the open is a good situation for armored cavalry. We were able to engage 'em very effectively. They did use rocket propelled grenades, and I do believe they struck us a time or two that day, but not to any huge effect. Once again, usin' the very aggressive tactic of using fire power to subdue them while you attack 'em, we were able to get right up on this bunch and inflicted a lot of damage on 'em, while protecting a very small American unit. I always wondered what that platoon was doin' wanderin' around by itself.

The award citation claims that we killed nine that day. Body counts, in the Americal Division were unusual for U.S. forces in Vietnam. The rule was you could count 'em, if you could kick 'em. You might shoot one right straight through the neck, and if his buddies drag him off, he didn't count as a kill. We counted only the ones they left behind. I don't think all infantry units did it that way.

Fortunately for me, my unit didn't do a lot of search and destroy. That was never our mission, so we didn't interact a great deal with the civilian population. Because of my training and that of my NCOs, I can personally attest that no violation of international law occurred against the civilians at our hands. But I did see angry American infantry units that had suffered booby trap injuries and had fallen into pits and been injured. They had taken injuries, without seeing their enemy, and when the next group of humans they saw were happened to be villagers, the villagers would suffer the brunt of that anger, in the form of disrespectful behavior or violence.

I don't recall ever seeing an assassination, but I did see some behavior their parents wouldn't have approved of. The 1st Battalion of the 20th Infantry was a neighbor, and that the incident that became so famous, in the 1970s: known as the My Lai Massacre was in my area. I had visited that Pinkville village many times. It was a dangerous place to be on foot, because of the nature of the enemy's way of booby trappin' it, but I was able to come and go through it in my APC.

Apparently, this guy William Calley lost control of his guys there, as the court pointed out to us all on television. His men murdered innocent women and children, and called it a military operation. I heard about it, in the scuttlebutt, but all I knew was that they'd engaged a hostile force in the pink village and defeated them. I knew no better, until I was in the United States years later. I heard about atrocities by other units, but unless I had my eyes on it, I'm not a big believer.

While I was there, there was a lot of tension between black soldiers and white soldiers. I saw it in infantry units that literally segregated. They changed platoons' personnel, so there'd be a black 3rd platoon and a white second and a white first. I thought what the hell's that? I saw it happen.

I would see groups of black soldiers giving their greeting sign, a clenched right-hand fist: The Black Power salute. The Caucasians sign was peace, the V sign made with the first and second fingers held vertically. Those two signs were greetings, but they were almost like greetings of two opponents.

I had black soldiers in my unit, but my unit was small and self-contained. We had eight armored personnel carriers modified and one mortar track. The crews were four or five men, with a minimum of four.

I saw American infantry and artillery units where heroin was a problem, for the command. It was so readily available, so reasonably priced that its use was widespread. When a Spec 4 artillery gun crew member can afford heroin, it must be pretty reasonable.

I saw it affect units' effectiveness. I stopped using American artillery from two fire bases, because I knew they were all hammered, and I wouldn't call them. I knew they wouldn't be effective. And I knew the contrary to be true of others, and, if I was over near those, I'd consider using artillery.

The first marijuana I ever saw was in that county, and it was pretty popular with guys that were from the northeast and California, 'cause it had been there. It just hadn't gotten down here to Georgia. I didn't quite see the danger in it. I didn't like the idea of someone not being alert, and so I let it be known that it would not be used in the field with us: figure out another time and place.

There was a Republic of Korea Marine detachment, a ROK Marine detachment, at landing zone Bronco, which was home of the 11th Light Infantry Brigade, with four rifle battalions. The ROK Marines had the only camp area on the premises without a fence, gate, chain, or any security around it. They would hang their clothes on lines and leave them out, and the locals absolutely knew better than to come and steal from them, because the ROK Marines were violently brutal with anybody they caught stealing from them.

The Vietnamese boys that stole were called slicky boys. They were very slick. The ROK Marines actually would tie kids caught stealing up to posts and leave them tied up for a couple of days. They didn't kill any in my presence. They just make them very uncomfortable.

I never worked with the ROK Marines. They would attach platoon-sized units of about 30 men to an American rifle company. I know that when they were involved in missions, it seemed like they had better luck interrogating captured Viet Cong guerrillas and North Vietnam soldiers than the Americans did. I'll leave it there.

I have my medal citations on a wall in an alcove in my house, and I have never thought about reading them by date. Then I thought, maybe I could remember better, if I did it that way. I did that, and it did jog a lot of memories, about soldiers I served with, which was good.

The medals and badges I received on active duty with the Army are the Distinguished Service Cross, the Silver Star Medals with two Oak Leaf Clusters, the Bronze Star Medal with V device and three Oak Leaf Clusters, Army Commendation Medal, the Purple Heart Medal with one Oak Leaf Cluster, the Vietnam Service Medal with three bronze campaign stars, Combat Infantryman Badge, Parachutist Badge, Sharpshooter Marksmanship Badge with Machine Gun and Rifle Bars, two Overseas Service Bars, National Defense Service Medal, Republic of Vietnam Campaign Medal with 1960 device, Republic of Vietnam Gallantry Cross with Palm Unit Citation,

I left Vietnam, in September of 1969 and came back to Ft. Lewis, Washington, by air, by way of Japan and Alaska. I was released from active duty, on September 16, 1969, and headed for home with Lt. Joseph Machen, an infantry Lieutenant, from the 1st Battalion of the 21st Infantry, 11th Light Infantry Brigade, who I'd served with the entire year. He was from Mobile, Alabama, and August 17th, the day we got back to the United States was the day Hurricane Camille came in the Gulf of Mexico and crushed his home town.

It was pre-cell phone, and there was no telephone to Mobile. He was having trouble getting ahold of anybody to let 'em know he was home. My folks in Atlanta, I could reach. He and I chose to go from Ft. Lewis to Las Vegas, where he was comped at the gambling halls, because that's the business his parents were in, in south Mississippi. They complimentarily gave him lodging, food, time at the table, for his father had an account, so to speak. We waited in Vegas for a day or two, and finally got ahold of some of his kinfolk who had driven out of the storm's way and were safe and sound in Tennessee. He proceeded to Knoxville to meet them, and I proceeded on to Atlanta.

When I came home, I enrolled in West Georgia College, in Carrollton, Georgia, and attended there for eight straight quarters without a break, and then saw an opportunity in the construction field and took it. Seven years after leaving West Georgia College, I started a small business of my own, which I operated for 35 years, till I sold it, in 2005. It was a commercial grass-planting business: highways, roads, airports, dams. Initially, the business was out of Alpharetta, Georgia, a stretch of time in west Georgia, and then back to Alpharetta. Since then, I've done part-time work to keep myself entertained mostly. I don't see me stoppin'.

My first bride was a lady I met in college. She was an Atlanta girl, born in Ozark, Alabama, right next to Ft. Rucker. I actually met her grandparents, at Ft. Rucker, long before I met her. We were married in 1976. She is the mother of my two sons and remains a friend. We drifted apart after a 20-year marriage. My first-born son is Sidney, born in '81. His younger brother is Hank, born in '87.

I went single for a bit, and then married again. That marriage ended in 2014. Then I met a girl that I had taken to a sports banquet, at age 14. She had married a high school friend of mine and had been widowed for a number of years. In a whirlwind fashion we were married 7 October 2015 and happy to be. Her name is Donna. I have no grandchildren, but I married into a nice bunch. My wife and I live at Big Canoe, in Pickens County, Georgia.

I have never been bothered by PTSD. I'm sure there's others that would testify otherwise: some women, in my life, along the way. I have no disability award and none requested.

I am a proud member of Free and Accepted Masons of Georgia, Alpharetta Lodge No. 235 and was master of the lodge, in 2007. I'm a member of the North Georgia Veterans Association, at Big Canoe, in Pickens County, Georgia, and I am a life member of the Military Order of the Purple Heart.

I'm about to do a public speaking thing for the Johns Creek Veterans' Association, at the portable Vietnam Memorial wall, at Newtown Park, on the 29th of March. I look forward to it. I've been told the subject on which to speak, and I argued I don't speak on me, but I will speak on patriotism, and that's my pitch.

Second Lt. Philip Leslie Spackman, before Vietnam

# The author

Norman Philip Black served, as a U.S. Navy Journalist, in the western Pacific; reported for *United Press International* and edited copy for *Associated Press*, both in New York City; and reported, in New Jersey, for the *Newark Evening and Sunday News*. He later worked in public relations, for major companies. His news reports, features, and commentaries have been published in many countries.

His first book is *Ice, Fire, and Blood*, a military history novel that tells about a period in the Korean War when the Chinese intervened and smashed U.S.-U.N. armies and the situation's rapid reversal. His other works are two volumes of autobiographical stories of *Combat Veterans' Stories of World War II*, and two volumes of *Combat Veterans' Stories of* the *Korean War*.

Made in the USA
Columbia, SC
04 April 2018